1974
PROGRESSIVE ROCK COMES OF AGE

Kevan Furbank

sonicbondpublishing.com

Sonicbond Publishing Limited
www.sonicbondpublishing.co.uk
Email: info@sonicbondpublishing.co.uk

First Published in the United Kingdom 2026
First Published in the United States 2026

British Library Cataloguing in Publication Data:
A Catalogue record for this book is available from the British Library

Typeset in ITC Garamond Std & ITC Avant Garde Gothic
Printed and bound in England

Graphic design and typesetting: Full Moon Media

1974
PROGRESSIVE ROCK COMES OF AGE

Kevan Furbank

sonicbondpublishing.com

The 1974 incarnation of Gong, featuring a youthful Steve Hillage (third from left).

1974: PROGRESSIVE ROCK COMES OF AGE

Contents

Introduction

'Welcome back my friends to the show that never ends', said Emerson, Lake & Palmer on their 1974 hit live album. They were wrong, of course. All shows must come to an end – but they are great while they last. For progressive rock, the show was never greater than in the glory years of 1972 to 1974, when it was a dominating force in popular music.

This book is very much a companion volume to the chronicles of 1972 – written by yours truly – and 1973, penned by my fellow Sonicbond author Geoffrey Feakes. Together, they chronicle the big three years of prog, when it was at its most creative and influential.

In these pages, I examine the albums and artists who made 1974 so prog and are still listened to and talked about today. Many of the long players contained in these pages are probably among your favourites of the genre – quite a few of them are mine, and it has been a joy to revisit them.

In these pages, you will find studio albums by such progressive rock giants as King Crimson, Camel, Gentle Giant, Gong, Jethro Tull, Frank Zappa and Mike Oldfield. What you won't find are any live albums because they usually document tours to promote a previous year's release (although King Crimson and Frank Zappa often mixed live and studio recordings), so I don't consider them to be distinct artistic statements. That means the album that provided my opening line ISN'T in the book! How perverse is that...

In making my selection of proggy platters, I have been influenced by chart success, longevity and general critical appreciation. But a fair amount of personal choice comes into it, too, so, inevitably, some of your favourite albums may not have made the cut. That's why I include a section that, as far as possible, gives a nod to all the other progressive rock albums released in 1974 that didn't quite claw their way onto the A-list.

The main chapters in this book look at how each album was conceived and produced, and why it is, in my inflated opinion, a prog landmark. They also include some history of the bands responsible, particularly the lineup changes and personal interactions that helped shape the music that emerged. After all, would *Relayer* have sounded the same if Patrick Moraz had not replaced Rick Wakeman in Yes? What challenging personal circumstances resulted in Robert Wyatt making *Rock Bottom*? And why did *The Lamb Lies Down On Broadway* ignite the departure of Peter Gabriel as lead singer of Genesis? All these questions will be discussed and, hopefully, answered.

I also take a brief look at what else was happening in 1974 – the social, political and musical events that may have influenced prog artists. After all, no music exists in isolation – it is shaped and moulded by what is going on around it, in the corridors of power as well as in the charts. Music is a living, breathing, ever-changing creature, and thank whatever deity you believe in (or not) for that.

So, join me in my wood-pulp De Lorean as I take you back to a year of two US presidents, two UK prime ministers, a rumble in the jungle, the rise of ABBA and, surprisingly, the invention of the Rubik's Cube. Let's go to 1974!

Freak Parade

If you don't like politics, look away now. The year 1974 was dominated by dramatic and often forced political change across the globe. In the United States, President Richard Nixon resigned over the Watergate scandal and was replaced by Gerald Ford (who, surprisingly, sometimes ranks WORSE than Nixon in the list of duff US leaders, even though he wasn't a crook).

There were two General Elections in the UK – a hung parliament in February saw Conservative leader Edward Heath quit as prime minister, replaced by Labour's Harold Wilson, who had to call a second election in October to get a small, three-seat majority. There was a new government in Turkey, a new female Argentine president in Isabel Peron and a new nuclear power in India, thanks to the rather inaptly named Project Smiling Buddha (because nuclear weapons are nothing to smile about).

A left-wing coup in Portugal – known as the Carnation Revolution after a restaurant worker handed flowers to soldiers – ended a 41-year dictatorship; a military coup in Cyprus was followed by an invasion by Turkey, occupying nearly half the island; and Emperor Haile Selassie of Ethiopia was deposed, sparking a 17-year civil war.

There were also the usual acts of terrorism and violence that seemed to mar practically every year in the 1970s. The Ulster Volunteer Force – a bunch of insane British murderers – bombed pubs in the Republic of Ireland, killing 33 people. They were swiftly followed by the Irish Republican Army – a bunch of insane Irish murderers – who bombed the 11th-century Westminster Hall in London and then killed 21 people by blowing up two pubs in Birmingham. In Italy, neo-fascists killed 12 people by bombing a train, and in Tokyo, the Mitsubishi Heavy Industries building was blown up by radical far-left terrorists, with a death toll of eight people.

But it wasn't all doom and gloom, so you can look again now. In 1974, the oil crisis came to an end, and sky-high petrol prices began to fall. The stunning Terracotta Army – thousands of figures buried with Qin Shi Huang, the first emperor of China, in 209BCE – was discovered. And a book called *Carrie* was published, the debut novel of an unknown horror writer named Stephen King. I wonder how he turned out.

It was the year Lord Lucan disappeared after his wife was attacked and their nanny murdered. He was never found. Labour MP John Stonehouse also disappeared – but he was found in an Australian love nest with his secretary. Meanwhile, Lucy was found after 3.18 million years – she was an early human ancestor whose fossilised skeleton was dug up in Ethiopia. She was named after the Beatles song 'Lucy In The Sky With Diamonds'.

An estimated one billion people tuned in to watch boxers Muhammad Ali and George Foreman (now better known as George Foreman Grill. Insert smiley face here) punch the stuffing out of each other in what was billed as The Rumble in the Jungle (because it took place in the capital of what was Zaire, but is now the Democratic Republic of the Congo in Africa, miles from any jungle). Dubbed the greatest sporting event of the 20th century, it saw underdog Ali defeat undisputed heavyweight champ Foreman by punching him to the canvas in the eighth round.

Lovers of screen drama also flocked to watch *The Towering Inferno*, the most successful movie of 1974, which united Paul Newman and Steve McQueen atop a burning skyscraper. Life tragically imitated art – in February, a fire at the 25-storey Joelma Building in São Paulo, Brazil, killed 177 people. Other big screen bangers included a double dose of Mel Brooks madness in *Blazing Saddles* and *Young Frankenstein* (puttin' on the riiiiitttz...), disaster movies *Earthquake* and *Airport 1975*, and the second (and best) instalment of the *Godfather* trilogy.

If anyone summed up the complicated and baffling nature of 1974 best, it was Hungarian inventor Erno Rubik, who in that year completed the first working prototype of his Cube, made of wood and held together by elastic bands. It didn't hit the market until 1980, but it went on to sell more than 500 million units by 2024. That's a lot of people sitting on their own, fiddling with a bit of plastic for hours on end. I guess it prepared us all for the invention of the mobile phone.

Zappa's live band in 1974. Most of them played on his most commercially successful album, *Apostrophe (')*.

Sound Chasers

It's a surprising fact that today's music industry is dominated by solo artists, and bands have topped the UK singles charts for just three weeks this decade (and one of those was The Beatles). In just one year, 1974, the biggest-selling single in the UK, 'Tiger Feet' by the band Mud, was number one for six whole weeks, and was joined at the top by Paper Lace, The Rubettes, The Three Degrees, The Osmonds and, of course, ABBA, who won the Eurovision Song Contest with 'Waterloo'.

It was the same story in the UK album charts. In fact, the year opened with Yes sitting comfortably at number one for two weeks with *Tales From Topographic Oceans*, released at the tail-end of 1973, and they were followed by The Carpenters, Slade and the Bay City Rollers.

In the US, the album charts churned over more rapidly, with hits by Jim Croce, Bob Dylan, Barbra Streisand and Eric Clapton. Another big seller was Marvin Hamlisch's soundtrack for *The Sting*. In the *Billboard* Hot 100, the Steve Miller Band sold five million copies of their number one single 'The Joker'.

In 1974, there was music for everyone, from Andy Williams and Charles Aznavour to Queen and Deep Purple. It was also a particularly good year for glam rock, which combined 1950s rock 'n 'roll, hard rock riffs and bubblegum pop with outlandish 1970s fashion. Some were obvious throwbacks to an earlier time, such as the aforementioned Mud, Suzi Quatro and Showaddywaddy. Others, including T. Rex, David Bowie and Elton John, made elderly TV watchers choke on their cocoa with what was then outrageous gender fluidity.

Beneath the make-up and glitter, however, some glam rock acts were pushing the envelope of their music as far as they could – and can almost be called prog. In particular, I point to Bowie and Queen as acts that bent genres as well as genders. Bowie's *Diamond Dogs* – his first proper album after retiring androgynous alter ego Ziggy Stardust – embraced soul, funk and proto-punk, while Queen created dramatic musical works of art such as 'Now I'm Here' and 'Killer Queen' on their third album, *Sheer Heart Attack*. Their second album – *Queen II*, also released in 1974 – has an even stronger claim to be prog but shows a band still searching for a musical identity.

Prog may not have had as many chart-toppers as glam rock, but it was still a dominating force in the album charts. Apart from Yes, both Rick Wakeman and Mike Oldfield had number-one hits in 1974, while Emerson, Lake & Palmer, Genesis and Roxy Music all took up residence in the top ten.

The US seemed more immune to prog's charms at this point (although Jethro Tull had a number two with *War Child*), but, as usual, it did very well in the rest of Europe. Genesis hit number one in France, Focus number five in the Netherlands, Zappa number six in Norway and King Crimson number seven in Italy.

What was prog, and where had it come from? It emerged from the psychedelic rock of the 1960s, when, thanks to the success of The Beatles, artists were taking control in the studios to indulge their musical fantasies. Perhaps the first prog album was The Moody Blues' *Days Of Future Passed*, in which psychedelic rock was merged with classical orchestral music to create a modern take on Antonín Dvořák's *New World Symphony*. That approach was pushed even further by Keith Emerson in The Nice, who deliberately rocked up Sibelius and Leonard Bernstein, and created a side-long epic in classical style, 'Ars Longa Vita Brevis'.

Other bands began incorporating folk and jazz into their work, while dispensing with old ideas about song structure, length and content until, in 1969, we got what is generally regarded as the most influential prog rock album – *In The Court Of The Crimson King*. After that, prog was on a roll as band after band embraced the genre and took it to even greater heights.

By 1972, the likes of Yes, Genesis and Jethro Tull had released what are still seen as progressive rock classics, albums that took the listener on a wild, often non-stop musical ride – or, at least, as long as a side of vinyl could last. *Fragile* and *Close To The Edge* (Yes), *Nursery Cryme* and *Foxtrot* (Genesis), *Aqualung* and *Thick As A Brick* (Tull), *If I Could Do It All Over Again, I'd Do It All Over You* and *In The Land Of Grey And Pink* (Caravan), *Acquiring The Taste, Three Friends* and *Octopus* (Gentle Giant) and the third Soft Machine album were taking rock to places it had never been before.

Then came 1973 and the most commercially successful progressive rock album of all time – Pink Floyd's *The Dark Side Of The Moon*. It galloped across genres and musical boundaries like Shergar on speed, selling 45 million copies worldwide by 2024, beaten only by AC/DC's *Back In Black* (50m) and Michael Jackson's *Thriller* (70m). Prog had not just arrived – it had seen, and it had conquered.

It's true that, by 1974, progressive rock was entering its final year as a major force in modern music. From now on, there would be a slow decline in importance but not in quality – some of the genre's best-loved albums were still to come over the next 50 years. And 1974 saw the release of some great albums that are still revered today. In fact, one can argue (and I will) that it was the year when King Crimson, Genesis, Gong, Robert Wyatt, the Strawbs and Supertramp released their finest works, and Frank Zappa his most commercially successful album in a career spanning more than 30 years and at least 100 releases.

In fact, most of the big beasts of prog produced new LPs in 1974, with the exception of Floyd, who were touring *The Dark Side...* and unveiling tracks that wouldn't be recorded for commercial release until 1977's *Animals*. Meanwhile, they were also playing about with wine glasses, rubber bands and brooms as they attempted to find a direction for a follow-up to their big hit.

Now, a few words on why some of your favourite artists that you regard as progressive are not here. Even though this was a good year for jazz-fusion – and, as you will discover, bands such as the Mahavishnu Orchestra and Return To Forever had a big influence on prog – their inclusion would make this book so big that it would have to be delivered by forklift. So, I have made an executive decision to sideline them.

The same goes for electronic music, but for the simple reason that I don't like it very much! Get your own book, Tangerine Dream! I make an exception for Kraftwerk because it doesn't send me to sleep.

Here, then, are my top prog albums of 1974. None of these send me to sleep – in fact, some are loud enough to wake the dead.

Mike Oldfield during the recording of *Hergest Ridge*.

Genesis – *The Lamb Lies Down On Broadway*

Key personnel:
Peter Gabriel: lead vocals, flute
Steve Hackett: guitars
Mike Rutherford: bass guitar, 12-string guitar
Tony Banks: keyboards, guitar
Phil Collins: drums, percussion, vibraphone, backing vocals
Recorded between August and October 1974 with the Island Studios Mobile at
Glaspant Manor, Capel Iwan, Carmarthenshire, Wales
Produced by John Burns and Genesis
Engineered by David Hutchins
Cover design: Hipgnosis
Record label: Charisma (UK), Atco (US)
Release date: 22 November 1974
Chart placings: FR: 1, UK: 10, IT: 14, CA: 15, FI: 17, NZ: 34, US: 41
Tracks: 'The Lamb Lies Down On Broadway', 'Fly On A Windshield', 'Broadway
Melody Of 1974', 'Cuckoo Cocoon', 'In The Cage', 'The Grand Parade Of Lifeless
Packaging', 'Back In N.Y.C', 'Hairless Heart', 'Counting Out Time', 'Carpet Crawl',
'The Chamber Of 32 Doors', 'Lilywhite Lilith', 'The Waiting Room', 'Anyway', 'Here
Comes The Supernatural Anaesthetist', 'The Lamia', 'Silent Sorrow In Empty
Boats', 'The Colony Of Slippermen – A) The Arrival B) A Visit To The Doktor C)
The Raven', 'Ravine', 'The Light Dies Down On Broadway', 'Riding The Scree', 'In
The Rapids', 'it.'

The Story So Far...

The band was formed in 1967 by Peter Gabriel, Tony Banks, Anthony 'Ant'
Phillips, Mike Rutherford and Chris Stewart, all pupils at Charterhouse public
school in Surrey and members of previous bands Anon or Garden Wall. An
early demo tape was given to record producer Jonathan King, another
Charterhouse alumnus, who named them Genesis and signed them to Decca
Records. It was, apparently, that easy. Early singles were unsuccessful, and

drummer Stewart left, replaced by John Silver (also from Charterhouse). The album, *From Genesis To Revelation*, released in 1969, sold fewer than 700 copies at the time. Dumped by Decca, they recorded more demos that were rejected by every record label in sight. So, not so easy after all. Silver left, replaced by John Mayhew.

Concentrating on live work, they were eventually signed by Charisma, who released their second album, *Trespass*, in 1970. It flopped in the UK but reached number one in Belgium. Phillips, suffering from stage fright, left the group, and Mayhew was fired. Replacements Steve Hackett, on guitar, and Phil Collins, on drums, joined to record *Nursery Cryme*, released in November 1971, which fared better in the rest of Europe than in the UK. *Foxtrot* (1972) changed that, reaching number 12 on the UK chart, while 1973's *Selling England By The Pound* went to number three and broke into the US *Billboard* Hot 100.

The Album

The sixth album by English prog band Genesis was based on a children's book by French writer Antoine de Saint-Exupery about a little prince who visits various planets, including Earth, and muses on life, love, loss and human nature. At least that's what COULD have happened. Certainly, if Mike Rutherford had had his way. When Genesis were searching for a concept for their first double album, it was he who suggested taking inspiration from one of the best-selling novellas in history.

It wasn't an altogether ludicrous idea. In fact, it would have fitted in very well with the band's brand of pastoral whimsy and folklore-ish flights of fancy that had given the world 'The Fountain Of Salmacis', 'Supper's Ready' and 'Firth Of Fifth'. Even when Genesis tackled serious subjects, such as corrupt landlords, consumerism and gangland criminals, they usually did so in an understated, very English way, with tongue firmly lodged in cheek, frequently to the accompaniment of tinkling 12-string acoustics, grand pianos and gentle flute.

The band's desire to make a double LP stemmed from the positive fan reaction to the long tracks on the last two albums. If people loved 40 minutes of Genesis, then they would surely wet their drawers over 80 minutes. But double albums needed a concept, particularly in progressive rock – look at The Who's *Tommy* and *Quadrophenia*, and Yes's *Tales From Topographic Oceans*. The Little Prince sounded like something Genesis could spin out across four sides of vinyl.

Yet, the diminutive royal was rejected in favour of a completely different protagonist – a streetwise Puerto Rican in New York who goes on a disturbing voyage of self-discovery. A surly, leather-jacketed thug armed with a bottle of gasoline who would probably torch you as soon as he saw you, and who 'don't believe in pain' – the Trailblazer, Rael, Electric Razor. Just the sort of thing you would expect middle-class English public schoolboys to come up with.

It was Peter Gabriel's idea, inspired by *West Side Story*, the Broadway-then-Hollywood musical that transplanted William Shakespeare's *Romeo And Juliet* into the 1950s multiracial Upper West Side of Manhattan, and *El Topo*, a 1970s Mexican film directed by its star Alejandro Jodorowsky and packed full of bizarre acid-drenched surreal scenes and dense religious symbolism. It was also deeply influenced by the band's first epic US tour to promote *Selling England By The Pound* – in Detroit, police had to confiscate guns from members of the audience – and the rugged, working-class 'heartland rock' persona of Bruce Springsteen.

Gabriel liked drama and telling strange stories. On stage, he would wear eye-catching costumes, including a black catsuit with bat wings, and his wife's long red dress with a fox's head. While Rutherford and Steve Hackett spent an eternity tuning their 12-strings, or during the frequent Mellotron breakdowns, he would weave surreal, tangled and slightly gross narratives to introduce the songs. And on the back cover of 1973's *Genesis Live,* he penned a deeply disturbing tale about a woman on an afternoon tube train who strips off her clothes and unzips her entire body, leaving a shimmering golden rod hovering above the floor of the carriage.

The rest of the band were a little nonplussed by it all, but recognised that Gabriel's cosplay and storytelling helped Genesis stand out from the crowd. Later, the costumes would become a distraction, particularly when Gabriel found he couldn't sing properly inside his grotesque outfits. And the storytelling would cause conflict with his bandmates – particularly with Tony Banks – because Gabriel wanted to take control of the lyrics, reasoning that few novels are written by committee.

So it was with some reluctance and trepidation that they gave in to Gabriel's vision for their next album. Collins, Banks, Hackett and Rutherford would come up with the musical ideas and pass them to Gabriel, who would scribble out the lyrics. His vision was encapsulated in the surreal story he wrote that was spread across the middle of the gatefold album sleeve: a young, leather-jacketed Puerto Rican called Rael – which came from the idea that a lot of early deities seem to have 'ra' in their names – is spray-painting graffiti on a wall in New York when a dark cloud descends on to Times Square and our hero is whisked off into an alternate world, imprisoned in a cage, sees his brother John screaming for help and finds his gang members turned into lifeless 'packaging'.

He reaches a chamber via a spiral staircase, is led to a cave by a pale woman and meets Death himself before entering a pool of pink water where snakelike creatures consume his flesh, turning him into an ugly, grotesque creature of lumps and stumps. He is reunited with his brother and discovers, to his understandable alarm, that the only cure for their condition is to be castrated! Handed his member in a plastic tube, a raven swoops down and steals it, dropping it into the rushing waters at the bottom of a ravine.

Rael gives chase and sees a skylight that could take him back to his real world. But then he sees John is drowning in the ravine, and he has to decide whether to save himself or his brother. Choosing the latter, he hauls John to safety, only to find he is looking at himself. He becomes 'one with everything', like the Dalai Lama's pizza. Gabriel told the *New Musical Express* in 1974: 'I think the main thing I was striving for was the contrast between character and fantasy. It's the idea of him being an outcast in a totally alien situation. I identify with him to a certain extent.'

So, The Little Prince it ain't, and it is unlikely that the rest of the band really bought into, or even understood, Gabriel's vision. Banks certainly felt the theme was too dark, too 'street' for a band that previously explored more romantic musical territory. But they all agreed it was ambitious and groundbreaking and would push the band to its very limits. It was also timely – in Hugh Fielder's 1984 *Book Of Genesis*, Gabriel said: 'This was 1974; it was pre-punk, but I still thought we needed to base the story around a contemporary figure rather than a fantasy creation. We were beginning to get into the era of the big, fat supergroups of the 1970s, and I thought, 'I don't want to go down with the Titanic'.'

Later, Gabriel would learn to his annoyance that The Who had used the name 'Rael' on their 1967 album *The Who Sell Out*, although it was a country, not a person, being short for 'Israel'. The name was also adopted by French journalist turned religious leader Claude Vorilhon in 1973, when he founded the extra-terrestrial-worshipping Raelian Movement.

In June 1974, Genesis moved into Headley Grange in Hampshire to write and rehearse, an 18th century former poorhouse where both Bad Company and Led Zeppelin had recorded – it was where Zep drummer John Bonham got his big drum sound on 'When The Levee Breaks'. But it was a grim, rundown place that seemed to be haunted by sad spirits. In his autobiography *Not Dead Yet*, Collins recalled:

Whichever band was in last has left it in a horrific, stinking state. Taking advantage of this are the rats. They are everywhere, leaping up and down the creaky staircase, rustling up the creepers covering the trees, scurrying up the vines covering the house. Dozens, hundreds of them. And that's just the ones you can see.

Steve Hackett, in his autobiography *A Genesis In My Bed*, adds:

One weird and freaky thing that happened was an occasion when I'd just washed my hands in a bathroom. The second I stepped back from the basin, the floor gave way on the exact spot where my feet had just been, leaving a gaping hole. Robert Plant told me later he was convinced the place was haunted, and Jimmy Page claimed he saw an apparition at the top of the stairs where Led Zep were recording there, just outside the room where I slept.

Adding to the sense of unease were the personal tensions in the band, the harder, denser nature of the music they were coming up with and the domestic issues many of them were facing: Hackett had just split from his first wife Ellen and their newborn son Oliver, while Gabriel was frequently away from the writing process, looking after his wife Jill, who had given birth to a child that wasn't expected to survive. In fact, doctors whisked the newborn away so her mother would not bond with a baby that was unlikely to make it. (That baby, Anna-Marie, is now an accomplished photographer and film director.)

Then the director of the year's most notorious horror movie, *The Exorcist*, put his oar in. William Friedkin had read Gabriel's short story on the back of *Genesis Live* and wanted to collaborate with him on a film project. Gabriel asked the band to put the album on hold, but the answer was no. In fact, says Collins, they gave him an ultimatum: You're either in, or you're out. Peter chose out, leaving the band wondering whether it could continue as a strictly instrumental four-piece. Mortified that he was apparently splitting the band up, Friedkin withdrew his offer, and Gabriel returned, but now with hidden resentment on all sides.

Recording was done in a barn at the remote Gaspant Studio in Wales before being mixed at Island Studios in London. Brian Eno was recording his second solo album, *Taking Tiger Mountain (By Strategy)*, in a studio upstairs, and he was drafted in to put effects on some of Gabriel's vocals. Collins recalled in his autobiography:

> During the mixing sessions at Basing Street, a schism develops between daytime Genesis and nighttime Genesis. Peter and I sometimes mix till two in the morning, then Tony comes in the next day, hates it and scrubs it. Sometimes we are still recording when we are supposed to be mixing. Time is short, the mood is tense and everyone is tired. There's too much music, too many lyrics, we're rushing to get finished, the narrative nuances of this double-vinyl concept album are a mystery to us all (including, we suspect, Peter) – and any minute now we're due to go on tour.

That was until Steve Hackett gripped a wine glass just a little too tightly at a party and smashed it, severing a tendon and a nerve. The injury needed stitches and time to recuperate, irritating the rest of the band but giving them a bit more time to polish off the album.

So the music on *The Lamb Lies Down On Broadway* was born out of tension, conflict and immense pressure – no wonder it contains some of the toughest music Genesis ever recorded. Sure, they could be noisy at times, but no Genesis album sounds as hard and brittle as *The Lamb*.... Of course, there are some beautifully melodic moments, too, and we'll come to them. But it is amazing how these five English fellas somehow managed to embrace the speed and noise of New York in their music.

The first thing you notice is that there are a lot of tracks – 23 of them spread across four sides of vinyl, most clocking in at between two and six minutes, and many having relatively simple structures. Only two of the 23 songs break the eight-minute mark, and there is no 'Supper's Ready', although some of the tracks segue into each other. Then you hear that the music is dominated by Tony Banks's keyboards – in fact, Hackett said he found it difficult to know where his guitar fit in. It is to his credit that it does. There are also a lot of vocals, although fewer than Gabriel initially wanted – he always had a tendency to fill up every moment with lyrics, while Banks would want the opposite, leading to (mostly) constructive friction between the two.

The keyboard player's dominance is clear from the very beginning. The opening title track starts with busy, ominous arpeggios from Banks on an RMI 68D Electra-Piano, which creates a harsh, metallic sound totally unlike the grand piano he used to open 'Firth Of Fifth' on *Selling England By The Pound*. It has a jaunty rhythm to it, created by Banks using a cross-handed technique, with each hand playing alternatively. It moves rapidly through a series of keys before the band come in with staccato musical 'hits'. Gabriel sings the title and then the song launches into a medium-fast 4/4 rhythm with a simple riff in E major, Rutherford playing fuzz bass and Hackett echoing the riff on guitar.

Gabriel sets the scene: it's 'early morning Manhattan, ocean winds blow on the land' (the Atlantic borders the city's eastern and southern shores). Homeless sleepers are turfed out of the 24-hour cinemas, shops' metal defences are unlocked and traffic rumbles along poorly-maintained roads. Then, here comes 'Rael Imperial Aerosol Kid', the hero of the story. It seems he has been on a bit of a graffiti rampage – he is hiding his spray gun in case he gets caught. Then he sees a lamb lying down on Broadway.

There have been entire books written about the imagery in 'The Lamb…' and what it all may mean. Does the lamb itself represent innocence and purity? Is it, in fact, inspired by the birth of Gabriel's first daughter, and is Rael's 'spray gun' a metaphor for his penis? There are, after all, an awful lot of sexual references in the album. Or is it simply the incongruity of it? If you have been to Broadway, which runs through the heart of Manhattan's theatre district, one thing you certainly do not expect to see is woolly livestock.

Whatever it is, the lamb is a catalyst for change. In a slower bridge between the second and third verses, Gabriel sings: 'The lamb seems right out of place … Somehow it's lying there brings a stillness to the air'. Then we crash back into the last verse, in which Rael reveals: 'Something inside me has just begun, Lord knows what I have done'. The song ends with misquoted lines from the opening of The Drifters' 1963 hit 'On Broadway', written by Barry Mann, Cynthia Weil, Jerry Leiber and Mike Stoller. The original says: 'They say the neon lights are bright on Broadway/They say there's always magic in the air'. Gabriel misquotes it as 'They say the lights are always bright on

Broadway'. There's no obvious reason for the change, so it may well be that Gabriel simply got it slightly wrong.

'The Lamb Lies Down On Broadway' is a great opening to the album and the last song Banks and Gabriel wrote together. In an interview for this book, Steve Hackett told me:

Harmonically, the way the title track progresses is very interesting. By the time you get to the chorus – and at that time, Genesis were not exactly great at writing choruses – the harmonic changes behind it tend to have more to do with big band and the writers that preceded us. You've got this keyboard introduction, and it's very florid keyboard work throughout, so you've always got a melodic heart running underneath the vocal, so there's no doubt you've got a strong keyboard-playing brain at the centre.

The title track fades into the gentle strummed guitar chords of 'Fly On A Windshield', sounding quite Eastern and mysterious. In the lyrics, a dark cloud is descending in Times Square – it is moving towards Rael, who seems to be the only one who can see it; he feels like he is 'hovering like a fly, waiting for the windshield on the freeway'.

Then the entire band come in with a slow, marching rhythm, with Hackett playing wailing lead guitar over the top. Hackett told me:

Some of the best moments on *The Lamb...* were improvised – Genesis in general didn't specialise in that. But 'Fly On A Windshield' was largely improvised, and I think it's one of the best moments on the album for me. I loved being able to play over the top of chords that Tony was coming up with, kind of classically-inspired chords, and for once, the single bass note from the bass pedal works very well. We were influenced by film music at the time. We were thinking of two things: the Ben Hur ramming sequence from the 1957 version, which is why the drums are terribly simple and just beating out a rhythm, and at the same time, we were calling it 'Pharaohs' because it had a slightly Egyptian feel to it. It addressed the extremes; it was both very classical, but it was very rock as well, very cinematic.

There are also elements of early 20th-century Italian composer Ottorino Respighi and Maurice Ravel's 'Bolero'. Meanwhile, Hackett is soaring over the top with long, sinuous guitar lines, occasionally using a slide – most of it is improvised, although he had to sit down and write the melody to go over the tonal shift. His guitar sounds like a cry of pain at the beginning – again inspired by Ben Hur.

The track moves seamlessly into 'Broadway Melody Of 1974', in which Gabriel lists some of what were then major cultural and political figures, including stand-up comedian Lenny Bruce (1925-1966), Canadian-born media commentator Marshall McLuhan (1911-1980), comedian and movie star

Groucho Marx (1890-1977), executed criminal and author Caryl Chessman (1921-1960) and famous reclusive billionaire Howard Hughes (1905-1976). Musically, the band play stabs of chords over Mellotron strings. By the way, the original 'Broadway Melodies' were a series of four MGM backstage musicals that stretched from 1929, just two years after the introduction of sound, to 1940.

A sequence of three gentle chords played on guitar leads into 'Cuckoo Cocoon', a pretty tune based on a fingerpicked guitar riff in D, pretty much a variation on all the tricksy things guitarists can do with a D chord. Written mostly by Hackett and his brother John, it also allows Gabriel a rare opportunity to play his flute and is one of the few tracks on the album that sound like 'old' whimsical Genesis. Hackett originally had lyrics for it, but they were, of course, replaced by Gabriel's. Hackett told me: 'I wasn't particularly precious about lyrics.' Good job, really.

It is followed by 'In The Cage', an outstanding track that continued to be part of the Genesis setlist long after they had ceased to be a progressive rock band. Penned by Banks, who presented it to the band in its almost completed form, it opens with thumping bass like a beating heart as new daddy Gabriel sings 'I've got sunshine in my stomach, like I've just rocked my baby to sleep'. But there are more sinister things happening here – Rael is locked in a cage formed by a cave's stalactites and stalagmites (tites go down, mites go up), and they are all moving towards him to crush him. Banks plays organ arpeggios with syncopated bass from Rutherford.

A brief major key bridge allows Rael a moment of optimism – 'If I keep self-control, I'll be safe in my soul' – before we head back to the minor-key angst. Later, there's an amazing keyboard solo from Banks, reminiscent again of his work in the main body of 'Firth Of Fifth' and the instrumental ending of 'The Cinema Show'. At about halfway through, we enter a section in which Rael sees his brother John trapped in one of the cages, over power chords from Hackett and keyboard riffs from Banks.

There's a short reference to the Burt Bacharach and Hal David song 'Raindrops Keep Falling On My Head' before we head back into the minor-key section, in which John disappears and Rael's body starts spinning like a top.

In the final track on side one of the original vinyl, Rael finds himself in a room containing old gang members and his brother John wrapped up as 'lifeless packages'. Musically, this offers some respite from the agony and frustration of 'In the Cage' – Banks plays simple synth chords in a marching tempo. This was one of the rare occasions when the words came first; in Mario Giametti's book *Genesis 1967-1975: The Peter Gabriel Years*, Banks revealed:

I just started playing these two chords, a dopey kind of riff really ... I just keep one note going through the whole thing and just change the chords underneath it, letting it build. Then what Pete did on top was kind of wild, and he didn't really make any use of the melodic content of the piece, but I think it works very well.

This is also where Brian Eno did his 'Enossification' on Gabriel's voice. In return, Collins agreed to play drums on one of Eno's songs.

Side two opens with the powerful 'Back In NYC', one of the most aggressive songs Genesis ever performed. Rael gets a vision of his old life on the mean streets of Manhattan and we learn what has shaped and motivated him – his membership of a 'chain gang' (presumably Gabriel means a street gang rather than a group of convicts chained together), a spell in Pontiac Correctional Center in Illinois, his feeling that he doesn't really belong and his arsonist activities.

Heading home after a raid, he finds himself cuddling a sleeping porcupine. It's an unlikely occurrence, so perhaps the porcupine symbolises a difficult, prickly person. Porcupines will huddle together for warmth and reassurance. Is Rael trying to love and understand himself? Things become even stranger as Rael imagines his heart covered in hair, being removed from his body to be shaved. 'No time for romantic escape,' sings Gabriel, 'when your fluffy heart is ready for rape'. In the absence of Gabriel explaining himself, as he doesn't tend to do, we can only assume what the image means. Does Rael have a heart that is too soft, too emotional, that must be shaved for him to survive? Or is that hair prickly and egotistical?

Mike Rutherford says the song was worked up during jam sessions at Headley Grange, while Banks insists it was mostly Rutherford's work with his help. The verse riff in D, D6, C and Bm certainly suggests it was written on guitar or a six-string bass while playing around with the standard D chord fingering, in a tricky-dicky 7/8 time signature. Both recall jamming it with the band and Gabriel doing a 'shouty' vocal on it, which surprised his fellow musicians.

The verses are punctuated by syncopated little riffs, while the minor-key porcupine-cuddling – which I guess acts as a chorus of sorts because it is repeated later – plays about with the time signature, adding extra beats in places. In a video to promote the 2025 album remaster, Tony Banks said:

> The song is a bit more complicated than it needs to be – I think there are a couple of little extra bits in the middle there, probably courtesy of me, in fact, which probably would be better off if they weren't there. But they are there, so that's what you got!

'Back In NYC' segues nicely into 'Hairless Heart', a beautiful, romantic instrumental with a comparatively simple structure that is very welcome at this stage. It is the fruit of a rare collaboration between Hackett and Banks – the former always felt the latter was a bit dismissive of his contributions, and, like George Harrison in The Beatles, he frequently had to fight to get his compositions onto the albums. *The Lamb…* was a particularly difficult album for him because he struggled to make himself heard. In a 2023 interview with *Ultimate Guitar*, he said:

> There seemed to be a competition between Peter and Tony to see how much audio space they could fill. And it means you've got very busy, crowded virtuosic keyboard work and very busy narrative-driven lyrics from Peter. And these two paths seemed to be at loggerheads to a large degree. It became difficult to define what the other instruments can do because there was less 'breathing space' as a result of this.

'Hairless Heart' contains two complementary melodies. The first, played initially by Hackett on nylon-stringed classical guitar, is a slow, stately and bittersweet Tudor-like tune in D minor. The second, composed by Banks, ups the romantic content with warm keyboard strings. The two pieces are repeated, with Hackett on electric guitar and Rutherford strumming 12-string before the track segues into what became the first single from the album.

In 1974, few progressive rock bands expected to have a hit single – in fact, some actively resisted it. Record companies tried to slip them out, but viewed them more as promotional devices to get their acts on the radio. Genesis had a surprise hit the year before in 'I Know What I Like (In Your Wardrobe)', so no doubt Charisma Records thought they could repeat the success. They chose 'Counting Out Time', a song that Hackett later dismissed as 'Benny Hill put to music'. (For non-British readers, Benny Hill was a British comedian whose TV shows ran from the late 1950s to the 1980s and used sexual innuendo and seaside postcard humour. Each show invariably ended with 'dirty old man' Hill being chased by scantily-clad women to the sound of the novelty instrumental 'Yackety Sax'.)

As the only song on the album solely written by Gabriel (although, like every track on *The Lamb…*, credited to all members of the band), it uses a well-worn, descending chord sequence to detail Rael's first sexual encounter, in which he tries to follow the instructions in a manual on how to please a woman, only for it all to go horribly wrong.

Apart from the incongruity of a Puerto Rican gang member in New York consulting The Joy of Sex, the lyrics reference erogenous zones and having 'my finger on the button'. Ooerr, missus! Finally, when all goes wrong, 'Mankind handkinds through the blues'. Yes, Genesis released a single about wanking. No wonder it couldn't penetrate the charts. Musically, it relies on simple keyboard chords (although in the unusual key of E flat), with the occasional guitar interjection and an instrumental break on what sounds like a kazoo (it's actually Hackett playing through an EMS Synthi Hi-Fi guitar synthesiser – he says he was attempting to play 'like Django Reinhardt with a demented sound').

Hackett told me: 'It was very much one of Pete's jokes, which is fine. I've done humorous things myself subsequently, and not everybody is thrilled with musical jokes, but, hey, it's just a bit of fun, and it's not worth being analysed to death. It's a little pop song with a cheeky little lyric.'

Paradoxically, the 'joke' song is followed by the second single from the album, and a classic Genesis ballad that was played live right up to the band's final performances. In fact, on 11 March 2022, it was the last song Genesis ever played. Originally named 'Carpet Crawl' on the album, it became 'The Carpet Crawlers' when it was released as a single in 1975 and has been known by that name ever since.

In the story, Rael finds himself in a red carpeted corridor among the same people he saw as lifeless packaging on side one. They are all moving towards a 'heavy wooden door' somewhere above them, behind which is a chamber with a 'harvest feast lit by candlelight' and the bottom of a spiral staircase. The song's chorus repeats the line 'We've got to get in to get out', suggesting that behind the door is freedom from some sort of captivity. The 'Crawlers' are ordinary, powerless people – 'mild-mannered supermen held in kryptonite' and 'wise and foolish virgins' seeking release – while their 'callers' are, we assume, their superiors or leaders dictating their movements.

Unlike most of the songs on the album, the lyrics came first; Gabriel had some action in the story that the band had no music for. Rutherford and Banks then found a simple chord sequence, while Gabriel then spent days on his out-of-tune piano at his in-laws' home trying to hone the melody. It opens with a reprise of the tune from the bridge section of the title track – Banks thought it deserved repeating – before settling into alternating D major and E minor chords for the verses. Hackett adds distant harmony guitar lines, trying to sound like a ghostly violin, an effect he had heard on a track by Jeff Beck and The Yardbirds.

The sparse chords and simple, folk song structure make this one of the most direct and affecting tracks on the album, as well as a long-standing fan favourite. It has been covered by several bands and was re-recorded by Hackett with final Genesis vocalist Ray Wilson in 2012.

Side two ends with another song that has been resurrected by Hackett in his live shows. Rael reaches the chamber to find there are 32 possible doors, only one of which is the exit. All the others lead straight back into the chamber. Meanwhile, the people are rushing around shouting at each other and arguing over which is the door to take. Rael doesn't know who to trust – 'the rich man' standing in front of him or 'the poor man behind my back'. In the song, he tries to explain his reasoning: 'I'd rather trust a countryman than a townsman', and 'I'd rather trust a man who works with his hands'. He ends the song huddled in a corner, not knowing what to do. 'Take me away', he pleads.

Musically, 'The Chamber Of 32 Doors' contains several different styles. There is the 'orchestral' opening with heavy Mellotron chords and Hackett's expressive electric guitar introduction, sustaining the notes to mimic some of the vocal lines that will come later. Then Gabriel sings the first verse to a steady rock backing, followed by a sparser section in which his voice is supported by little more than organ and occasionally drumbeats.

There follows a surprise country feel as Gabriel sings about his trust issues, Hackett strumming his treated electric guitar in Eb major and Banks playing almost honky-tonk piano, sounding like the chords to Pat Boone's 'Love Letters In The Sand'. Hackett told me: 'Back in the day, I used to use an Echoplex, and the dirtier the wheel got, the more it sounded like chorusing ... it's one of the strange guitar sounds on *The Lamb....*' Finally, Gabriel sings 'Down here, I'm so alone with my fear', again with little more than sustained organ chords behind him, before a reprise of the orchestral opening.

The entire musical sequence is repeated, but the last section is even more sparse – just piano and what sounds like single, bell-like vibraphone notes under Gabriel's voice. The final 'take me away' is accompanied by a few piano notes that turn the minor key into a surprise major.

Phew! That's the first two sides of the double LP, generally regarded as the best single album Genesis ever made. Indeed, Gabriel is of the opinion that *The Lamb...* should have stopped there. As with many double concept albums, the band struggled to maintain the quality throughout. But there are still some great songs to come.

They include the side three opener, 'Lilywhite Lilith' – Rael, still stuck in the crowded chamber, is approached by a blind woman with pale skin who helps him find the way out. 'She gonna lead you right', says the chorus. Mostly written by Collins, the verse melody dates back to an earlier unrecorded composition called 'The Light' that Genesis performed live in 1971. A very poor-quality audience recording from a gig in Belgium shows Hackett already had some of the guitar phrases that precede the verses. Collins later composed the chorus.

The song also reprises 'The Broadway Melody Of 1974' from side one, but with new lyrics – Lilith leaves Rael in a big, round cave to face his fear. As he sits in the darkness, two golden globes float into view. This leads into 'The Waiting Room', a collage of sounds and music that came out of a jamming session at Headley Grange – indeed, it was originally called 'Evil Jam', which is what it was titled when it was used as the B-side to 'The Carpet Crawlers'. Banks told Peter Morton, Jonathan Dann and Alan Hewitt for their book *The A To Z Of Genesis*:

We just sat there and tried to frighten ourselves! Some of the early versions of that were just great before we started to record it and began to think about it too much. The first time we ever did it, and I went into that sort of melody, it sounded great because it came out of nowhere, and suddenly, there was this incredible thing going on. By the time we put it down, it had all been thought about, and it didn't sound half as good.

In the video interviews DVD in the *Genesis Box Set 1970-1975*, Phil Collins added:

Our brief on 'The Waiting Room' was darkness to light … we started off making noises, Steve with his darkness and lots of rain sticks and eerie noises, and suddenly Tony would start playing these chords – duh-duh, duh-duh, duh-duh – and, literally, it was pouring with rain outside, and suddenly Tony put these chords in and it started changing rhythm, and there was a rainbow and it stopped raining and the sun came out … it was the most cosmic thing.

And that sums it all up, really – three minutes of strange noises (including what sounds like howling cats) concluding with an explosion, followed by two minutes of pounding, mostly major key chords with a spooky keyboard lead over the top.

Track three on side three is one of the oldest compositions on the album, originally written with different lyrics to accompany an unreleased 1970 BBC documentary on Michael Jackson – no, not THAT Michael Jackson, but the British painter. It was part of a longer piece called 'Frustration', and its original lyrics were about a mad scientist making a humanoid sex doll – quite prescient, really. It even included the word 'Anyway', which became the new title when the band needed something more straightforward to come out of the sound collage.

It's a pretty piano tune by Banks that follows the pattern of the earlier version – repetitive arpeggios that move from G minor to E flat to C. Transpose it down to E minor, and what have you got? The James Bond Theme, folks, originally composed by Monty Norman (with a lot of help from John Barry) in 1962! But I digress … what's added for *The Lamb…* is a magnificent guitar solo by Hackett that pierces its way into the song and changes it from a pretty melody to something altogether darker and more dramatic.

Like 'Cuckoo Cocoon', Hackett was involved in writing both music and words for 'Here Comes The Supernatural Anaesthetist', a short interlude based mostly on the repetition of the chords G and D, played on guitar by Mike Rutherford. Once again, Gabriel threw out Hackett's lyrics and replaced them with four short, succinct lines of his own to describe the moment Rael meets Death, who is wearing a light disguise he made himself. Death delivers, well, death by puffing from a canister. Gabriel and Collins sing in unison for about 30 seconds, followed by two minutes of sprightly, fun guitar soloing from Hackett. This is probably the most cheerful Death you will ever meet.

A little Mellotron link that sounds distinctly Beatles-ish leads into the undoubted highlight of side three and, possibly, the most beautiful song on the entire album. 'The Lamia' was mostly composed by Tony Banks, although its heart lies not in his melodies or Gabriel's words but in the exquisitely melodious guitar solo from Hackett. Without it, 'The Lamia' could come across as, well, slightly creepy, but Hackett gives it heart; he provides the emotional balance the song needs.

Emerging unscathed from his encounter with Death, Rael smells a strange scent, following it into 'a long passageway lit by chandelier' to a magnificent chamber, within which is an ornate pink-water pool 'shrouded by fine mist'. He thinks he is alone, but he's not – this is the lair of The Lamia, snakelike creatures with the heads and breasts of beautiful women, who lure him into the pool and then proceed to, erm, 'taste, test and judge all that is mine'.

Unfortunately, his blood is toxic to them – 'with the first drop of my blood in their veins, their faces are convulsed in mortal pains'. They tell him they love him as they die – he then eats their dead flesh (it's garlicky). As he leaves, the lights change and 'the stage is set for you'.

So far, so Freudian. This is sex and death entwined – la petite mort, as the French call orgasm. The little death. The Lamia have their origins in Greek mythology, originally as a reference to an insane queen of ancient Libya who hunted down and devoured children. Then, by the 1st century AD (or CE as we are supposed to call it now), the myth morphed into serpentine creatures who seduced young men and ate their flesh.

The song's melody is based on a beautiful (and challenging) descending chord sequence from Banks, full of flats and sharps, sixths and sevenths. At first, the arrangement is sparse, just a grand piano and Gabriel's voice. Additional keyboards are added to separate the first two verses, then bass, drums and guitar come in for the pre-chorus as Rael 'stands astonished, doubting his sight/struck by beauty, gripped in fright'. Bass pedals supply added drama for what I guess you could call the chorus, as 'muted melodies fill the echoing hall … Rael, welcome, we are the Lamia of the pool'.

We're back to the grand piano playing more exquisite arpeggios before the sequence of two verses, pre-chorus and chorus is repeated. The Lamia are really tucking into him now, but, as we have already seen, this is an act of suicide as well as lust. Piano and keyboards provide a second interlude, with what sounds like distant seagull calls over the top, before Gabriel sings a short final verse leading into Hackett's lead guitar.

Most Genesis fans would probably rate Hackett's solo on 'Firth Of Fifth', from 1973's *Selling England By The Pound*, as his supreme instrumental contribution to the band's output. But in my view, his solo on 'The Lamia' comes a very close second. Hackett told me:

I always thought that 'The Lamia' as a song perhaps belonged on an earlier Genesis album because it is outright romanticism. Pete had a way of writing things that managed to sound both poetic and challenging in terms of his writing about stuff that's sexual, but in a very metaphorical kind of way. So it's a real pre-Raphaelite of a song … [in the solo] I tried to write something romantic for it. It's a written melody. I've always struggled to make that sequence fly; it's all over the place on the fretboard because originally that sequence was written on keyboard, so whenever I play it live, I'm always thinking, 'Are my fingers in the right place?'

'The Lamia' is followed by a musical interlude called 'Silent Sorrow In Empty Boats', taken from a line in the preceding song but originally titled 'Victory At Sea'. It is three minutes of ambient music based on a repetitive guitar phrase that sounds like it was played backwards because each note fades in, with Mellotron strings and vocal chorus over the top. After the psycho-sexual drama of 'The Lamia', it provides a moment of haunting respite and contemplation before we head into one of the most dense and complicated tracks on the album.

'The Colony Of Slippermen', which opens side four, is the second-longest song, beaten by 'In The Cage' by just one second, and is the only one to be divided into sections like a proper prog song. The narrative background is that Rael has found himself in some kind of 'freaks ghetto' populated by distorted figures covered in ugly lumps and stumps (titled 'The Arrival'). He soon discovers they have all made the acquaintance of the Lamia and their disfigurements are the result of their ordeal – and that 'you yourself are much the same as what you see in me'.

While there, he meets his brother John, who explains the only way out of their predicament is a visit to Doktor Dyper, who will, er, cut off their willies, which are then hung around their necks in yellow plastic tubes ('A Visit To The Doktor'). So, after sex and death, we have castration. Peter, are you feeling okay? Unfortunately for Rael, a big black raven swoops down and takes the dismembered member, flying off to a ravine with our hero in close pursuit ('The Raven').

Musically, 'The Colony Of Slippermen' is a Tony Banks tour de force – no-one else really gets much of a look-in. It is certainly difficult to detect much in the way of electric guitar beyond chords with a bit of phasing and chorus on them. It opens with a mysterious 105-second little tune that the band called 'Chinese Jam' before the song properly starts, introduced by Gabriel's words 'buppity-bump'. He borrows from English poet William Wordsworth for his opening line – 'I wandered lonely as a cloud' – over a jaunty synth backing in F# major, creating a nursery-rhyme effect.

It's during the first verse that Gabriel uses my favourite word on the album: slubberdegullions. It's a real word, dating back to at least 1612, and is defined as a filthy, slobbering person. As the verses unfold, we get some vivid descriptions of the creatures Rael has encountered: 'His skin's all covered with slimy lumps/With lips that slide across each chin'. As Rael realises he is the same, he cries, 'Me? Like you? Like that?', over a keyboard flourish that seems somehow to inject a bit of pathos.

This slips instantly into Part II, a more dramatic, minor-key section in which Rael learns he has to visit the Doktor to 'dock the dick' (a rather literal example of Gabriel's claim that *The Lamb...* is all about Rael finding his femininity). Then we are into Part III, in which the raven steals the severed todger. This has an insistent 'travelling' momentum as Rael chases the bird, with what is regarded as one of Banks's most celebrated synth solos that flies like the raven, swooping up and down the keyboard. Like 'Lillywhite Lilith', this section was adapted from the rare 1971 track 'The Light'.

Most of the remaining tracks on side four support the argument that *The Lamb…* may have worked better as a single album. The band were rushing to finish the recording at the time, so some of the songs may not have received the attention they really deserved. There's 'Ravine', a two-minute soundscape of spooky synth and monk-like chanting. The track was improvised by the band, with Hackett creating 'windy' effects with a fuzz box and wah-wah pedal.

'The Light Dies Down On Broadway' is a reprise of 'The Lamia' in the verses and the title track's chorus, but this time slowed down and bathed in strings. It is the only track on the album with lyrics NOT written by Gabriel – instead, Banks and Rutherford do the honours, with Gabriel laying down the story.

'Riding The Scree' is a funky workout notable for its extended solo, a fast and furious example of Banks's virtuosity and melodic invention. Hackett is notable by his absence – Rutherford plays both bass and guitar on this – while Gabriel has just a few lines of lyric. The tricky time signatures were a challenge to reproduce live, particularly for Banks, who would play his solo in 4/4 and hope he met the band at the end! 'In The Rapids' is a pretty guitar-based ballad – Hackett plays particularly beautifully here with some gorgeous major sevenths – that ends with Rael saving his brother John and then realising he is looking in his own face.

Which brings us to the closing track, 'it.' Genesis couldn't come up with a finale they all liked, and time was ticking away. Eventually, they based it on an instrumental by Banks and Hackett, with some furious strumming and a perky little guitar riff in G major. In the lyrics, Gabriel gives 32 definitions of 'it' – a reference, perhaps, to 'The Chamber Of 32 Doors'?

Perhaps. But what is 'it'? 'It is chicken, it is egg/It's in between your legs', claimed Gabriel, among other things. He also told music paper *NME* in 1975: 'It's an attempt to form substance out of negatives.' No, the *NME* didn't understand it, either. As the final song fades out, Gabriel repeats: 'It's only knock and knowall, but I like it' – a reference to the Rolling Stones album and single that had been released that year. Here he is explaining that in the *NME* article:

That's partly aimed at the Press, and it's partly a throwaway in story terms. It gets back to the thing about art. While it's fun to be pompous and sermonise, it's still an illusion, a grand illusion. If you can retain your sense of humour and be cynical, it's better. I go right inside my lyrics and laugh at them at the same time.

The band were so far behind, 'it' was recorded while the rest of the album was being mixed. In fact, *The Lamb…* wasn't released until a few days after Genesis went out on tour, playing the entire album to people who hadn't listened to it yet. When it was eventually released in late November – clad in a stark black and white sleeve showing scenes from the incomprehensible story, spread across the inner gatefold, and with a new Art Deco band logo – it baffled some critics, with *Melody Maker* calling it a 'white elephant'. But all the reviewers praised the ambition, vision and musicianship of the band, and more recent assessments have rightly placed it high in the lists of the greatest progressive rock albums of all time.

The 102-date live tour across the US and Europe brought its own difficulties and helped hasten the departure of Peter Gabriel. In the 2007 reissue interview, Phil Collins said:

> I was starting to feel that the music was being overshadowed by the visuals, which were getting a little bit out of hand … There were two things. One was 'The Lamia', where this thing came down, and Peter was in the middle of it, and sometimes the microphone cord would get caught up with the top and the bottom of it, and either it didn't move, or he had to move with it. It was almost Spinal Tap. And the worst was the Slipperman, where he came out of this inflatable dick, dressed in this horrible outfit, which sometimes got a little bit stuck on the way out, and when he did get out, the microphone could barely get near his throat, and then he was out of breath because there were a lot of words in that song.

It was on one of the early dates in November 1974 that Gabriel told the band he was leaving. He stayed until the end of the tour in May 1975, then released a statement confirming the rumours that he was out of Genesis, claiming 'the vehicle we had built as a co-op to serve our songwriting became our master and had cooped us up inside the success we had wanted' and that he wanted to spend time being a daddy and growing vegetables. His departure has undoubtedly coloured his bandmates' view of the album – Hackett told me:

> I think it was Genesis's most difficult album because when there's the uncertainty of whether you have a singer or not, that does rather colour things. Plus, when you are functioning in a series of derelict houses, or ones being built, that presents its difficulties, too … I look back on it very fondly musically, but by that time, we had all either become fathers or about to become fathers, which presented difficulties because you are thinking about taking care of children and wives and mothers … Some of us were functioning like we did when we were teenagers, but by the time you are 24, the priorities change.

But the fans' devotion to *The Lamb …* was illustrated in their reaction to the news that Hackett would feature some of the album live in concert in 2024 – nine songs including the title track and the closer, 'it.'. The only criticism was that Hackett didn't play ALL of the double LP. For me, it's the band's crowning glory and nothing else in the Genesis catalogue comes close. Indeed, I will humbly suggest that no other album in 1974 was as maddening, as inspired and as musically fascinating as *The Lamb Lies Down On Broadway*.

Genesis during the recording of *The Lamb Lies Down On Broadway*, Peter Gabriel's last album with the band.

King Crimson – *Starless And Bible Black & Red*

Key personnel:
Robert Fripp: guitars, keyboards
John Wetton: bass guitar, vocals
Bill Bruford: drums, percussion
David Cross: violin
Starless And Bible Black recorded on 23 October, 15 and 23 November 1973
(live) and January 1974 at Air Studios, London
Produced by King Crimson
Engineered by George Chkiantz and Peter Henderson
Cover design by Tom Phillips
Record label: Island (UK), Atlantic (US)
Chart placings: IT: 7, FR: 8, UK: 28, US: 64
Release date: 29 March 1974
Tracks: 'The Great Deceiver' (John Wetton, Robert Fripp, Richard Palmer-James),
'Lament' (Fripp, Wetton, Palmer-James), 'We'll Let You Know' (David Cross, Fripp,
Wetton, Bill Bruford), 'The Night Watch' (Fripp, Wetton, Palmer-James), 'Trio'
(Cross, Fripp, Wetton, Bruford), 'The Mincer' (Cross, Fripp, Wetton, Bruford,
Palmer-James), 'Starless and Bible Black' (Cross, Fripp, Wetton, Bruford),
'Fracture' (Fripp).
Red recorded on 30 June (live) and between 8 July and August at Olympic
Studios, London
Produced by King Crimson
Engineered by George Chkiantz and Rod Thear
Cover artwork by John Kosh
Record label: Island (UK), Atlantic (US)
Chart placings: UK: 45, US: 66
Release date: 6 October 1974
Tracks: 'Red' (Robert Fripp), 'Fallen Angel' (Fripp, John Wetton, Richard Palmer-
James), 'One More Red Nightmare' (Fripp, Wetton), 'Providence' (David Cross,
Fripp, Wetton, Bill Bruford), 'Starless' (Cross, Fripp, Wetton, Bruford, Palmer-James)

The Story So Far...

In 1967, brothers Michael and Peter Giles advertised for a singing organist and got non-singing guitarist Robert Fripp, from Minster, Dorset, England, to form Giles, Giles and Fripp. After several singles and an album, the band failed to make a breakthrough, so they recruited Ian McDonald on keyboards, his then girlfriend and singer Judy Dyble (ex-Fairport Convention) and songwriting pal Peter Sinfield. Fripp also recruited old friend Greg Lake, a singer and guitarist. Sinfield named the band King Crimson after a phrase he had used in a set of lyrics. The group bought a Mellotron and made their debut at the Speakeasy Club, London, in April 1969 (Dyble had left by then). Their second gig was a free Rolling Stones concert in Hyde Park in front of 500,000 people. Their debut album, *In The Court Of The Crimson King,* was an instant smash, but its overnight success and a gruelling US tour led to the band's break-up. Most members, apart from McDonald, helped record follow-up *In The Wake Of Poseidon* (1970), with the addition of Mel Collins on sax, Keith Tippett on piano and Gordon Haskell on vocals for one track. Haskell doubled on bass, and the band brought in drummer Andy McCulloch for *Lizard* (1971), which also featured Jon Anderson on vocals.

Haskell and McCulloch quit during tour rehearsals, so Fripp recruited drummer Ian Wallace and Raymond 'Boz' Burrell on bass and vocals to record *Islands* (1971). The band broke up during rehearsals in 1972, leaving Fripp as the only remaining member of King Crimson. His next recruits were Yes drummer William Scott Bruford from Sevenoaks, Kent, Derbyshire, bassist and singer John Kenneth Wetton from Family, Plymouth violinist David Cross and percussionist Jamie Muir. This lineup released *Larks' Tongues In Aspic* in 1973.

The Albums

In 2024, I went to a venue in Edinburgh and saw Robert Fripp enjoying himself. The moodiest man in prog was playing in a band with his unstoppable wife, Toyah Wilcox, and having a whale of a time – fresh from the success of their Sunday Lunch blogs in which Mr Fripp mocks being a rock guitarist and Mrs Fripp wears, ahem, revealing tops.

Why do I make this observation about the Frippster's newfound happiness? Because this is the man who once said: 'My life as a professional musician is a joyless exercise in futility.' He also pointed out, in a documentary marking the band's 50th anniversary, that the final King Crimson conglomeration was the first time he had been in a lineup in which at least one person didn't actively resent him.

We could simply dismiss him as music's Victor Meldrew if it were not for one slightly important fact: he has been responsible for some of the greatest rock music produced in the last half-century. King Crimson are the quintessential prog band – a term Fripp hates, but how else to describe a beast that embraces jazz, metal, folk, industrial, musique concrete, new wave and Indonesian gamelan?

The two albums they released in 1974 are part of a trio widely regarded as the pinnacle of their musical achievement, along with their powerful 1969 debut. In fact, it's more of a plateau than a pinnacle because there are so many albums to squeeze onto it, including *Discipline* (1980) and 1995's *Thrak*. If I am ever summoned to BBC Radio 2's desert island, those are the only possessions I would take with me (along with *The Lamb...*). Stuff Shakespeare and the bible.

What all the KC albums seem to have in common is that they were all born out of turmoil and division – in fact, no lineup lasted more than one album until the 1980s. Someone was always quitting or getting the sack. One reason is undoubtedly Fripp himself – a demanding perfectionist, he admits he can be difficult to work with. Disciplined, intellectual and relentless, with a strong vision of the music he thinks King Crimson should make and the musical knowledge and technical prowess to deliver it, he can come across as stubborn, intimidating and short-tempered with those who fail to match his high standards.

But many who have worked with him also praise his support and encouragement, and his willingness to step back and let the other musicians fulfil their potential. It was, said Bill Bruford, the only band where you could play what you liked (so long, I suspect, as Fripp liked it, too). Recently, Fripp has also revealed that, surprise, surprise, he has a sense of humour and the ability to mock himself, whether it's donning a multicoloured Mohican for his Sunday Lunch excursions or urging fellow band members NOT to say nice things about him in interviews.

But enough about the man. Let's talk about the music the band created in 1974 by going back to the end of 1973, after the release of *Larks' Tongues In Aspic*. The name of that album was coined by percussionist Jamie Muir, who was a wild and unpredictable stage performer, with a percussion kit that seemed to consist of piles of rubbish from a tip – horns, whistle, shells, balloons, kitchen utensils, baking sheets, anything that could be hit to make an interesting sound.

He also liked to thrash steel plates with metal chains, and it was reported that during some enthusiastic flailing, a part of his body got in the way, forcing him to pull out of a tour. Later, Muir gave a different reason for his departure in Sid Smith's book *In The Court Of King Crimson: An Observation Over 50 Years*. He had, he said, read Paramhansa Yogananda's book *Autobiography Of A Yogi* – indeed, he had recommended it to Jon Anderson, so Muir is responsible for Yes's *Tales From Topographic Oceans*. He went on:

After reading about two pages of this book, the tears just started pouring down my face and they just wouldn't stop. I didn't really know what was going on. I read a bit of that book each night before I went to bed, and every time I started reading it, I just started crying and crying. It was extremely bizarre, and it went on for months. It felt like it was a flood just going through and washing my personality, my past and everything away …

So it wasn't an injury that needed healing (that was management bullshit) – it was his spiritual self. Exit Jamie Muir, crying. Another departure that affected the band's recorded output was the sacking of co-founder, lighting engineer and lyricist Peter Sinfield. He had not only given the band its name but had provided the words for the first four albums – indeed, by 1970, he and Fripp were the core of King Crimson. Together, they wrote all the material on *Lizard* and *Islands* until Fripp announced he could not work with him anymore. In a 2014 interview with *Uncut* magazine, Sinfield revealed:

Robert works in a very strict, concrete, disciplined way … I'd been to Spain, and was rather full of Mediterranean fields, warmth, dusty roads, sunsets … and wanted a softer, Ahmad Jamal/Miles Davis-y feel to the music, while Robert wanted to do [harder music]. I wanted something more relaxing. In that situation, you start becoming disrespectful to your partner. And this was what happened. I started cutting him off, and he quite rightly got tired of that, to the point where he said, 'One of us has got to go, and I'm not leaving.'

The departure of Sinfield affected Fripp's output – without a lyricist to work with, his self-penned contributions would be mostly instrumental fragments that needed to be fleshed out in rehearsals. Bruford complained in Sid Smith's book: 'Had there been greater output from Robert, we'd have got on quicker and faster.' Fripp's point of view was that he was never given the time to write.

That's why a year after making *Larks Tongues In Aspic*, the only new tune to have appeared in the band's set was 'Doctor Diamond'. A frantic, riff-heavy song with a hint of Eastern scales and sinister gabbled lyrics about being the 'driver of an underground train … I shake your houses and then I'm gone' (although it's supposed to about a drug dealer, like The Beatles' 'Dr Robert'), the band could never settle on the perfect arrangement – it was either too fast or too slow – so it disappeared by September.

The lyrics had been written by Richard Palmer-Jones, a guitarist who was one of the founders of British band Supertramp. Before that, he had played in several groups in the south of England that included Wetton on bass and vocals, so the two were good friends from their early teens. In the absence of Sinfield, it became the vocalist's job to come up with lyrics for King Crimson songs.

On that album, he contributed words to a cassette of demos, but for the next release, KC had a three-week holiday in July 1973 (Fripp complained he only had three days) during which Wetton went to Munich, where

Palmer-James was living, and, in time-honoured songwriting duo style, they faced each other with a guitar or piano and a notepad to try out musical and lyrical ideas.

When KC met up in August to rehearse a new set, they had three tracks that were complete enough to play live a month later. They included 'Fracture' – solely written by Fripp – a 'Lament' about the ephemeral nature of rock fame, and 'The Night Watch', inspired by Rembrandt van Rijn's painting *Militia Company of District II under the Command of Captain Frans Banninck Cocq*, displayed in Amsterdam's Rijksmuseum.

'Fracture' is notorious for being one of the most difficult King Crimson instrumentals to play. Fripp wanted to write something that would stretch his incredible guitar talents to their absolute limits, and this fiendishly complex piece of music certainly does that. One section contains about 1,700 notes played without any break across three minutes. It has a strong resemblance to the two parts of 'Larks Tongues In Aspic' in its use of dramatic dynamics: delicate, filigree guitar notes that erupt into crunching riffs, the chords ascending in thirds, the chugging, staccato rhythm and even some blatantly similar melodies. In many ways, it is the true 'Larks Tongues In Aspic Part III'. The ultra-heavy section in the last third of the piece also heralds the later title track of *Red*.

'Lament' sounds like at least two songs bolted together – not surprising because it is made up of musical fragments dating back to 1971. Wetton sings a plaintive tale about a guitarist's rise from obscurity to his fleeting moments of fame and back again, with gentle digs at the music industry. Oh, pity the poor, exploited rock star! Gentle, stroked electric guitar chords underlie his sad croon about the rise ('I'd take the crowd with my guitar/And businessmen would clap their hands/And clip another fat cigar') and fall ('But now it seems the bubble's burst').

Perhaps Palmer-James was writing about himself – as plain Richard Palmer, he was the guitarist and main lyricist for Supertramp when they released their debut album in 1970, but quit after falling out with the rest of the band. His lyrics for 'Lament' were originally written as a downbeat country and western ballad with Supertramp's then tour manager, John Andrews. Later, Palmer-James wished he had found new words for King Crimson's song.

After two verses, the song takes a sudden left turn into metal riff territory, as Wetton belts out the lyrics over Fripp's descending guitar phrases, punctuated by sudden stops in which the guitarist moves through some chords to get back into key. Then there is a THIRD section in which everything is played at twice the speed for about 20 seconds to the end. Disjointed and unpredictable, it is probably the least effective track on the album, but it has some great aggressive interplay between guitar, bass and drums.

The third composition to appear after the August rehearsals was 'The Night Watch', one of the most delightful and musical moments on the *Starless And Bible Black* album. This illustrates an interesting dichotomy about the allegedly spiky Mr Fripp, that he is capable of composing both noisy, disturbing heavy metal monsters, and gentle, wistful ballads in minor or major-seventh keys.

'The Night Watch' demonstrates Fripp's sentimental side and his almost Beatle-like ability to pluck exquisite melodies out of thin air. Like 'Lament', this song appears to be pieced together from separate musical ideas: a slow, major-key 'overture' that builds up out of silence, beginning with gentle interplay from Fripp and David Cross; and the minor key main section containing plucked harmonics from guitar and bass. Sensibly, the 'overture' is used to bookend the song, so it feels more planned and structured.

The lyrics once again came from an earlier song Palmer-James had written with John Andrews. I said it was inspired by Rembrandt's painting, but it is more than that; it's a commentary on what it depicts, how it was staged and who was in it. One of the most famous works of art from the Dutch Golden Age of the late 16th and early 17th century, the 14ft wide painting was commissioned by Captain Cocq and his troop to hang in a banqueting hall. Completed in 1642, it uses light and shadow to turn what is, of course, a static picture into something that seems to be full of drama and movement.

Palmer-James's lyrics delve into the construction of the painting, and it is well worth looking at them in conjunction with the artwork. The opening line is 'Shine, shine, the light of good works shine', and the central characters do indeed shine as a shaft of sunlight illuminates them. 'The watch before the city gates depicted in their prime/The golden light all grimy now/Three hundred years have passed/The worthy Captain and his squad of troopers standing fast'. The painting was covered in a dark varnish for most of its life, leading to the mistaken notion that it depicted a nocturnal gathering (which is why it became known as 'The Night Watch').

'The artist knew their faces well/The husbands of his lady friends/His creditors and councillors/In armour bright, the merchant men' – Rembrandt would indeed have known the main characters in the painting, while minor figures in the background would be given the faces of other acquaintances.

'So many years we suffered here/Our country wracked with Spanish wars/ Now comes a chance to find ourselves/And quiet reigns behind our doors/We think about posterity again' – the militias were set up to guard the Protestant city against attacks from the Spanish in the Eighty Years War, which was coming to end around the time Rembrandt completed the painting.

'And so the pride of little men/The burghers good and true/Still living through the painter's hands/Request you all to understand...' – it's a lovely ending to the song, in which we stop looking at the painting, and the characters reach out to us. See what we are protecting, our comfortable, bourgeois way of life.

We've spent a bit of time on this song, but it is worth it because it is an example of the perfect synthesis of music and lyrics and one of the lasting classics of the King Crimson catalogue. Palmer-James is particularly proud of it as one of the few rock songs about a painting.

The three new tracks were played live from September 1973 before the band took a well-earned Christmas break and reconvened at Air Studios in January 1974 to work on the new album. But they discovered that some of the songs they had sounded better live than in the studio. In fact, only two tracks were wholly studio recordings, the aforementioned 'Lament' and a new one that took shape that month, 'The Great Deceiver'.

It began life as a fast and furious bass riff from Wetton – according to Sid Smith's book, he wanted Fripp to double up on guitar, but the latter was not convinced. So, after everyone else had gone home, Wetton doubled up the bassline on his own Stratocaster guitar and presented it the following day. Fripp approved, and the recording formed the opening of the song.

Most of the lyrics came from Palmer-James again, except for the line 'cigarettes, ice cream, figurines of the Virgin Mary', which were supplied by Fripp, his caustic observation on the tat being sold (and still being sold) along the Via della Conciliazione leading to St Peter's Square in Rome. That became part of the chorus and clearly influenced Palmer-James in his choice of subject matter – the Great Deceiver is Satan, the Devil. Oh, and the reference to 'health-food faggot' is not a slur on homosexuals – PJ was actually thinking of the meaty balls mixed with herbs and breadcrumbs.

With 'Lament' and 'The Great Deceiver' under their belts, the band decided to use the live version of 'Fracture' from their show at the Concertgebouw, Amsterdam, on 23 November, cutting out the audience reaction and applying a few studio tweaks and overdubs to tighten it up. They also plundered the same concert for part of 'The Night Watch'. In 2012, Wetton told website *Classic Rock Revisited*:

We couldn't do that one in the studio. We tried and tried, but it just didn't happen. So we took the introduction from the Concertgebouw in Amsterdam, where it was perfect. It might have been a little scratchy here and there, but the atmosphere was bang on. When the edit goes into the formal tune with the guitar harmonics, I thought that was very, very cool to go from a live recording into a studio recording, which was typical of Crimson in those days. Rather than most bands who would be adding applause to studio tracks to make them sound live, we were subtracting the applause from live tracks to make them sound like they were done in the studio.

The band found two more album tracks from the Amsterdam concert – improvised pieces that became 'Trio' and the title track 'Starless And Bible Black'. King Crimson were always an improvising band, right from the start in 1969, and every night of the Fall Tour in 1973 contained music that was made up on the spot by four supremely talented players. Again, we go to John Wetton's *CRR* interview to find out how it was done:

We had one golden rule that was essential, and that was that if one person started something, then the rest would follow. We wouldn't take anything away from the person who started it; we would follow them and provide support. That was absolutely brilliant because it always sounded like we knew what we were doing … Then, when it was going completely over the top and about to crash 'n' burn, we'd pull the ripcord and go into a formal piece. This was not only a relief for us onstage, but also for the audience as well, who were probably just about to commit hari-kari. Sometimes, they'd be visibly relieved when we'd go into a formal song. It did tread a very fine line that could go either way at any minute, but that's what I thought the beauty of the beast was.

Sometimes, the best contribution a band member could make was to play nothing at all. That's exactly what happened in 'Trio', a slow, delicate weaving of sound between Fripp on Mellotron, Wetton and Cross. Bruford thought about playing something, but decided instead to cross his sticks across his chest and let the others take control. He was given a credit on the song purely for his masterly self-restraint.

The title track, named after a line in Dylan Thomas's 'Under Milk Wood', is a nine-minute beast that opens slowly and hesitantly with Fripp on guitar and Cross on Mellotron and electric piano. As it builds in volume and intensity, Wetton supplies biting stabs of bass and Bruford some varied percussion before settling down to a solid 4/4 drumbeat with a slight funky feel. Fripp plays angry, atonal lines on electric guitar, and Cross switches to violin towards the end to add long, lyrical lines to a quieter ending. By the way, the full Amsterdam concert was released in 1997 under the title *The Night Watch*.

More improvisations were taken from two further gigs. 'We'll Let You Know' was an edit of a longer piece that segued into 'The Night Watch' at the Apollo Theatre in Glasgow on 23 October. Similar in style to 'Starless And Bible Black', it is a track that builds from delicate beginnings to a duel between Wetton's stabbing bass, Fripp's guitar and Bruford on percussion. Then, from the Zurich Volkhaus on 15 November came 'The Mincer', originally sandwiched between parts one and two of 'The Law Of Maximum Distress' (released in 1992 on *The Great Deceiver* box set). It's a Fripp and Wetton duel again over two alternating chords played by Cross on heavily-distorted electric piano. Vocals were added in the studio by Wetton, double-tracking himself, from Palmer-James's lyrics about a coiffured stranger the band met in Los Angeles. The track stops abruptly because the tape ran out.

So *Starless And Bible Black* turns out to be a heavily disguised, mostly live album. I know what I said about live albums, but I think this one is the exception that proves the rule. Certainly, no-one knew it was mostly live when it was released on 29 March in a striking cream cover with the words looking as if they were stamped in metal. *Rolling Stone* called it 'stunningly 'powerful', while modern reviewers such as Sea of Tranquillity describe it as 'savage, adventurous King Crimson at its very best.'

One track that was worked on during rehearsals but never made it onto the album actually had the title in the lyrics. 'Starless' was brought in by Wetton – at that stage, he just had the vocal section, which he played on acoustic guitar – but neither Fripp nor Bruford was impressed, so it was put to one side. It was resurrected for the band's early 1974 tour and unveiled at Brescia in Italy, where it already had a lot of the elements that would make it a classic King Crimson track on *Red* – the slow, moody Mellotron opening with Cross's sinuous violin melody, written by Fripp; Wetton's slow, sparse vocals and repetition of the album title; the solo bassline after the last verse, originally composed by Bruford on piano; Bruford's tinkling percussion; Fripp's one-note repetition; and, finally, the full-on, freakout coda that restates the main theme and brings the track to a triumphant climax.

The studio version would be augmented with soprano sax from Mel Collins, a frequent KC collaborator, and alto sax from 1969 member Ian McDonald. It also replaced Cross's violin with Fripp's lead guitar. Another song that debuted in March 1974 was 'Guts On My Side', which lasted for just one night, then disappeared.

In April 1974, King Crimson set off on a US tour that ultimately led to the band's demise. David Cross was the first to crack. Wetton and Bruford were getting louder and louder – Fripp described it as playing with a 'flying brick wall' – and Cross felt he couldn't keep up. He told the *Let It Rock* website in 1999:

There was less and less room for musical doubt, ambiguity, vulnerability; the more sensitive expressions that had been sustainable at the beginning of the band were not there at the end. There was also less humour. On the other hand, Bill and John achieved an incredibly powerful and imaginative coalition; they couldn't understand why their frontline didn't want to constantly wail over the top of it.

Had he possessed the technology to make himself heard over the 'flying brick wall', then perhaps Cross may have felt more part of the band. Instead, he felt detached and alienated, suffering from anxiety, and the other three sensed that, too – at the end of the tour, they took a vote and asked him to leave (although he wasn't told until the morning of the first day of rehearsals for *Red*).

This left King Crimson as a trio, the three guys on the front of the cover. Their tour over – in fact, KC wouldn't play live again until 1981 – they started recording the band's seventh studio album just seven days later on 8 July at Olympic Studios in London. 'Starless' was an easy one to get down. After all, they had played it live more than 50 times. But some of the other tracks took a little bit of work.

Fripp brought in another guitar instrumental, the heavy metal workout that gave the album its title. Yet again, he utilises the so-called 'Devil's Interval' – also known as a tritone, which means moving from, say, C to F# (as Wetton does on bass in the second half of 'Starless'). The result is a sinister, unnerving dissonance that became known as diabolus in musica – the Devil in music – during the late Middle Ages and was frequently used by heavy metal bands such as Black Sabbath (and, strangely, Daevid Allen in Gong).

In 'Red', Fripp created a stomping monster that is as low down as you can get on a basic guitar, in the key of E, before moving up into surprising chords such as Bb. It opens with a bold, rising melody line that finishes up on an unnerving flat note before the main riffs enter, employing the repetition of two or three harsh, dissonant notes to a relentless, chugging rhythm. There is a central section in which bass and Mellotron double up on a deep, ominous melody before everyone ploughs back into the main riffs again, ending on the intro melody.

It is one of the most alarming and effective opening tracks any band has employed, and the listener is left in no doubt as to what *Red* is going to do. It's going to beat you to a pulp with sound. Surprisingly, Fripp seemed unable to decide whether he liked it or not – and Bruford was unsure about its merits, even though the drummer plays like a man possessed, a cracked, discarded cymbal giving the track a unique, Fracktured quality.

In fact, Fripp was not making things easy for his bandmates – he had adopted a position of what Bruford called 'radical neutrality' that put all the decision-making responsibility on the shoulders of the drummer and bass player. In his autobiography, Bruford said:

Robert neglected to tell us that, a few days before the sessions, he had undergone a spiritual awakening comparable to the one that Jamie Muir had undergone two years earlier … Our Fearless Leader decided to withhold his opinion on all proceedings in the studio, so a minor chord was as good, or not, as a major chord, and take four was as good, or lousy, as take five. All this spiritual awakening certainly wasn't making the music any easier to produce, and with the input of gurus and seers such as Paramhansa Yogananda and JG Bennett, it is indeed a miracle that any of these records were made at all.

Instead, it was Wetton who made the decision to use 'Red'. Two more tracks were created during the Olympic Studios sessions. 'Fallen Angel' was based on a distorted guitar arpeggio Fripp came up with during rehearsals for *Larks' Tongues In Aspic* and played live as an improvisation during late 1972. Wetton composed a pretty, melodic vocal section, and Palmer-Jones wrote the lyrics. Running slightly over six minutes, the song covers 16 years in the story of a man whose brother is stabbed to death in a knife fight in the back alleys of New York. It is a moving condemnation of the waste of a life, cut short by the blade of a knife. As I write this, a 15-year-old boy has just been stabbed to death in a Sheffield school by a youth of the same age, the fourth knife murder in little more than a month. It seems angels are not just falling in New York.

'One More Red Nightmare' features a repetitive opening guitar riff of E-Ab-Bb – that ol' Devil's Interval again – that was played by Fripp and Wetton in several improvisations during the 1974 tour. Wetton wrote the lyrics for the surprisingly swinging verses, about a plane crash scare that turns out to be a nightmare – he was asleep on a Greyhound bus all the time. The track ends with another guitar arpeggio driven by Wetton's slapped bass and distorted hand claps, with Ian McDonald blowing over the top on alto sax. Like 'The Mincer', it comes to an abrupt halt after seven minutes of amazing music.

The album was completed by another live improvisation from 30 June 1974, named after the town of Providence, Rhode Island, where it was recorded. This is the only track on *Red* to include the recently-sacked David Cross and, like a lot of KC improvs of the time, it opens with his solo violin before the rest of the band slowly make their presence felt. There are undoubtedly some overdubs here as Fripp appears to be playing both a Mellotron on the flute setting and a Hohner Pianet keyboard at the same time. It takes a while to get going – Bruford waits until the track is nearly five minutes in before providing a rhythm for Wetton and Fripp to play to, and, once again, Cross is pretty much drowned out by the flying brick wall.

Released in October 1974, *Red* fared worse than its predecessor in the charts – perhaps because, by then, King Crimson had ceased to exist. The mercurial Fripp had tried to replace himself with Ian McDonald and Steve Hackett from Genesis before finally pulling the plug, announcing that the band was 'completely over forever and ever.' There was one more album in 1975, a live recording of gigs in the US.

Despite disappointing sales, *Red* was well-received at the time, and its stature has grown considerably over the years, helped by Nirvana's Kurt Cobain citing it as a major influence and *Q* magazine naming it one of the 50 Heaviest Records of All Time. Indeed, it has been described as the first heavy metal record and is certainly the heaviest King Crimson release and one that Bruford is proud to have played on. In his autobiography, he said:

> I love *Red*. It was my third attempt at recording with the band and, despite the confused and genuinely upsetting circumstances surrounding its creation, the record has a coherence and a gritty consistency that has translated well across several decades of rock and an influence beyond the pain of its making.

Even professional curmudgeon Fripp felt able to praise Bruford's drumming on the title track, and the emotional response he felt after playing 'Starless' live, telling Sid Smith in the liner notes for the 50th anniversary box set: 'There were times playing it live when I was in tears, but I've said before, and I'll say it again – the musician doesn't write the music, music writes the musician. And if you're fortunate and manage to get yourself out of the way, sometimes music like that can happen.'

King Crimson in 1974. By the time they recorded *Red*, the band had slimmed down to a three-piece following the departure of violinist David Cross (second from left).

Yes – *Relayer*

Key personnel:
Jon Anderson: lead vocals, acoustic guitars, piccolo, percussion
Steve Howe: acoustic and electric guitars, pedal steel, electric sitar, backing vocals
Chris Squire: bass guitar, backing vocals
Patrick Moraz: piano, electric piano, Hammond organ, Minimoog, Mellotron
Alan White: drums, percussion
Recorded in 1974 at New Pipers, Virginia Water, Surrey, aka Chris Squire's house
Produced by Yes
Engineered by Eddie Offord
Cover design: Roger Dean
Record label: Atlantic
Chart placings: UK: 4, US: 5, FR: 9, NL: 10, AU: 15, IT: 17, NO: 18
Tracks: 'The Gates Of Delirium', 'Sound Chaser', 'To Be Over'
All tracks written by Yes

The Story So Far...

Formed in London in 1968 by singer Jon Anderson (originally from Accrington, Lancashire), bassist Chris Squire (Kingsbury, London), guitarist Peter Banks, drummer Bill Bruford and keyboard player Tony Kaye, it took Yes three albums and a change of guitarist to Steve Howe from Holloway, London, to hone their distinctive sound. Early releases *Yes* (1969) and *Time And A Word* (1970) showed promise, but it was *The Yes Album* (1971), *Fragile* (1971) – which saw the departure of Kaye and the arrival of Rick Wakeman – and *Close To The Edge* (1972) that established them as the UK's premier prog band. Bruford left and was replaced by Alan White, from Pelton, County Durham, for 1973's *Tales From Topographic Oceans*.

The Album

On 18 May 1974 – on his 25th birthday – Rick Wakeman told Yes manager Brian Lane he was quitting the band. He later told Yes biographer Chris

Welch: 'I'd heard some of the material being put together and it wasn't the kind of music I envisioned Yes doing. 'I can't be part of something I can't contribute to, so I'm out', I told him.'

It was the first but definitely not the last time Wakeman would throw his toys out of the pram and exit Yes. But it was probably the departure that caused the most pain, both to him and the band. Yes had just had their first UK number one album in the sprawling, divisive *Tales From Topographic Oceans* and were going to start making some real money. They were all set to capitalise on their success by recording their seventh album.

But Wakeman was adamant. On the very same day, he learned his solo album *Journey To The Centre Of The Earth* had reached number one (see the chapter on that album). So that was nice. Two months later, he had a heart attack. That wasn't nice.

It is no secret in Progland that Wakeman was unhappy with *Tales From Topographic Oceans* – he called it 'Tales From Toby's Graphic Go-Kart' and famously ate a curry on stage during a lengthy Steve Howe instrumental break. He thought there were too few good ideas spread too thinly across too many sides of vinyl. There is no doubt in my mind that *Relayer* is a superior album – the prog excess was dialled down to one side-long track instead of four, and there were two songs on side two. In Yes terms, that's practically pop music.

His band members knew he wasn't thrilled by Toby's Graphic Go-Kart, but his sudden departure still came as a surprise. Drummer Alan White told *Classic Rock* magazine in 2012:

Morale was low, and obviously, people were disappointed he'd gone because Rick was an important part of the band. I think we'd started working on some of the *Relayer* material before Rick left, but he had a bad taste in his mouth after playing and touring *Tales From Topographic Oceans*, and I guess he just wanted to carry on with his own music. We all got a grip and obviously started looking for a new person, and started working as a four-piece to get the flow going. We spent a long time rehearsing and getting the basic ideas for *Relayer* together.

The hunt for Wakeman's replacement led them first to Vangelis Papathanassiou, who, with the wobbly-voiced Demis Roussos, was a member of Greek prog giants Aphrodite's Child before their 1971 split (although their best album, *666*, was released posthumously in 1972). By 1974, Vangelis had two solo albums and a couple of film soundtracks under his belt – one of which, *L'Apocalypse Des Animaux*, was very much appreciated by a certain Jon Anderson. The keyboard player was invited to jam with the band at Chris Squire's house. But things did not work out as well as they had hoped. In a 2015 interview with the website *Hit Channel*, Steve Howe revealed:

Vangelis couldn't work with song structures. Every song has its structure. When you think of Yes music, you think about our songs, which are very highly arranged. He didn't want to follow the structure. In other words, he could play one thing one day, and the other day he could play something different. We couldn't do that … I believe that Vangelis didn't want to tour. He preferred being in the studio, in a controlled environment where he could improvise. We wanted to follow the arrangement because you had to play that thing, at that time, with that way, with that sound, with that harmony, at that time.

So Yes had to say 'Adio' to Vangelis (that's informal Greek for goodbye, for all you cunning linguists). Steve Howe also recalls having a chat with Keith Emerson, who understandably pointed out that he had his own extremely successful band. So how did Patrick Moraz then enter the picture? According to former *Melody Maker* journalist Chris Welch in his book *Close To The Edge: The Story Of Yes*, it was he who recommended Moraz to the group's manager Brian Lane. Moraz himself also credits a friend, Ray Gomez, for putting him in touch with Jon Anderson.

Born in Morges, Switzerland, Moraz was practically a child prodigy as a jazz pianist, winning awards at 16 and taking lessons from French violinist Stephane Grappelli. He formed his first band, Mainhorse, in the UK in 1969 before joining ex-The Nice bassist Lee Jackson and drummer Brian Davison in Refugee. They had released their one and only album in 1974 when Moraz got the call to audition for Yes, using the keyboards left behind by Vangelis. The very next day, he was invited to join the band as an equal member – Steve Howe told *Prog* magazine in 2014: 'Once we had Patrick there, we were up and running. With his flamboyance, he brought something like fresh blood to the thing.'

By this stage, the four-piece of Howe, Anderson, White and Squire had already written and rehearsed most of the material for *Relayer*. The 22-minute track that occupies side one, 'The Gates Of Delirium', was inspired by Leo Tolstoy's 1869 novel *War And Peace* and was first played to the band by main composer Anderson on piano, 'very badly'. The other inspiration was Vangelis, the fellow who wouldn't play the same thing twice – the pair had been hanging out together a lot, and Anderson was impressed by his friend's ability to create a symphony in half an hour. Anderson told Aymeric Leroy in a 2019 interview: 'I wanted to be Vangelis. I had my keyboards creating all these ideas, and then I could still work within the flavour of the band because they were still very helpful and eager to be part of something different.'

The aggression in the track came, he said, from his anger over the Watergate scandal, Vietnam and the oil crisis. 'It was really that period of time when it was all coming to an end – you were seeing the people climbing up, trying to get on the helicopters in Vietnam, and the incredible corruption that was going on.' He had also written a beautiful minor-key ballad, 'Soon', that he thought would make a good ending to the piece, a sort of cry for hope after the tumult and destruction. 'But,' he said, 'I knew that to get to that song

I had to go through hell. And how do you create hell? You manifest it through a very dagga, chikka-chikka, a very out of control thing feeling.'

Anderson also credits a disturbing piece of electronic music called 'Wings Of The Delirious Demon' by Turkish-American composer Ilhan Mimaroglu, which consists mostly of weird and terrifying sounds – crashes, bangs, scrapes, whooshes – whizzing between the speakers and conjuring up a hellish, nightmarish soundscape. That spurred the idea that, in the Yes track, one would be entering the gates of delirium to find the light.

Like 'Close To The Edge', the first time Yes created a side-long prog epic, 'The Gates Of Delirium' opens with an overture that contains melodic hints of what is to come later – Howe plays ringing harmonics on guitar over a busy, swirling keyboard backing, with frequent stabbing chords that would be reprised later. The overture builds up until Anderson enters, singing a surprisingly upbeat verse over strummed major chords on acoustic guitar (in G if you want to try it at home). This sequence has two verses, a bridge, a third verse and a further bridge before we enter a sprightly lead guitar break mostly over alternating chords of A and C.

It moves seamlessly into a slightly more sombre minor-key section in which Anderson sings, 'Listen, should we fight forever? Knowing as we do know, fear destroys'. A second 'Listen' section gets darker: 'Slay them, burn their children's laughter', he sings, 'on to hell!' We head back into a reprise of the alternating A and C chords before plunging into the 'battle' section – pounding drums and bass, fast keyboard passages and piercing, almost screaming notes from Howe's Fender Telecaster.

At this point, Yes borrow from Mimaroglu's aural playbook by drenching the music in random percussive noises, including the sound of a rack of old car parts being pushed over. In the liner notes of the 2003 remaster of the album, Alan White explained:

Jon and I used to travel together to Chris's home studio, where we recorded the album. We would stop at a junkyard along the way and pick up parts of cars. We'd just go there and bang on things. There were springs and pieces of metal, brake and clutch plates. We'd buy them and bring them back to the studio. We built a rack and hung all these things off it, and we'd bang on them. During the recording, I pushed the whole thing over. That crash is what you hear on the album.

Breaking out into an almost triumphant section that mirrors the A to C chord sequence (only this time in E and G), Moraz and Howe trade riffs to a point where it is difficult to tell who is playing what. Eventually, this slows and almost stops – there's just a long, slow, discordant chord from Moraz that introduces the 'Soon' ballad at the end. The heart-wrenching minor key melody is played first by Howe on a ghostly, echoey slide guitar before Anderson sings the lyrics: 'Soon, oh soon the light/Pass within and soothe this endless night'.

We have entered the gates of delirium, we have passed through hell and here we are with a song of hope – 'our heart is open, our reason to be here'.

Howe returns to sweep the melody into the stratosphere, Anderson repeats the final verse and then Howe and Moraz take us home with exquisite chords and that slide guitar again.

'The Gates Of Delirium' is almost a textbook example of how to write an epic prog song – where some of the 'Tales...' tracks (particularly 'The Ancient') meander aimlessly, 'Gates...' has direction, purpose and a surprisingly simple structure. There's the overture, the upbeat song, the battle sequence and the closing ballad, and that is it.

'Soon' was deemed commercial enough to be released as a single – it didn't appear in any charts because why would you buy it when you could get the album version in its full glory? The single was backed by 'Sound Chaser', the opening track on side two. In a 2002 interview with website *Notes From The Edge*, Moraz told interviewer Tim Morse it was the first composition the band played to him on the very first day he turned up to audition:

They started to play whatever they had composed of 'Sound Chaser' at the time, which was the song part of it, and I was absolutely knocked out! I was sitting in the middle of the four of them, and even though I had seen quite a few of their shows, being a couple of yards from them was an unbelievable experience, which I will always cherish. I was so impressed, and maybe I wasn't sure if I wanted to play with them after all! It was extremely vibrant. Steve explained a few things, and I played a bit on Vangelis' keyboards. Of course, any keyboard at that time would be out of tune, except the electric piano or the organ, so I was tuning the Moogs, and I took my time while Steve was explaining the few chords and structure of that part of 'Sound Chaser'.

The band asked Moraz to come up with an introduction for the song. Thankfully, the few moments of tuning had allowed him to think of something suitable. With the band gathered round him to listen, he played the bluesy, unpredictable Fender Rhodes tinkles that open the song, sounding more like free jazz than Rick Wakeman. The band loved it, and the whole track was recorded within 30 minutes.

'Sound Chaser' shows better than 'The Gates Of Delirium' what Moraz brought to Yes. If Rick Wakeman hadn't quit, he may have offered up something cod classical – what Moraz did was to take the band into unfamiliar experimental jazz territory, and his influence rubs off on the song, which is hard and atonal, with stop-start drum and bass interjections. Both Squire and White seem to revel in this newfound musical freedom, and both rise to the occasion, with the former providing a fast, distorted bass run – he composed the main riff that runs through the track – and White playing a frantic drum solo.

Even the vocals punch out of the speakers with an untypical aggression, and Howe's Fender Telecaster adds a gritty bite to his playing. He takes a lengthy solo in the middle that's reminiscent of what he did in 'Yours Is No Disgrace' on *The Yes Album*, sometimes with gentle string backing punctuated by orchestral drums.

Anderson gets a quiet, contemplative moment, and then the song bursts into what is almost country and western – Howe was, after all, a big fan of Chet Atkins – with Moraz playing a high-pitched, screeching Moog solo that sounds like he is trying to communicate with dogs. Then everything stops for a punching chant of 'Ta-ta-ta, ta, ta', accompanied by heavy breathing, before Moraz takes another fantastic solo over Squire's funky bass. The song ends with a fast Howe guitar riff over strings and a repeat of the chant.

Wow! What a track. And what an exciting new direction for the band, less Yes, more the Mahavishnu Orchestra or Return To Forever. That's down to Moraz – the band would never have attempted something like this without him, and it's what makes *Relayer* a unique album in the band's catalogue. If it wasn't for Jon Anderson's vocals – and his sometimes incomprehensible other-worldly lyrics – you wouldn't think it was Yes at all.

Final track 'To Be Over' is more like the Yes of old – a gentle ballad combining simple, repetitive melodies from Moraz's piano and Howe's guitar and electric sitar. Anderson sings fairly cliched lyrics about 'sailing down the calming streams' and 'go gently, holding doors will open every way', sounding like a stage hypnotist. There's a pretty slide guitar melody that turns into a country-influenced solo, and a vocal section that hints at 'Awaken' on the next album, *Going For The One*. Moraz gets a little Moog solo, but it's more the sort of thing you would have expected from Wakeman. Eventually, the song returns to the opening riff over deliberately gibberish vocals before fading out.

'To Be Over' is not a Yes classic by any stretch of the imagination and is a rather pedestrian ending to the album after a side and a half of truly surprising music. It's a shame the band and Moraz didn't work together on something more musically adventurous to end side two. But that doesn't detract from the overall quality of the album.

Despite a trademark Roger Dean cover – albeit less colourful than his previous Yes artwork – *Relayer* did not sell as well as its predecessor, and Howe professed himself disappointed with the album (although it is one of Anderson's favourites). I believe the poorer sales were more of a reaction to the disappointment of Yes fans to *Tales...* and, perhaps, a reaction to the departure of Wakeman. But that didn't stop the album from getting glowing reviews from contemporary critics. Perversely, Rick Wakeman said he liked it because he DIDN'T like it – it was too freeform and jazzy for him. Had his old bandmates made a more Yes-like album, he would have been more miffed.

Would *Relayer* have been different if Wakeman hadn't quit? There would probably have been more classical flourishes and less of the experimental jazz, resulting in a softer, more symphonic sound than the abrasive touch his replacement brought to the band. He would also have been involved in the initial writing process of the album, which may have resulted in less Howe – he is all over the record with overdubs up the wazoo. But one of the things that makes *Relayer* my second-favourite Yes album (*Going For The One*, in case you are interested) is that it sounds tougher and nastier than their usual output. *Relayer* is to Yes what *Animals* is to Pink Floyd – an album with balls.

Yes in 1974, featuring Swiss keyboard player Patrick Moraz, who lasted just one album (far right).

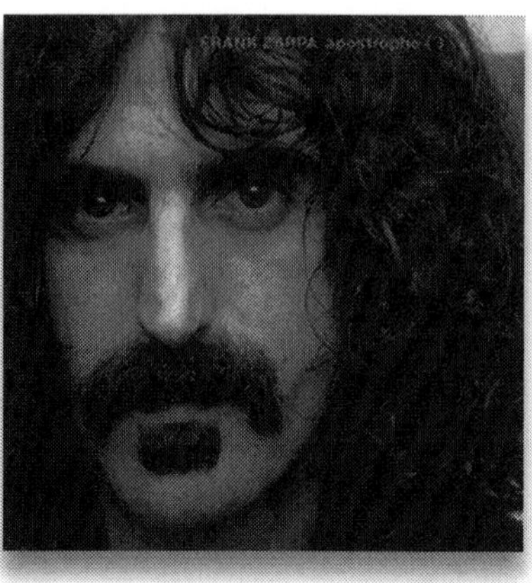

Frank Zappa – *Apostrophe (')*

Key personnel:
Frank Zappa: vocals, guitar, bass, bouzouki
Sal Marquez: trumpet
Ian Underwood: saxophone
Napoleon Murphy Brock: saxophone
Bruce Fowler: trombone
Tom Fowler: bass guitar
Don 'Sugarcane' Harris: violin
Jean-Luc Ponty: violin
Ruth Underwood: percussion, vibraphone
George Duke: keyboards
Tony Duran: rhythm guitar
Harper May: bass guitar
Erroneous (Alex Dmochowski): bass guitar
Jack Bruce: bass on 'Apostrophe'
Ralph Humphrey: drums (side one)
Johnny Guerin: drums on 'Excentrifugal Forz'
Aynsley Dunbar: drums on 'Uncle Remus' and 'Stink-Foot'
Jim Gordon: drums on 'Apostrophe'
Recorded between 1969 and 1974 at various locations, including Electric Lady
Studios, New York; Bolic Sound, Inglewood, California; and Paramount
Recording Studios, Hollywood, California
Produced by Frank Zappa
Engineered by Barry Keene, Kerry McNabb, Steve Desper, Terry Dunavan and
Bob Hughes
Record label: DiscReet
Release date: 22 March 1974
Chart placings: NO: 6, US: 10
Tracks: 'Don't Eat The Yellow Snow', 'Nanook Rubs It', 'St Alfonzo's Pancake
Breakfast', 'Father O'Blivion', 'Cosmik Debris', 'Excentrifugal Forz', 'Apostrophe'

(Frank Zappa, Jim Gordon, Jack Bruce), 'Uncle Remus' (Zappa, George Duke),
'Stink-Foot'
All tracks by Frank Zappa unless otherwise noted
'Don't Eat The Yellow Snow'/'Cosmik Debris' (single)
Released: August 1974
Chart placings: US: 86

The Story So Far...

Born in Baltimore, Maryland, in 1940, Frank Vincent Zappa was a
precociously intelligent young man inspired by R&B, doo-wop, the
modernist classical music of Igor Stravinsky and the sound experiments of
Edgard Varèse. Beginning his musical career as a drummer, he switched to
guitar, moved to Los Angeles and tried to make a living as a composer and
producer. He was briefly imprisoned after recording a fake erotic audio tape
with a female friend. In 1965, he took control of local band The Soul Giants,
calling them The Mothers. They were spotted by record producer Tom
Wilson, who signed them to Verve/MGM Records, renaming them The
Mothers of Invention. Their debut, *Freak Out!*, was only the second rock
double album. Between 1966 and 1971, Zappa released no fewer than 12
albums, including *We're Only In It For The Money*, with its *Sgt Pepper*-
pastiche cover; the UK hit, *Hot Rats*; and the film and accompanying
soundtrack album, *200 Motels*. In December 1971, Zappa was pushed
offstage by a jealous fan at the Rainbow Theatre in London, suffering
serious fractures and a crushed larynx. As he recuperated in a wheelchair,
he recorded and released jazz-influenced albums *Waka/Jawaka* and *The
Grand Wazoo*, both in 1972. In 1973, Zappa and his business manager, Herb
Cohen, formed DiscReet Records and released *Over-Nite Sensation*, which
went gold.

The Album

There have been many so-called geniuses in the field of popular (and not so
popular) music, but few deserve the label as much as Frank Zappa. In a
30-year career that saw him working almost non-stop, even while
recuperating from his fan-inflicted injuries in 1972 and fighting the prostate
cancer that eventually killed him in 1993, he recorded and released more than
60 albums. A further 67 were released posthumously by his family and the
Universal record company.

Most of his albums – encompassing pop, rock, jazz, orchestral and musique
concrete – are utterly brilliant, and a few achieved some small degree of
commercial success. But none did as well for his bank balance as his 1974
release *Apostrophe (')*. Indeed, if I were to recommend any albums as a
starting point for Zappa newbies, it would be three he released between 1973
and 1975: *Over-Nite Sensation*, *Apostrophe (')* and *One Size Fits All*. No need
to thank me.

Zappa considered himself first and foremost a composer – he wrote all the time. But he had to create his own band to play his music, because no-one else was capable of doing it (including the London Symphony Orchestra), so he was playing and gigging all the time, too. In the *Classic Albums* documentary on the 1973/74 albums, singer Napoleon Murphy Brock said, 'He was completely ahead of his time. Years, decades ahead of time. Even now, I think his music is still ahead of his time.' And guitarist Warren Cuccurullo, who worked with Zappa from 1977 to 1980, said: 'He was the mad scientist of music, period. He was the Mozart of the 20th century. He was a free-thinker, and he had an incredible intellect.'

Thanks to Zappa's work rate and the fact that he squirrelled recordings away to be used years later, it is sometimes hard to see where one album ends and another begins. In the case of *Apostrophe (')*, bass and drums for one song were laid down in 1970 for a completely different track. In fact, mixing elements from different recordings to make something new was a Zappa speciality – he called it xenochrony.

Over-Nite Sensation and *Apostrophe (')* were mostly made at the same time, and they overlap with sessions for *The Grand Wazoo*. So, on 24 May 1972, Zappa laid down the basic track for 'Uncle Remus', along with 'Eat That Question' for *The Grand Wazoo* and 'Psychosomatic Dung' for George Duke's 1974 solo album *Faces In Reflection*. In July that year, he put overdubs on Johnny Guerin's 1972 drum track for what would become 'Excentrifugal Forz'; 'Apostrophe' started life as 'Energy Frontier (Bridge)' on 8 November; 'Rollo' became part of 'St Alfonzo's…' on 10 November; 'Cosmik Debris', which – along with 'Father O'Blivion' – was played live at the end of 1972; and the whole 'Yellow Snow' sequence, which makes up most of side one, was part of the live set by May 1973.

It's clear that most of the time, Zappa had no definite idea which tracks would appear on which album, and that he tended to try them out live first before taking core members of the band to record in the studio. Generally, however, an album credited to The Mothers of Invention (or just The Mothers, as Zappa preferred), such as *Over-Nite Sensation*, had a set lineup of musicians, while a 'Frank Zappa' album, such as *Apostrophe (')*, could have a changing cast. Rehearsals could be intense – five days a week, six hours a day, with Zappa conducting proceedings and demanding a level of perfection that few musicians could hope to reach. It was a serious commitment, a full-time job with plenty of unpaid overtime.

It wasn't until June 1973 that the *Over-Nite Sensation* tracklist was finalised and the recordings mixed and edited. After that, Zappa concentrated on the *Apostrophe (')* songs, but, even then, they were mixed up with compositions that wouldn't appear until *One Size Fits All* in 1975. Central to *Apostrophe (')* is what we could call the 'Yellow Snow' sequence, four tracks that segue into each other in a sort of mini-suite that, played live, could stretch for nearly 20 minutes. In an Australian TV interview recorded in June 1973, Zappa explained:

It's about an Eskimo and his seal and an evil fur trapper. And then the evil fur trapper has something terrible happen to him, and then he has to get repaired, and in order to get repaired, he has to trudge across the tundra so that he can get to St. Alfonzo's parish at the juncture of the Columbia River delta. And he has to seek out the representative of St. Alfonzo, who is the patron saint of the smelt fishermen of Portuguese extraction. And uh, he has to find St. Alfonzo's only authorised representative here on Earth, Father Vivian O'Blivion, man of the cloth.

Over an insistent, repetitive nine-note motif, the opening song, 'Don't Eat The Yellow Snow', introduces Nanook (a stereotypical Eskimo name made popular by the 1920 movie *Nanook Of The North*) and his mother's warning, 'Watch out where the huskies go and don't you eat that yellow snow'. Why shouldn't you eat the yellow snow? Because it's got husky wee-wee in it, of course. This goes immediately into 'Nanook Rubs It', in which he comes across the fur trapper clubbing his favourite seal to death. Nanook disables the fur trapper by rubbing the yellow snow into his eyes, blinding him.

A sudden faster tempo change takes us into 'St. Alfonzo's Pancake Breakfast', which was inspired by a TV commercial in the US. Zappa told the Australian interviewer:

There's a margarine in the United States called Imperial Margarine, and they have this commercial that is in such bad taste it makes you wanna die every time it comes on. There's a young black gentleman sitting in a bed, and he's just woken up, and he's got his covers up like this. And then his young girlfriend comes trudging into the room; she's carrying a tray. She walks in, and he goes, 'Oh, boy! Pancakes and butter!' And she says, 'Good morning, your highness! No, it's not butter!' And as soon as she says 'Your highness', this crown appears on his head. It goes, 'ding!', like that. And he takes a big mouthful of these pancakes and starts shovelling it in and goes 'Mmm ... this really tastes better than butter', you know. God, it's horrible! We used to see that two or three times a night, watching science-fiction movies, and that would come on, and I would just roll all over the couch, you know. Just loathsome. So it turned into a song.

The track contains some astonishing tuned percussion playing from Ruth Underwood, who, as Ruth Komanoff, had joined Zappa's band in 1968 and married his saxophonist Ian Underwood. Zappa seemed to delight in writing seemingly impossibly fast marimba passages for Ruth, who nevertheless took them in her stride.

In Alex Winter's 2020 documentary *Zappa*, she said: 'There was no doubt that there was a person who could write music. Fantastic music. Who cared that it be played properly. And what I'm hearing was put on this Earth for me.'

The instrumental second half of 'St Alfonzo's…' was originally a standalone piece of music called 'Rollo', composed in 1971 while Zappa was recuperating from his stage plunge. Initially, it had lyrics about a man and Rollo, his dog, coming across a couple in the act of lovemaking, and was played live in late 1972 before ending up as part of the 'Yellow Snow' sequence.

We end with the frantic 'Father O'Blivion', in which the titular cleric serves up the pancakes and reveals his sexual encounters with a leprechaun and his sock. The suite fades out on the band singing 'Good morning your highness' from the margarine ad.

So far, so … uncommercial. Yet, it was this mini-suite that was to help propel *Apostrophe (')* up the US *Billboard* chart – that and a DJ in Pittsburgh. He had edited 'Don't Eat The Yellow Snow' and 'Nanook Rubs It' into a single to play on his radio show; Zappa heard it while on tour and immediately released his own version that adds the intro to 'St Alfonzo's…'. Backed with 'Cosmik Debris', it became Zappa's 17th single but the first to break into the US *Billboard* Top 100.

As for 'Cosmik Debris', that was the closing track on side A, a bluesy, stomping putdown of Eastern gurus and the gullible people who follow them. So-called 'Transcendental Meditation' had become popular among the trendy people, thanks to The Beatles and The Beach Boys helping to promote TM's creator, Maharishi Mahesh Yogi. Zappa was deeply cynical about a lot of things that attempted to exercise control over people, and was particularly scathing about politics and religion, so it was only a matter of time before he turned his savage humour on Eastern mysticism.

The lyrics of 'Cosmik Debris' begin with the 'Mystery Man' offering his services to Zappa for 'his regular fee' to help him reach nirvana. Zappa is dubious – in the chorus he sings: 'Who you jivin' with that Cosmik Debris?'. Eventually, Zappa gets fed up with the fraudulent mystic's gibberish and tells him to 'take your meditations and your preparations and ram it up your snout'. He then proceeds to hypnotise him, rob him of all his belongings and enjoy a sex act with his wife.

Zappa talks through most of the song – as he did on 'Montana' and 'I'm The Slime' from *Over-Nite Sensation* – for reasons he explains in the *Classic Albums* video:

If you try and sing a complicated text – I mean, not a collection of words that are readily apparent. If you start talking about 'the leaves', 'the love', 'baby' – those are words you've already heard a million times. The text doesn't matter because you can take those words and sing them all over the place, and people will still understand the idea. But if you are talking about concepts or using phrases that are unfamiliar, it's hard to get that information across if you are singing elaborate musical lines at the same time. I do that every once in a while just to be nasty, but most of the time, if the idea goes out there some place, I try and talk it.

In fact, Zappa frequently said he would rather just write instrumental music, but he recognised that the average music fan wants words to sing along to. So he sang stuff, too, but not about the usual teenage preoccupations of cars and girls – Zappa explored his own interests and gave an honest reflection of his point of view. Exactly what he is singing about on 'Excentrifugal Forz' is anyone's guess – the lyrics seem to be little more than wordplay. Even the title is made up of a mixture of words: 'Eccentric' and 'centrifugal' with 'Forz' spelt and pronounced more like German or Italian.

The basic track of Johnny Guerin on drums, Jean-Luc Ponty on violin and Zappa on bouzouki was recorded in July 1972 (some say 1969, with Sugarcane Harris on violin, but I'm following the exhaustive session details on the Information Is Not Knowledge website) with Zappa overdubbing guitar, bass and vocals in the summer of 1973. The lyrics mostly defy understanding – 'The clouds are really cheap the way I seen them through the forts/Of which there is a half-dozen on the base of my resorts'. Eh?

There is a reference to 'Korla Plankton' and a 'Hammond organism', which Zappa experts have linked to 1950s Hammond organ player Korla Pandit. But I'm not sure if this is anything more than a stream of consciousness over a pounding beat and lightning-fast riffs. Anyway, it's over after just 93 seconds.

The title track is a busy instrumental recorded in November 1972 with Zappa and Tony Duran on guitars, Jim Gordon on drums and Jack Bruce on bass. Gordon was a session drummer who played with Delaney & Bonnie, Derek & The Dominoes and Traffic. Sadly, he murdered his mother during a psychotic episode in 1983 and was locked up until his death 40 years later. Bruce was best known as one-third of Cream, the 1960s supergroup that also featured Eric Clapton and Ginger Baker. The music is pretty much a jam based on a simple riff and two or three repetitive chords. Most of the lead work is actually down to Bruce playing high up on his bass. Apparently, Zappa didn't enjoy playing with Bruce because the latter's style was 'too busy'.

'Uncle Remus' came about when Zappa produced a demo of tunes he had composed with George Duke, originally for a Duke solo album, before deciding he would use it himself. It's almost a pop song, with a gorgeous piano opening by Duke, but no pop song would have lyrics like these – Zappa pens an anti-racism song that appears to be from the standpoint of a black man being sprayed from a police water cannon. 'Have you seen us, Uncle Remus?' he sings, a reference to the fictional narrator of African-American folk tales in Joel Chandler Harris's controversial 1881 book, and in the equally problematic *Song Of The South*, a 1946 film by Walt Disney.

There is also a reference to 'knocking the little jockeys off the rich people's lawn' – these were statues frequently depicting racist caricatures of black jockeys that were originally placed in front gardens as hitching posts for horse riders in the US, but later became associated with wealthy white American racists.

There's a slight melancholic feel to the track, which reminds me of something Carole King might have composed for one of her solo albums (although she wouldn't have sung such politically-charged lyrics). Zappa's vocal is supported throughout by 'Tina, Debbie & Lynn' – alias Tina Turner and her 'Ikettes', Debbie Wilson and Linda Simms.

The album ends with a Zappa classic, the hilarious 'Stink-Foot' – bromodosis has never been so entertaining. The music comes from a completely different track, a bluesy cover of Muddy Waters's 1950 song 'I'm A Rollin' Stone' (itself a remake of 'Catfish Blues', which dates to the 1920s), recorded in March 1970 with Sugarcane Harris on violin, Ian Underwood on keyboards and sax, Max Bennett on bass and Aynsley Dunbar on drums. In early 1974, Zappa erased everyone from the tracks except Harris and Dunbar, overdubbing new vocals, keyboards, sax and bass.

The hilarious lyrics explore the dangers of wearing tennis shoes or a python boot for too long, and the 'exquisite little inconvenience' that can result. He sings: 'Y'know, my python boot is too tight/I couldn't get it off last night/A week went by and now it's July/I finally got it off and my girlfriend cried 'You got Stink-Foot!'' We then delve into something that Zappa labelled 'Conceptual Continuity', the idea that everything in his music is somehow linked. So in 'Stink-Foot', we are introduced to Fido the poodle, a breed of dog that Zappa found so ludicrous he mentioned it in several other songs. In fact, Zappa owned a poodle that he called Thrunobulax.

'Stink-Foot' contains plenty of examples of Zappa's most underrated talent – his guitar-playing. He could create a piercing, ugly sound from his Gibson SG, coupled with a lightning-fast fingering style that enabled him to wrench out unpredictable bluesy melody lines.

Apostrophe (') was not just a commercial success in the US, it was critically-acclaimed, too, with *Rolling Stone* magazine calling it 'a Mother of an album', and even the curmudgeonly Robert Christgau, usually contemptuous of anything even slightly clever, admitting: 'Disillusioned acolytes are complaining that he's retreated, which means he's finally made top ten, but that's just his reward for professional persistence.'

Of course, Zappa probably couldn't have cared less if the critics loved it or hated it. In fact, I think he quite enjoyed watching his (mostly right-wing) detractors get their knickers in a twist over his music – although it angered him that one phone call from an arrogant, outraged little philistine could get him banned from the radio waves. As he said in his autobiography, *The Real Frank Zappa*:

It's never mattered to me that 30 million people might think I'm wrong. The number of people who thought Hitler was 'right' did not make him 'right'. The same principle should be applied to everyone who has an individualistic attitude. Why do you necessarily have to be wrong just because a few million people think you are?

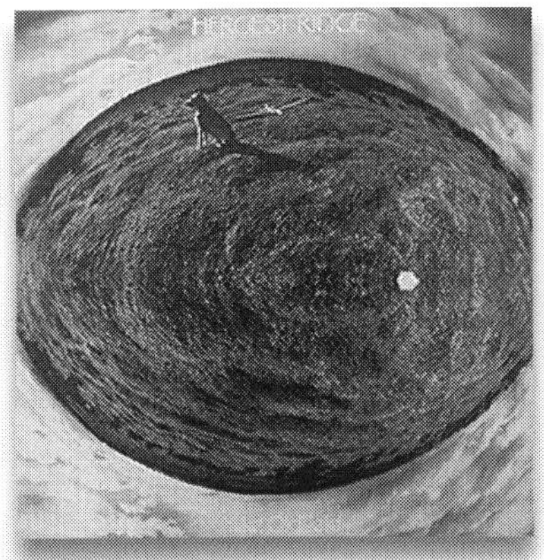

Mike Oldfield – *Hergest Ridge*

Key personnel:
Mike Oldfield: electric and acoustic guitars, bass guitar, glockenspiel, sleigh bells, mandolin, nutcracker, timpani, gong, Spanish guitar, Farfisa organ, Lowrey organ, GEM Gemini organ
June Whiting: oboe
Lindsay Cooper: oboe
Ted Hobart: trumpet
Terry Oldfield: flute
Chilli Charles: snare drum
Clodagh Simonds: vocals
Sally Oldfield: vocals
David Bedford: choir and strings conductor
Recorded in the spring of 1974 at The Manor Studio, Shipton-on-Cherwell, Oxfordshire
Engineered and produced by Mike Oldfield and Tom Newman
Record label: Virgin
Release date: 30 August 1974
Chart placings: UK: 1, NL and AU: 12, US: 87, CA: 91
Tracks: 'Hergest Ridge (Part One)', 'Hergest Ridge (Part Two)'
All tracks written by Mike Oldfield

The Story So Far...

Born in Reading, Berkshire, in 1953, Michael Gordon Oldfield started learning guitar aged ten, and by 12 was playing in folk and youth clubs. In 1968, he formed a duo, The Sallyangie, with his sister, Sally, releasing their sole album *Children Of The Sun* in 1969. After they broke up, he was briefly in the band Barefoot with brother Terry before joining ex-Soft Machine Kevin Ayers' backing group, The Whole World, as a bass player. He appeared on Ayers's albums *Shooting At The Moon* (1970) and *Whatevershebringswesing* (1971) before leaving to become a session musician and bassist for the Arthur Louis Band, recording at Richard Branson's studios in Oxfordshire. By this time, Oldfield had a demo tape of a lengthy instrumental he called 'Opus One' – Branson heard it and gave him a week to record what became part one of *Tubular Bells*. Part two was recorded two years later, and the album became the first release on Branson's newly-formed Virgin Records label. It rocketed to number one in the UK, Canada and Australia, and was a hit in the US, Spain, New Zealand, Germany and the Netherlands.

The Album

Mike Oldfield was in a bad way. Hunkered down in a rundown house in north-west Herefordshire, a few miles from the Welsh border, he was downing booze and swallowing Valium in a desperate attempt to conquer crippling panic attacks, while smothering the telephone with a pillow. In his 2007 autobiography *Changeling*, he said:

All the guilt, the emotional anger, the loss that I'd experienced in the past, it was all there inside me, like a ball of emotional energy. Many situations would bring back memories of my childhood: key moments like the fight with my dad would be triggered by certain things, like if I felt physically threatened. If I felt an injustice, that was a big one; it plugged into lots of things. I would often feel completely out of control, almost working on automatic due to my deep-seated fears and psychological conditioning.

The trigger was fame – sudden and overwhelming. Seemingly overnight, the fragile 20-year-old had been catapulted from virtually unknown session musician to world-famous British rock star, facing pressures and demands that, thanks to a difficult childhood with a mentally ill, alcoholic mother and bouts of depression, he was ill-equipped to cope with. Everyone wanted a piece of Mike Oldfield – while he was rapidly going to pieces.

The sudden fame was all thanks to *Tubular Bells*, the album he recorded almost single-handedly at Richard Branson's country house studio in the picturesque English village of Shipton-on-Cherwell. Released in May 1973, it initially sold slowly despite fulsome praise from critics. Then the sinister, tinkling opening notes to part one (in 15/8, time signature fans) were used as the theme to the head-turning demon-possession horror movie *The Exorcist* – and all hell was let loose.

Tubular Bells soared into the UK top ten in March 1974 and stayed there for a year, reaching number one for a week. Eventually, it would sell 15 million copies worldwide, three of those millions in the UK. Virgin were, of course, cock-a-hoop as the success of the album helped establish the label as a serious player in the music business, and Branson understandably wanted to milk it for all it was worth. This was while Oldfield was earning just £25 a week plus luncheon vouchers. In his autobiography, he revealed:

Before I knew it, I was hanging on for dear life to my sanity. Richard wanted me to take *Tubular Bells* on tour, but I just couldn't imagine it; I was fending off panic at every second … I would get phone calls from him saying, 'They really want you in the States!' I was getting requests from just about everywhere to go and perform concerts, but I just wasn't psychologically capable of doing that.

There were a few live performances, starting with the album launch. Reluctantly, Oldfield agreed so long as Branson gave him his Bentley (he did) and, with the help of musicians such as composer and conductor David Bedford, Mick Taylor of The Rolling Stones and Fred Frith from Henry Cow, he played both parts without a break at the Queen Elizabeth Hall in London. Oldfield thought it was a disaster, so he was shocked when the 800-strong audience gave him a standing ovation.

Virgin also wanted a follow-up as quickly as possible – his contract was for ten albums – but Oldfield's musical cupboard was bare after putting every idea he had into *Tubular Bells*. In a bid to escape the pressure cooker, he and his then-girlfriend jumped into Branson's clapped-out Bentley and went searching for a house in the country. They went west, then north, finally coming upon a little house for sale in the Herefordshire village of Kington. It was called The Beacon, it was 800ft up Bradnor Hill and it cost £12,000 – Branson bought it for him and deducted the cost from his royalties. It had amazing views of the brooding Black Mountains and, in particular, a large, elongated hill called Hergest Ridge.

The girlfriend didn't stay long – the house was bitterly cold and the small log fire fought a losing battle against the wind that whistled through the walls. But Oldfield loved the seclusion and the spectacular views, and he would sit absorbed in the scenery, playing traditional tunes with a local musician at a nearby restaurant in exchange for free wine and flying model gliders – while wondering what the hell to do with his difficult second album.

It was at the restaurant that he learned about the legend of the black dog of Hergest (pronounced 'Hargest' with a hard 'g') Ridge – a legend that may well have inspired the Sherlock Holmes story, *The Hound Of The Baskervilles*.

The legend claims that back at the tail-end of the 15th century, an evil squire called Thomas Vaughan – who lived at Hergest Court, which can still be seen today – was decapitated at the Battle of Banbury in 1469, fighting for the Yorkist cause in the War of the Roses. As his severed bonce bounced on the ground, there was a fearsome howling, and his faithful black bloodhound bounded up, seized the head in its powerful jaws, and ran home with it to Hergest Court.

Vaughan was buried in Kington church (along with his wife, who was just as evil – she was known as Ellen the Terrible for killing her cousin), but locals claimed his ghost roamed abroad in the shape of a black bull, accompanied by his spectral bloodhound. Ironically, for Oldfield, 12 priests attempted to carry out an exorcism at Hergest Court, for which his debut album would have provided a suitably chilling soundtrack.

Branson kept up his campaign to unclog the tap of Oldfield's creative juices. What do you need to start writing again, he asked. Oldfield wanted a Farfisa organ – and he looked out of his window one day to see Branson staggering up his drive with the heavy, monstrous instrument in his arms. Virgin also delivered a mixer and four-track recording machines. Oldfield now felt obliged to sit down and piece together what would become his second album, *Hergest Ridge*. He didn't want to do it, but didn't think he had any choice. In his autobiography, he explained:

> *Hergest Ridge* was a real struggle to begin with, but having pushed myself to get started, it was like piling twigs on a fire. It took on a life of its own, with its own momentum, and it became self-sustaining. Musically, it was nothing like *Tubular Bells*. It had trumpets and tin whistles, all different kinds of influences that were in some way echoes of the place I was living in … I was running on nearly empty tanks when I was putting it together, but I managed to cobble together some kind of album.

With the demos done, he moved to Branson's studios and, with the help of Tom Newman, who had worked on *Tubular Bells*, he turned his rough musical ideas into two sides of a long-playing record. He said: 'My heart just wasn't in it. I had to squeeze it out; it was like getting the last bit out of the toothpaste tube.'

Split into two parts, *Hergest Ridge* opens with a single, drone-like keyboard chord in E major. A distant tin whistle seems to call from the hills, like wind blowing through the rocks. Slowly – very slowly – a gentle marching rhythm develops as the keyboards cycle between E major, D major and F sharp minor. Electric guitars and bass take over, cycling through a series of mostly minor chords before Oldfield ramps things up with his trademark lead guitar sound, over a wordless choir conducted by his friend from the Kevin Ayers days, David Bedford.

After cycling through virtually the same chords for about seven minutes, the music builds to a crescendo, with spiky lead guitar improvisation and pounding timpani before fading into a delicate, almost medieval soundscape of acoustic guitars, sinuous oboe and muted trumpet. This develops with the help of electric guitar into interlocking melodies, none of which really stand out, until a squeal of guitar heralds a complete change in mood. A bass plays a repetitive riff in two minor chords, then a series of descending notes under gentle organ chords, before electric guitar picks out a lyrical melody, probably the first memorable tune we've heard so far.

Everything slows down for a big finish as Oldfield's high-pitched lead guitar gives way to the wordless choir, sounding all church-like as it blends some exquisite harmonies over acoustic piano. And then – yes, some tubular bells, clanging away until we return to the tin whistle sound over gentle keyboards from the opening.

Part Two opens as Part One leaves off, with a sombre, introspective introduction of minor-key acoustic guitar chords and muted keyboards. The acoustic guitars take over a bit with a tin whistle melody (probably played on a keyboard because there is no mention of the instrument in the liner notes) before Clodagh Simmonds and Sally Oldfield sing what appears to be nonsense words (and foreshadow Oldfield's work on the later *Incantations*). The melody is very pretty, particularly when it hits a major key and sounds like the sun coming out.

Electric guitar takes over briefly, then a tinkling mandolin is played over acoustic guitars, followed by a slow, quieter section on bell-like keyboards. Things burst into sudden life with the addition of powerful organ chords and a heavy minor-key riff on guitar (the same one the bass did in Part One), while Oldfield improvises over the top.

The heavy stuff comes to a sudden stop, and we're back into the gentle, folky acoustic guitar and indistinct keyboards before Part Two exits with a repeat of the earlier choral section, this time augmented by Bedford's orchestra, fading into a few seconds of Spanish classical guitar.

Gentle, pastoral, even morose, *Tubular Bells II* it ain't. Indeed, I would challenge anyone – even Oldfield himself – to hum any of the themes from memory. But there is an honesty and openness to *Hergest Ridge* that is very appealing – the overall sound does evoke the British countryside, allied to a sense of yearning or searching. In many ways, it is early New Age music, more of a soundscape than a series of distinct melodies linked together.

The album was released to lukewarm reviews – the critics felt it was a pale imitation of *Tubular Bells*. That didn't seem to stop the fans, who sent *Hergest Ridge* to number one – indeed, Oldfield became only the second artist in history to replace himself at the top of the album charts when the new album made way for a surprise comeback by its predecessor. (The first artist? The Beatles, of course.)

The problem, I guess, is that Oldfield really didn't have enough good ideas for 40 minutes of music, an issue he would rectify for 1975's *Ommadawn*. It was also recorded in a rush, so some of the melodies are buried in the mix. An orchestral version taken on tour later in 1974, with Steve Hillage of Gong playing guitar, reveals its melodic beauties more readily.

But it is still an amazing achievement considering its creator was still in his early 20s and teetering on the edge of a breakdown. Perhaps the only way to really listen to it is while walking Hergest Ridge, with a view of the wild, rolling hills, the breeze in your hair and the distant ghostly sound of Black Vaughan and his faithful bloodhound.

Robert Wyatt – *Rock Bottom*

Key personnel:

Robert Wyatt: vocals, keyboards, percussion, slide guitar, James' drum, Delfina's wineglass, Delfina's tray and a small battery

Mike Oldfield: electric guitar

Gary Windo: bass clarinet, tenor saxophone

Ivor Cutler: voice, baritone concertina, harmonium

Alfreda Benge: voice

Mongezi Feza: trumpets

Fred Frith: viola

Hugh Hopper: bass guitar

Richard Sinclair: bass guitar

Laurie Allan: drums

Recorded between February and May 1974 at Delina's Farm, Little Bedwyn, Wiltshire; The Manor Studios, Oxfordshire; and CBS, London

Producer: Nick Mason

Engineers: Steve Cox (Delfina's Farm & The Manor, Dick Palmer & Tony Bird (both at CBS, London))

Record label: Virgin

Release date: 26 July 1974

Chart placings: US Billboard FM Action: 13

Tracks: 'Sea Song', 'A Last Straw', 'Little Red Riding Hood Hit The Road', 'Alifib', 'Alife', 'Little Red Robin Hood Hit The Road'

All songs by Robert Wyatt.

'I'm A Believer' single recorded at The Manor Studios shortly after the Rock Bottom sessions

Producer: Nick Mason

Record label: Virgin

Release date: September 1974

Chart placings: UK: 29

Tracks: 'I'm A Believer' (Neil Diamond), 'Memories' (Hugh Hopper)

The Story So Far...

Born in Bristol in 1945 but living near Dover (and going to school in Canterbury), Wyatt was taught drums by visiting US jazzer George Neidorf. He became friends with Australian beatnik Daevid Allen, who lodged with his parents in 1961 and formed a trio with bass-playing friend, Hugh Hopper. When Allen left, Wyatt and Hopper formed The Wilde Flowers with guitarist/vocalist Kevin Ayers, Richard Sinclair and Hugh's older brother Brian. Allen returned, and the band split into two – half went on to form Caravan, while Wyatt, Allen, Ayers and keyboard-player Mike Ratledge became The Soft Machine, named after the 1961 novel by William Burroughs. Their first and only single, 'Love Makes Sweet Music', was released and flopped in 1967. Allen left after being denied entry back into the UK following French appearances, leaving the band as a three-piece to record a debut album. Ayers left after a 1968 US tour supporting Jimi Hendrix, replaced by Hugh Hopper for a second album, imaginatively titled *Volume Two*. Their third album (called, wait for it, *Third*) added a horn section but showed a growing split between instrumental jazz and Wyatt's quirky songs. Wyatt recorded a solo album, *An End Of An Ear*, before leaving Soft Machine following their all-instrumental album, *Fourth*. With David Sinclair (ex-Caravan) on organ, Dave MacRae on keyboards, Phil Miller (ex-Delivery) on guitar and Bill MacCormick (ex-Quiet Sun) on bass, he formed Matching Mole (the name a pun on the French translation of Soft Machine) and released a debut album in 1972. Second album *Matching Mole's Little Red Record* soon followed. Then, during a birthday party for Gong's Gilli Smyth and musician June Campbell Cramer (aka Lady June), he fell out of the fourth-floor window of the latter's Maida Vale home and broke his spine.

The Album

It was the alcohol that saved him. Doctors said it had relaxed his body, so when he hit the pavement, he went *flump* instead of *ker-rack*. Of course, you don't walk away from falling from a fourth-floor window (or it may have been from a drainpipe while trying to escape a 'scene' in the bathroom). So Robert Wyatt ended up in a wheelchair for the rest of his life.

The accident was shocking but, to some people, not entirely surprising. Wyatt was the sort of person things happened to. He liked a drink – I mean, a lot of us do, but he *really* liked it. Being drunk was almost like a normal state – being really drunk meant he was so inebriated that he was hallucinating.

And he was physically quite reckless. On stage, he would perform stripped to the waist, arms flailing about like an octopus plugged into the mains – Mike Oldfield recalled trying desperately to keep up with him when Wyatt filled in as the drummer for Kevin Ayers's band, describing his playing as 'like having an epileptic fit'.

Being turned into a wheelchair-bound 'incontinent giant', as he once called himself, would have dampened the spirits of anyone, not least someone as physically active as Wyatt. But, by all accounts, he seemed to come to terms with his situation very quickly. In his authorised biography *Different Every Time*, written by Marcus O'Dair, he is described as actually enjoying being bedbound in hospital: 'People bringing me breakfast, making my bed like Little Lord Muck … this is the life!', O'Dair quotes him as saying. Later, Wyatt added: 'I think if God had invented wheelchairs, he would have presented them as a natural alternative to legs for those who preferred the choice.'

The strange thing is that, almost thanks to the accident, he produced what is regarded as his musical masterpiece. Wyatt puts it down to the fact that, unable to play drums, he had to focus more on his singing and keyboard-playing. He told Martin Aston for *Q* magazine in 1991: 'If anything, being a paraplegic helped me with the music because being in hospital left me free to dream, and to really think through the music.'

He was also lucky to have poet Alfreda 'Alfie' Benge as his partner. She was at the party with him when he went on his drunken plunge; she sat beside his bed for months as he recuperated at Stoke Mandeville hospital in Aylesbury, Buckinghamshire; she married him and became his carer, his lyricist, his muse, his everything. They met when Matching Mole performed a benefit gig at the Roundhouse in London for the Upper Clyde Shipbuilders consortium, which had gone into liquidation. Wyatt spotted a 'cool, very hip and very beautiful girl' in the crowd and made a beeline for her.

Soon, they were living together in Alfie's London tower block flat, but it was in Venice that Wyatt started composing the music that was intended for the third Matching Mole album but would become *Rock Bottom*, using a cheap Riviera keyboard she bought him while she was filming Nicolas Roeg's psychological horror movie *Don't Look Now*. The keyboard had a function that was a key influence on the music Wyatt was creating. He told Aymeric Leroy in 2001:

I could control the speed of the vibrato. Generally, where you have a fixed vibrato on, for example, the Hammond organ, you've got a yo-yo-yo-yo-yo-yo … whereas on this keyboard she had, it was a cheap one, almost like a toy, about three octaves, not much more, but I could find a vibrato on it that kind of matched the natural vibrato when I'm singing so that I could really write notes and immediately imagine them sung, and part of the chord, and place my voice in it. This was a real breakthrough and, I think, the words came during that time … a lot came from being surrounded by waters in the lagoons of Venice.

After the accident, he spent six weeks in a virtual coma, pumped full of painkillers – even when he woke, he seemed to be drifting in a dreamlike state, with jumbled, disconnected words floating through his head, and it is from that experience that the hazy, disorientating atmosphere of *Rock Bottom* comes from. Later, when he was allowed to move around the hospital in his wheelchair, he found an upright piano in the visitors' room, where he shaped the album, committing 40 minutes of music to memory.

When he left hospital in January 1974, friends rallied round to help. Pink Floyd and Soft Machine raised £10,000 from two benefit shows, while model Jean Shrimpton donated her car and actress Julie Christie bought them a flat in London.

By far the most influential act of charity came from wealthy Spanish philanthropist and arts patron Delfina Entrecanales, who knew Wyatt through his half-brother. Her father had sent her to England at the end of the Spanish Civil War, where she bought a farm in Little Bedwin, Wiltshire, and offered it to Wyatt and Alfie as a place to both recuperate and create. A van full of recording equipment was parked outside, and cables ran through the windows.

So in the peaceful surroundings of Little Bedwyn – population 250 in 2011, so it must have been practically empty in 1974 – Wyatt began recording, mostly with his Riviera organ and piano but adding random percussion using a tin tray and a toy drum owned by one of Delfina's sons. He was not an accomplished keyboard player, certainly not compared to the ivory ticklers he had worked with in Soft Machine and Matching Mole. Inspired by Richard Wright's work in Pink Floyd, he concentrated on creating an atmospheric backdrop for his voice with chords and simple harmonies.

There was nothing really intellectual or planned in his approach – the musical ideas he had were little more than basic sketches. His approach was to simply try to create something he would want to listen to, and perhaps others would enjoy it, too. If it sounded all right, he went with it – and stopped when he got bored. He told Leroy: 'If you have a rhythmic device or a chord sequence that sounds nice, you think, yeah, a lot of things are nice for about two minutes, but if you keep playing it morning and night for about two weeks, over and over again, if you still think it's nice, then you're on to something.'

So Wyatt was on to something, but he needed some help to flesh out his solo efforts. Before his accident, when he was planning to put together a new Matching Mole lineup, he had contacted Pink Floyd's Nick Mason and asked him to produce the third album. The two drummers had known each other since 1967, when Floyd and Soft Machine were regulars at the UFO club in London. But on the very same day Mason received the invitation, he also learned about Wyatt's accident the night before.

Six months later, Wyatt was back in touch, asking Mason to produce the overdubs for *Rock Bottom*. A veritable who's-who of Canterbury Scene musicians and great British eccentrics was assembled at Richard Branson's Manor Studios, all keen to help Wyatt resurrect his career.

There was Richard Sinclair on bass, who was in Canterbury origin band Wilde Flowers with Wyatt in the early 1960s, followed by Caravan and, in 1974, Hatfield and the North. Another bassist was Wyatt's old Soft Machine pal Hugh Hopper, while Laurie Allan, ex-Delivery, Gong and a former Alfie boyfriend, provided drums at CBS Studios.

Mike Oldfield, who was hanging around the Manor Studios after recording *Tubular Bells*, played electric guitar and made some crucial suggestions about the tracks. Fred Frith – ex-Henry Cow – played viola, while another Henry Cow contributor, South African Mongezi Feza, brought his trumpet, and Gary Windo, who was earmarked for the new Matching Mole lineup, played sax and bass clarinet.

Wyatt also made use of Scottish poet and musician Ivor Cutler, known to Wyatt through his broadcasts on the BBC Home Service and his appearance as Buster Bloodvessel, the conductor in The Beatles's *Magical Mystery Tour* movie.

The results sounded like no-one else on earth. Indeed, it still sounds like no-one else except Robert Wyatt. First, there is his voice – straightforward, plaintive, unshowy, sometimes delicate and childlike, with a very English, self-deprecating tone. Then there are the lyrics, which couple the simplicity of nursery rhymes with the surreal imagery that can only come from being stoned on painkillers for weeks on end, with plenty of watery references from gazing into the lagoons of Venice. They are also drenched in love and yearning for Alfie.

Like his old Soft Machine playmate, Daevid Allen, Wyatt is not afraid of sounding childlike and vulnerable, and of injecting dashes of self-deprecating humour. Like Richard Sinclair, he will also dispense with words entirely and use his voice almost like a muted trumpet.

Finally, the music. Led by simple piano and keyboard chords rather than drums and bass, it is almost the antithesis of progressive rock at the time, eschewing instrumental dexterity for a slightly ramshackle and tortured approach that nevertheless seems to bypass the ears and go straight to your heart. This is Wyatt exposed in all his gentleness, neediness and vulnerability.

The album opens with what is generally regarded as Wyatt's greatest work, the sublime 'Sea Song', a gentle, swaying ballad based on piano and keyboard, with gentle taps from Wyatt on James's toy drum. It opens in Ab with a pretty, melodic intro that is repeated later as a sort of middle-eight – Wyatt contrives to end up in E major and, from then, shifts unexpectedly into F#m for the vocal.

Wyatt sings amusing lines comparing Alfie to a creature that is 'partly fish, partly porpoise, partly baby sperm whale' but he can't understand her in the morning 'when it's time to play at being human for a while'. She is a 'seasonal beast' this sea creature, he realises, 'your madness fits in nicely with my own'.

The two verses are separated by a strange, discordant piano improvisation that only someone who can't play very well could have come up with, and after the second verse, there is a lengthy outro taking up half the length of the track in which Wyatt sings wordless vocal noises over alternating D major and E major chords. Sinclair is in there somewhere, playing (for him) very simple basslines.

'A Last Straw' opens with a similar, dreamlike approach, with gentle piano notes over Hopper's slow, seductive bass and unobtrusive percussion from Allan. Then it builds into something with a bit more urgency and pace, belying the humorous nature of Wyatt's lyrics, once again dedicated to Alfie, in which he suggests 'seaweed tangled in our home from home reminds me of your rocky bottom'. The line gives the album its title, although some fans thought it was a general reference to Wyatt's condition after the fall – and perhaps there is an element of that, too.

In 'Little Red Riding Hood Hit The Road', we get a discordant opening of duelling trumpets – all played by Feza – with a driving rhythm led by piano and Sinclair's bass. Wyatt provides wordless cries before singing disjointed lyrics in which he seems to be protesting about both his accident and a row with Alfie – 'Stop please, oh deary me/What in heaven's name?/Oh blimey, mercy me, woe are we/Oh dear, oh stop it, stop it'. He adds: 'I didn't mean to hurt you/But I'll keep trying/And I'm sure you will too'. Towards the end, Ivor Cutler provides a spoken word verse of what appears to be total nonsense – 'I lie in the road, try to trip up the passing cars/Yes, me and the hedgehog, we bursting the tyres all day'. The song fades out on another trumpet cacophony.

'Alifib' is a string of childish endearments to Wyatt's wife, the sort of things one would normally keep to oneself, but here he guilelessly opens his heart and mixed-up brain. 'No nit not/Nit no not/Alifie my larder', he sings. 'I can't forsake you/Or forsqueak you'. It's set to a slow, melancholy drone with amateurish keyboard flourishes over stately bass from Hopper. This segues seamlessly into 'Alife', which becomes darker in tone, with squeaky sax from Gary Windo and Wyatt playing the lowest notes he can find on his Riviera keyboard. Here, Alfie gets her right to reply: 'I'm not your larder/Jammy jars and mustard/I'm not your dinner/You soppy old custard … I'm Alife your guarder'. I suppose Alfie was both his lover and larder, the supplier of all his basic needs, and his guarder.

Finally, we reach 'Little Red Robin Hood Hits The Road' – again, a dark, mysterious tune based on minor chords from the Riviera, but this time augmented by some excellent and occasionally wild *Tubular Bells*-ish lead guitar from Oldfield, bass from Sinclair and Laurie Allan's drums. Wyatt's lyrics are downbeat and surreal, in which he bemoans the fate of … moles. 'In the garden of England', he sings, 'Dead moles lie beside their holes/The dead-end tunnels crumble/In the rain, underfoot/Innit a shame?' Then he double (or maybe triple) tracks his voice in a long chant of 'Can't you see them?'

After about three minutes of this, Fred Frith strokes his cello in a sparse musical interlude before Ivor Cutler intones strange poetry over the top about smashing his telly with a broken telephone and demanding a crust of loaf for his 'lunch-tea'. The song ends with a repeat of the 'hedgehog tyre bursting' from 'Little Red Riding Hood Hits The Red' and Cutler's maniacal laughter.

With a subdued pencil-drawn cover by Alfie – deliberately designed to contrast with the overblown Roger Dean artwork favoured by some progressive rock bands at the time – *Rock Bottom* was released to universal acclaim from the critics, who praised its 'strong statement of mood' (the *NME*) and its 'honesty, wit and identity' (*Record Mirror*). Today, it usually features in most music publications and websites' Top 500 and can be found nestling somewhere in the top ten of any list of the best prog albums of 1974.

The album was promoted by a concert at the Theatre Royal, Drury Lane, in September, released on CD some 30 years later. Introduced by cult DJ John Peel, it featured all the musicians who played on the album, with the addition of Canterbury Scene keyboardist Dave Stewart. They played some Hugh Hopper and Matching Mole songs before performing *Rock Bottom* in its entirety, finishing with a barnstorming version of Wyatt's 1974 hit single 'I'm A Believer'.

During an interview to promote the album, he mentioned that he really liked pop music, 'the folk music of the industrial age' (*Uncut* magazine, 2014), so Virgin suggested he record and release a pop song. Wyatt loved The Monkees' debut single 'Last Train To Clarksville' but got muddled up and suggested their second single 'I'm A Believer' by mistake – written by Neil Diamond, it topped the UK and US charts at the end of 1966 and was the bestselling single of 1967.

With Nick Mason producing and drumming, and with the help of Sinclair, Frith and keyboard player Dave McCrea, the song was swiftly recorded at the Manor Studios and released in September 1974, when it reached number 29 in the UK chart. Led by piano rather than guitars – and with Frith providing an adventurous violin arrangement in the middle – the song has amazing energy and more interesting musical ideas than the original.

The single led to two appearances on *Top Of The Pops* – the second time involving a run-in with a stuffy BBC producer. Wyatt told *Uncut* magazine:

The producer said, 'I'm embarrassed by that wheelchair, it's not entertaining, can you go and sit in this wicker-work thing?' I told him to fuck off, and he said, 'You will never work on this programme again' – but as I just told you, I am too posh to care, frankly. I mean, I can't wheel a wicker chair, and I need to be able to get out quick in case the cops are coming, for fuck's sake!

In the end, Branson bought an antique wheelchair for Wyatt to sit in, reasoning the BBC couldn't possibly object to that. Later, Wyatt and several of the musicians he had worked with on the album and concert were pictured on the front of the *New Musical Express* – all sitting in wheelchairs. Some readers complained that it was tasteless.

Over the following five decades, Wyatt continued to pursue his unique musical muse, based on the template he had set with *Rock Bottom*, and has earned a place in the affections of open-minded British music lovers as a truly original artist. His influence has spread to more recent bands such as Tears For Fears, who wrote the Wyatt-ish 'I Believe' for their 1985 album *Songs From The Big Chair*, releasing it as a single backed with their rendition of 'Sea Song'.

He has also inspired a new verb. 'Wyatting' means to play unusual tracks on pub jukeboxes to annoy other customers. Wyatt himself was honoured at becoming a verb, but Alfie, as usual, rushed to his defence. 'The man who coined it, I'd like to punch him on the nose', she said.

Robert Wyatt recording *Rock Bottom* following the accident that left him partially paralysed. The album was produced by Pink Floyd's Nick Mason.

Camel – *Mirage*

Key personnel:
Andrew Latimer: guitars, flute, vocals
Peter Bardens: organ, piano, Minimoog, Mellotron, Fender electric piano, Hohner clavinet, celesta, vocals
Doug Ferguson: bass
Andy Ward: drums, percussion
Recorded in November 1973 at Island Studios, Decca Studios and AIR Studios, London
Produced by David Hitchcock
Engineered by Phil Ault, Richard Collins, Richard Elen and Howard Kilgour at Island, Mike Jones, Nick Raymonde and John Burns at Decca, Denny Bridges, Pete Henderson, Sean Milligan, John Punter and Bill Price at AIR
Cover design by Modula
Record label: Decca/Gama in the UK, New Zealand and most of Europe; Janus in the US and CA; PAX in Israel; Nova in Germany
Chart placings: US: 149
Tracks: 'Freefall' (Peter Bardens), 'Supertwister' (Bardens), 'The White Rider – a) Nimrodel b) The Procession c) The White Rider' (Andrew Latimer), 'Earthrise' (Bardens, Latimer), 'Lady Fantasy – a) Encounter b) Smiles For You c) Lady Fantasy' (Bardens, Latimer, Andy Ward, Doug Ferguson)

The Story So Far...

The band was formed as The Brew in 1971 in Guildford, Surrey, by local guitarist Andrew Latimer, drummer Andy Ward from Epsom, Surrey, and Carlisle-born bassist Doug Ferguson. The trio backed singer/songwriter Phillip Goodhand-Tait on his album *I Think I'll Write A Song* before advertising for a keyboard player, finding Peter Bardens (born Westminster, London, 19 June 1945) through *Melody Maker*. Renamed Camel, they toured through 1972, signing with MCA Records and releasing their unsuccessful eponymous debut the following year.

The Album

There can't be many progressive rock bands who have been threatened with legal action by a cigarette company. Or who promoted their music by offering free packs of cancer sticks. But that was the fate of British group Camel when they released *Mirage*, which some fans believe is their best album in a career spanning nearly 50 years.

Camel had named themselves after the animal, not a pack of fags. Someone – no-one can remember who – came up with it as they sat in a pub. They thought, 'Why not? They are loveable, funky animals'. So, initially, they had nothing to do with the cigarette brand, founded in the US in 1913 and so called because it attempted to imitate then-fashionable Egyptian cigarettes. But it was inevitable that they would come to the attention of the company, which was looking for ways to promote itself to younger people.

According to the 2003 Camel documentary *Curriculum Vitae*, it was manager Geoff Jukes's idea to do a deal with the Swiss branch of the cigarette company to get money for equipment – Andy Latimer said: 'He could see big dollars!' The band's side of the deal was to ape the cigarette branding on the cover of their next album and distribute mini-packs of cigarettes sporting the artwork and track listing at gigs. Peter Bardens said in the video: 'It was somewhat politically incorrect. Even then, it didn't feel quite right.' Andy Ward added: 'We put a stop to that as soon as we could. It's not a great association, rock music and lung cancer.'

Company execs even visited the band in the studio to persuade them to change the album track titles to something that would reflect the new partnership, such as 'Twenty To The Pack'. The Camel website reveals: 'The band were getting belligerent and a sarcastically amusing Peter Bardens suggested an album song title of 'Twenty Sticks Of Cancer'. Thus ended the association twist the beast and the leaf.'

Camel cigarettes in America took a different view and insisted that the band issue the album with a different cover. So, the US version of *Mirage* shows a rearing dragon, with no camels or cancer sticks in sight.

Despite half a century of great music, Camel never quite reached the A-list of progressive rock bands. Perhaps it was because a lot of their material was instrumental, or because they were not terribly gifted in the vocal department when they deigned to add lyrics to their compositions. Or perhaps it was because they were so shy and retiring that they were almost invisible.

What made Camel distinctive was Andy Latimer's guitar sound – bluesy, jazzy and packed with melodic earworms. Like David Gilmour, Andy Latimer played guitar solos you could sing along to. Like Peter Gabriel in Genesis and Ian Anderson in Jethro Tull, he could also toot a bit of flute. Sure, Peter Bardens was also an important element, and his keyboard playing enriches all those early albums. He and Latimer were the main songwriters, and Bardens has two solo compositions on *Mirage*.

As for bassist Doug Ferguson and drummer Andy Ward, they were solid, dependable players who laid down the foundation for Latimer and Bardens' musical pyrotechnics – although Latimer was soon to discover, after sacking him for not being jazzy enough, that Ferguson also helped provide the social 'glue' that kept the band together.

But that was in the future. In 1973, when our story starts, Camel had issued an excellent but commercially unsuccessful debut album on MCA Records. The eponymously-named release contained the track 'Never Let Go' that was to become a Camel classic, but that didn't stop it sinking without a trace like a dromedary in quicksand. MCA decided they could carry on without Camel and declined to pick up on the option for a second album.

This was even though Camel had built up a bit of a reputation as a live act, supporting bands such as Barclay James Harvest and Wishbone Ash on gruelling and seemingly never-ending tours. Undeterred, Camel's manager, Geoff Jukes and his business partners, Richard Thomas and Max Hole, formed their own record company, Gama (an acronym of Gemini Artist Management Agency), and made the band their first signing, installing them in Island Records' studios in Basing Street, London, to record a follow-up. In an interview with the website *Magenta*, Latimer said:

Mirage was ... well, first of all, it was a reaction against the first album because the first was very heavily arranged, and we worked out all our parts, kept solos to a minimum. I think *Mirage* was a slight reaction against it because when we played live, everything was much longer and our solos were much more extended. So maybe it was a little bit of self-indulgence. I mean, we went in and kept things as we did them on stage. And so there were a lot of lengthy passages, so long, which was a reaction against, as I say, the first album. Also, we were starting to get into other areas of our writing – I started writing about certain areas, like books. I was reading *Lord Of The Rings* at the time, which you know everyone in the band was reading at the same time – it's a great book. And I wrote a piece called 'The White Rider', about Gandalf.

Some of the *Mirage* tracks had made their live debut a year earlier – the 13-minute, three-part 'Lady Fantasy' was part of their setlist during their 1973 UK tour and has become the band's most-played track. Drummer Andy Ward told me: 'Lady Fantasy developed as the band's musicianship did. It was mostly written by Peter and Andy with contributions by Doug and me.'

Part one, 'Encounter', opens with a commanding organ arpeggio and Latimer's heavy, meaty guitar notes, before the song settles into a repetitive minor-key chord sequence over a slightly funky beat. Latimer sings lyrics about a mysterious woman who is beautiful but unattainable – 'a lady I've seen but never could hold'. Latimer has been known to sing this with tears in his eyes, so perhaps it was inspired by a real lost love. There's a chorus of sorts – 'I can see clearly, face in the sky, moon's in your eye, you're passing me by'.

Bardens takes a keyboard solo before the chorus is repeated. Then we enter a fast-riffing section, called 'Smiles For You', which allows Latimer to take off with a powerful guitar solo, while Bardens and Ferguson double up the bass riff. We return to the intro melody before a quieter, sombre section in which Latimer recalls seeing his mystery woman 'riding on a moon cloud', 'walking on a whirlpool' and 'sitting on a sunbeam'. He neglects to say whether he also saw her shopping at Aldi.

Then we launch into the title section, a fast guitar workout over repetitive bass and keyboard backing, ending proceedings with a restatement of the opening guitar melody.

Another early live track to make its way onto the album was 'Earthrise', an instrumental by Bardens and Latimer. A mysterious, spooky wind is joined by baroque-style electric guitar picking before a church-like organ chord in D major introduces a pretty keyboard tune with a medium-paced backing from drums and bass. There are nice, melodic riffs doubled up on keyboards and guitar, and Andy Ward gets a chance to take a brief solo. Like 'Lady Fantasy' but on a much shorter scale, 'Earthrise' appears to be made up of several different sections, but they fit together well in a tune that maintains the same pace and upbeat character through its nearly seven minutes.

By mid-July 1973, the band had demoed all the tracks that would be recorded with Genesis producer David Hitchcock in November, with the exception of album opener 'Freefall', which didn't appear in the setlist until August. A Bardens composition, it marries lyrics about being 'like a snowflake falling, down, down, down, down, down' with a thumping bass and drums backing and stabbing electric guitar. It's a great opener, but it exposes the only Camel weakness, their vocals. Indeed, legend has it that producer Hitchcock – or Scratch, as he is known to his friends – heard the track and asked: 'Which one of you is the singer? Because none of you can sing!'

'Supertwister' is a catchy instrumental showcasing Latimer's flute skills – mostly sprightly and agile, but with a sombre central section. It was named after Dutch band Supersister, who frequently toured with Camel in the early 1970s. The track ends with the opening and pouring of a can of something fizzy and no doubt alcoholic.

Mirage is completed by another multi-sectioned beast, 'The White Rider', written after Latimer had read the JRR Tolkien trilogy *The Lord Of The Rings*. The title comes from the second book, *The Two Towers*, in which an old man clad in white and riding a horse is revealed to be none other than notorious hobbit-botherer Gandalf. The lyrics tell his story: 'Once he wore grey/He fell and slipped away from everybody's sight/The wizard of them all/Came back from his fall, this time wearing white'.

The track opens with 'Nimrodel', a short, spooky introduction on electric guitar and ghostly keyboards – the name is a river in Lothlorien, a land of elves created by Tolkien. It is followed by a brief marching tune, 'Procession', played to the background of cheering crowds. At the two-minute mark, we reach part three, the title song, which resembles a slower 'Lady Fantasy' until it suddenly picks up speed for a Moog solo over Latimer's swiftly strummed guitar. It ends with a magnificent instrumental section in which Latimer lets rip on slide guitar over a deep, funky bassline that will shake the screws out of your speakers.

Two more compositions were either demoed or played live in 1973, but didn't make the final cut. 'The Traveller' is a pounding, nine-minute opus with nice duet vocals from Latimer and Bardens. It does sound like bits of the other tracks put together, and would have required the loss of two of the short numbers to fit on the album, so it is no surprise that it didn't make the cut. 'Autumn' is a pretty ballad that sounds very Genesis in its use of guitar arpeggios and tinkling percussion. Both were made available on the 2023 *Air Born* box set.

Mirage didn't chart in the UK but surprisingly hit number 149 in the US *Billboard* Top 200, despite very little promotion. It was also given the thumbs-up by critics, who praised the 'well-oiled machine' of Ward and Ferguson. It was Album of the Month in *The Beat* magazine.

Today, it is seen as an essential progressive rock release and marks the moment Camel found their feet. Yes, they went on to make even more celebrated albums, but *Mirage* proved that their musical talent wasn't a mirage.

Camel in 1974, around the recording of their second album, *Mirage*.

PFM – *L'isola Di Niente* & *The World Becomes The World*

Key personnel:
Franco Mussida: guitars, lead vocals
Flavio Premoli: keyboards, lead vocals
Mauro Pagani: violin, flute, vocals
Patrick Djivas: bass, vocals
Franz Di Cioccio: drums, percussion, vocals
L'isola Di Niente recorded between November 1973 and February 1974 at
Advision Studios, London, and Fonorama Studios, Milan
Produced by Claudio Fabi and PFM
Engineered at Advision by Martin Rushent and Declan O'Doherty
Engineered at Fonorama by Piero Bravim and Ambrogio Ferrario
Cover by Fabio Nicoli Associates
Record label: Numero Uno
Release date: March 1974
Chart placings: did not chart
Tracks: 'L'isola Di Niente', 'Is My Face On Straight' (Franco Mussida, Flavio
Premoli, Peter Sinfield), 'La Luna Nuova', 'Dolcissima Maria', 'Via Lumiere'
(Mussida, Premolia)
All tracks by Mussida, Premolia and Mauri Pagani unless otherwise stated.
The World Became The World recorded between November 1973 and February
1974 at Advision Studios, London, and Fonorama Studios, Milan
Produced by Claudio Fabi and PFM
Cover by Fabio Nicoli Associates
Record label: Manticore Records
Release date: June 1974
Chart placings: did not chart
Tracks: 'The Mountain, 'Just Look Away', 'The World Became The World'
(Mussida, Pagani, Sinfield), 'Four Holes In The Ground', 'Is My Face On Straight'
(Mussida, Premoli, Sinfield), 'Have Your Cake And Beat It' (Mussida, Premoli)
All tracks by Mussida, Premoli, Pagani, Sinfield unless stated

The Story So Far...

Italian progsters Premiata Forneria Marconi (translation: Award-winning Marconi Bakery) grew out of I Quelli (translation: The Them, or Those Guys), formed in 1968 by guitarist Franco Mussida (born in Milan in 1947), keyboard player Flavio Premoli (born in Varese in 1949), drummer Franz Di Cioccio (born in Pratola Peligna in 1946) and bass player Luciano Dovesi. By 1970, their name had changed, inspired by a bakery shop sign. In 1971, they won a music competition and signed to Numero Uno Records, releasing the hit single 'Impressioni Di Settembre' and, in 1972, their debut album *Storia Di Un Minuto*, which topped the Italian charts (and also introduced new bass player Giorgio Piazza). A second album, *Per Un Amico*, came out the same year. In 1973, they were signed to Emerson, Lake & Palmer's new Manticore record label after being spotted by Greg Lake when ELP were on an Italian tour. Manticore released *Photos Of Ghosts,* mostly consisting of tracks from the first two albums, rerecorded with English lyrics by King Crimson writer Peter Sinfield.

The Albums

For some bands, it was drugs that kept them going during gruelling weeks on the road. For The Beatles, it was Benzedrine and Preludin (and, off the road, LSD). For Miley Cyrus, it was marijuana and MDMA. For Premiata Forneria Marconi, it was spaghetti.

Now, I know what you are thinking. Lazy stereotyping, Furbank. They're Italian, so they must love spaghetti. But, cliché or not, it happens to be true. Where other bands were smoking, snorting and mainlining, PFM were cooking. And it wasn't crack cocaine. Bass player Patrick Djivas told *Classic Rock* magazine in 2018:

> Our big thing was food. The bands we were playing with would often stay at the same hotel and would come over to our room, attracted by the smell. We'd be cooking spaghetti; we'd have a little wine, and all start singing. Aerosmith used to come to our room every night for spaghetti. Steven Tyler would be singing and laughing all the time … Girls would be going past our room: 'Hello, is there a party over here?'

Perhaps that's why PFM are still going today, 55 years after they were formed. A little portlier, perhaps, from all the calorie-packing pasta, but all still alive. True, there are only two members left in the band from the lineup that recorded the two 1974 albums – and only one founding member – but the PFM sound remains the same, with their most recent release, *I Dreamed Of Electric Sheep*, appearing in 2021.

Back in 1974, they were probably at their commercial peak as the only Italian progressive rock band to achieve modest success in the US and UK. That is because they were the first Italian prog band to release albums aimed at the English-speaking market. *Photos Of Ghosts* contained the whole of *Per*

Un Amica, plus one track from *Storia Di Un Minuto* and a newly-penned instrumental. It was Manticore's decision to ask Peter Sinfield, who had worked with Greg Lake in King Crimson, to pen new English lyrics.

Later, the band would fall out with Sinfield. But *Photos Of Ghosts* – one of four English-singing albums by PFM released on the Manticore label almost simultaneously with their Italian-language versions – established the band in the UK and America. And it was Sinfield who encouraged them to abbreviate their name to make it easier to pronounce. The move paid off, as it allowed British music papers such as *Melody Maker* and *New Musical Express* to place them high in their end of year polls without having to worry about how to spell their name.

PFM were riding high – but it was at the peak of their success that they lost bass player Giorgio Piazza. There is a certain amount of mystery surrounding his departure – in Franz di Cioccio's book on the band *Due Volta Nella Vita* (*Twice In A Lifetime*), Piazza is there one moment, gone the next. He doesn't appear to have decamped to another band and did little of any note until many years later, so perhaps he simply wanted out of the music business. Di Cioccio said his nickname was 'Fico', which translates as 'fig' because he was as 'soft as the fruit' – was he too soft for the rock 'n' roll lifestyle?

However, there are also hints that the decision was the band's rather than Piazza's. His replacement was Yan Patrick Erard Djivas (from Cannes, France), who was one of the founder members of Area, the Italian avant-garde group. In his book, Di Cioccio told how he first played with Djivas at a jam session at L'Altro Mondon in Rimini:

Patrick Djivas had no desire to play that evening. He had arrived at the last moment, practically by chance, and he didn't have his bass with him. This was an important detail because Patrick used a fretless bass. I think it was Demetrio Stratos, who was with him in the Area lineup, who convinced him. Patrick was taken to the hotel, took his instrument and came back in time to go up on stage with Demetrio and have the final big jam session … They also invited Mauro [Pagani] and me, and from the first bars I realised that the feeling with Patrick was remarkable. We already felt like a well-matched rhythm section.

Later, at dinner, Djivas was invited to join PFM. It was good timing because the bass player was becoming uncomfortable with the increasing politicisation of Area's music, and was impressed by PFM's international standing. Di Cioccio added: 'We were more 'just musicians' than Area were, and Patrick came with us.' Djivas added a jazz influence that, in Di Cioccio's view, improved PFM's improvisational techniques. In contrast to his predecessor, he was also a bassist who could sing (Sinfield had originally suggested King Crimson's John Wetton).

But his new role caused Djivas some difficulty because Piazza was his former student – there would surely have been no difficulty if it had been the latter's choice to go. Whatever the reason, in September 1974, Djivas became the new PFM bass man and is still there today.

In November, the band went into Advision Studios in London to record two albums simultaneously – *L'isola Di Niente* for the Italian market, and *The World Became The World* for, well, the rest of the world. There were four new tracks that had identical musical backing but different lyrics and titles. Sinfield's words weren't a direct translation of the original Italian – he created brand new lyrics for each song. A fifth track, 'Is My Face On Straight', was sung in English on both LPs.

Both albums open with a powerful 11-minute prog beast that displays all the influences PFM had soaked up from the British bands they loved. Called 'L'isola Di Niente' (The Isle Of Nothing) on the Italian version – and 'The Mountain' on *The World Became The World* – it begins with two minutes of dramatic chorale work recorded at the Accademia Paolino de Milano, under the direction of producer and composer Claudio Fabi.

This leads into stabbing minor-key guitar chords, busy drums and what sounds like two bass parts – the first pounding on the root note of D, the second bubbling up and down the frets in an impressive display of four-string virtuosity. Well done, Patrick. The vocals are full of passion and meaning, about loss and despair, although they lose something in the translation: 'Fables and lies that talk about God ... stupid soldiers who ask about me ... only in the gardens of minds sits the time that will come'. Thank you, Google Translate.

But Sinfield's new lyrics for the English version are not necessarily any better as he channels his King Crimson bombast: 'Red bellows of flame have blackened my stones/Convulsing my frame and cracking my bones'. All together now ... 21st century schizoid man!

At about the three-and-a-half-minute mark, the backing changes into a series of fast, almost funky chords that lead to a pretty major-key vocal melody with some very Yes-like synth passages, followed by gentle, sparse acoustic guitar picking that is soon joined by strings from the mighty Mellotron. Pagani's flute conjures up images of birds singing in the trees, and Mussida and Premoli play contrapuntal arpeggios on guitar and keyboards. Then we get another dramatic blast of the choir before the track plunges back into those stabbing minor key chords. The song ends with a lyrical guitar solo over shifting fingerpicked acoustic guitar chords before fading out.

This is a bold and brilliant piece of music played by a band confident in its ability to weld together several separate pieces, with different tempos and moods, into one glorious whole. Yes, it's derivative, drawing mainly from Mr Jon Anderson's merry crew, but there's a well-developed sense of melody and drama here that helps it stand alone as PFM's finest moment on the album – and possibly the best track they ever recorded.

'Is My Face On Straight' is the only song that appears unchanged on both the Italian and English albums, where it is sung in English with Sinfield's lyrics. 'Inflate your waistcoat, wind down your eyes', he penned, a useless bit of advice unless you happen to possess a very rare inflatable waistcoat. 'We have ways to make you cheer/As long as you're not sick or poor/A negro or a queer', the last word sung in some sort of falsetto screech.

I guess the song is about hiding our true feelings behind a bland face. Musically, it starts as a slow ballad punctuated by fast, guitar-led riffs before getting a bit rhythmic and funky, Pagani offering some improvised jazz flute. Then, after the screech of 'queer!', the song changes into something more rapid, more like a psychedelic track from the 1960s before settling into a stately chorus. 'Thank you for joining, here are your pills', they sing, although the song sounds like they were already taking them. There are plenty of great melodic ideas here, but it jumps about too dramatically between styles.

'La Luna Nuova' is a spirited, up-tempo and catchy track that swiftly became a fan favourite on the subsequent US tour. It is credited to Mussida, Premoli and Pagani, but the liner notes for the Japanese 2009 release claim new boy Djivas had a hand in it. They cite the strong Mediterranean influence in some of the melodies that were characteristic of Djivas's previous band, Area. Certainly, there's a folkie feel in the opening percussion and the jig-like melodies that switch between the key of C and A, all in (mostly) the time signature of 5/4.

A short drum solo leads into a galloping minor-key section with improvs from flute and keyboard before a return to the 5/4 folk melody, which then jumps into a slower section about halfway through the track for some vocals.

Sinfield does little better in the English version, retitled 'Four Holes In The Ground'. He starts well, by suggesting that 'what remains of truth and real value/Is wine shared with friends'. But he spoils it all with lines such as 'But if life is just a well-stuffed purse/It couldn't get much worse/For me and you/Chicken in a zoo'. Yes, a chicken ... in a zoo.

But back to the track. As is PFM's wont, there are still more musical sections to throw into the mix. There's a galloping, funky vocal section, a return to the folkie melodies interspersed with guitar pyrotechnics and, finally, a magnificent ending that builds up to a crescendo of keyboard and guitar before finishing with a brief restatement of the opening theme played on what sounds like a low tuba.

'Dolcissima Maria' is a pretty ballad, with soft vocals over fingerpicked acoustic guitar and gentle keyboard and electric guitar accompaniment. 'Sweet Mary', they sing, but in Italian. 'Forget the flowers painted by time on your face'. Charming. The English version, called 'Just Look Away', changes gender to an old violinist scraping his bow out of tune, 'blues on his fingers'. If they see the pain in his eyes, they just look away. It is a condemnation of our ability to turn a blind eye to misery and suffering, whether it's on our street or in places such as Ukraine and Gaza. The song boasts a beautiful, soaring chorus and a pretty repetitive outro melody played on flute.

The Italian album ends with the only track wholly recorded in the Milan studios. 'Via Lumiere' is a jazz-rock instrumental that has Djivas's fingers all over it, not least in the intricate fretless bass solo that opens proceedings. Jaco Pastorius, eat your heart out. After a minute of prime Djivas, he is joined by tinkling keyboards and electric guitar playing jazzy licks and chords. At the 1:42 mark, a slashing guitar chord kicks things off properly as the band propel into a Crimson-like sound battering in six-time, Premoli's keyboard screaming like a banshee.

There's a sudden lurch into what could be a cop show soundtrack – a mixture of laidback menace and melody – before another sound battering, Pagani blowing hell out of his flute. Another sudden shift takes us into a stately ending section based on the organ repeating the chords of A7, B and D. Yes, it all sounds mad, but it works, and is a glorious ending to the Italian album.

It is also the closing track on the English album, where it is retitled 'Have Your Cake And Beat It'. But English-speaking PFM fans got one more track than the Italians, a reworking of 'Impressioni Di Settembre' that was on the band's debut album in their home country but was never given a release elsewhere. For *The World Becomes The World,* it became the title track with new lyrics from Sinfield.

The track was requested by ELP's company, Manticore Records, and you can understand why, because it sounds just like a Greg Lake ballad, opening with vocals over acoustic guitar backing with Lake-era King Crimson Mellotron and guitar interludes between the verses.

L'isola Di Niente and *The World Became The World* were released separately but with covers that tied them together. Both had a bold wash of colour with a circular central image – the Italian version green with an island mountain in the middle, the English one blue with what looks like an overhead view of the island as a pizza. The band name and album titles were also depicted in the same olde worlde font.

Sadly, none of these tactics managed to push either of PFM's 1974 releases into the charts, but sales were enough to justify a US tour that resulted in the band's third offering that year, the live album *Cook*. Because, in 1974, Premiata Forneria Marconi WERE cooking – and it wasn't just good spaghetti they were dishing up.

Supertramp – *Crime Of The Century*

Key personnel:
Rick Davies: vocals, keyboards, harmonica
Roger Hodgson: vocals, guitar, pianos
John Anthony Helliwell: saxophones, clarinet, backing vocals
Dougie Thomson: bass guitar
Bob Siebenberg (credited as Bob C. Benberg): drums, percussion
Recorded between February and June 1974 at Trident, Rampart and Scorpio
Sound studios, London
Produced by Ken Scott and Supertramp
Engineered by Ken Scott and John Jansen
Record label: A&M
Release date: 25 October 1974
Chart placings: UK and CA: 4, DE: 5, NZ: 12, AU: 15, NL: 25, US: 38
Tracks: 'School', 'Bloody Well Right', 'Hide In Your Shell', 'Asylum', 'Dreamer',
'Rudy', 'If Everyone Was Listening', 'Crime Of The Century'
All tracks by Rick Davies and Roger Hodgson
'Land Ho' single recorded between July and September 1973 at Maximum Sound
Studios, London, and Kitchen Studios, London
Produced by Supertramp
Remixed by Ken Scott
Record label: A&M
Release date: March 1974
Chart placings: did not chart
Tracks: 'Land Ho', 'Summer Romance'
All tracks by Davies & Hodgson

The Story So Far...

Keyboard player Richard Davies was in several bands in the Swindon area
before ending up in The Joint, recording soundtracks for German films. In
Munich, he met Dutch millionaire Stanley August Miesegaes, who offered to

bankroll a new band with Davies in it. An ad in *Melody Maker* in August 1969 found Portsmouth multi-instrumentalist Charles Roger Pomfret Hodgson – yes, Pomfret! Also auditioned and chosen were guitarist Richard Palmer and drummer Keith Baker. Originally calling themselves Daddy, they changed their name to Supertramp, inspired by *The Autobiography Of A Super-Tramp*, published in 1908 by Welsh writer William Henry Davies. Signed to A&M Records, their self-named debut album in 1970 was critically praised but sold poorly. Dave Winthrop joined on flute and sax for the Isle of Wight Festival, but Palmer and Millar quit soon after, eventually replaced by Frank Farrell (bass, piano, accordion) and Kevin Currie (drums). This lineup released *Indelibly Stamped* (1971), which sold even less than the debut. Gradually, everyone quit except Davies and Hodgson, and Miesegaes withdrew funding. It looked like Supertramp's demise was indelibly stamped…

The Album

Pity poor Rudy. Who? He's the fella whose sad, lonely life is picked apart and displayed to the prying public on Supertramp's third album, *Crime Of The Century*. But who is Rudy? If you believe Roger Hodgson, it is his one-time songwriting partner, Rick Davies – if you believe Rick, it's a composite of all the miserable people he's ever met.

Whoever he is, he's not living his best life. His individuality has been crushed by his repressive school, he's shunned and ignored by society, damned for being a dreamer hiding in his shell and then deemed insane and committed to an asylum. The album cover shows him behind metal prison bars, floating in space. Let's just say it's not the story of Happiness Stan. Yet, this relentless portrayal of human misery resulted in what many believe is Supertramp's best album and the one that saved their career.

Most people know Supertramp for their multimillion-selling 1979 release *Breakfast In America*, which was number one all over the world. But what they probably don't know is that a scant six years before, the band were teetering on the edge of oblivion. In fact, if it wasn't for Dave Margereson, you probably would never have heard of them except as a very short footnote in the history of progressive rock.

You see, back in 1973, there was just Rick Davies and Roger Hodgson – everyone else was gone, including Dave Winthrop, who walked off at a motorway café on the way home from a gig. (In the case of drummer Currie, Davies and Hodgson told him the band was over because it was the easiest way to get rid of him.) Eventually, there was no band, no money and, seemingly, no future. Roger Hodgson told website *In The Studio With Redbeard*:

So it really felt like we were going nowhere. Certainly, we weren't being managed too well … We all decided that was it, we've had it, and we actually split up for two days. Yep, I decided I was off to India – I desperately wanted to go to India anyway at that time, and I thought, this is the opportunity. I don't know how it got back together again. I think it was the bass player or our sound engineer who said, listen, this is crazy. There is too much music here to throw it away. The chemistry between you and Rick is too valuable. We've got to give it one more go.

Then along came Dave Margereson. He was the next-door neighbour of Derek Green, who became Managing Director of the UK arm of A&M Records. He asked Dave to review the company's list of artists and decide who should stay and who should be given the heave-ho. By any criterion, Supertramp should have gotten the boot. They had signed a two-album deal, and both releases had gone straight into the bargain bins.

When they visited A&M's offices with demos for their next album, they discovered no-one on the label had heard of them. Hodgson told Redbeard: 'We said, we're on your label. And they said, are you? They didn't even know we were.' But there was something about them that Margereson liked. He went to see them live, and there were a few new songs that caught his attention – 'School', 'Bloody Well Right' and one about a dreamer … He bonded with Hodgson and offered to support them while they rebuilt the band and made one last attempt at rock stardom. Eventually, he would leave A&M to become Supertramp's manager.

The first new signing was Glasgow bassist Douglas Campbell Thomson, who had auditioned in 1972 as a temporary stand-in before receiving the dubious honour of becoming a full-time member of a practically non-existent band. Thomson was responsible for bringing in Yorkshire sax player John Anthony Helliwell; the pair had briefly worked together in The Alan Bown Set in the 1960s. The lineup was completed by California drummer Robert Layne Siebenberg, also known as Bob C. Benberg. Even though he hailed from the US, they bumped into him playing in a local bar.

Margereson rented Southcombe, a farmhouse in Somerset, and the entire band and crew, with their partners, moved in together to work on their make-or-break third album. In a 2022 video by *Total Classic Rock*, Helliwell said: 'We all got together, we lived together, worked together, all in the same place and made a really big effort to make something solid, and it seemed to work because it laid the foundations for our career from then onwards.' Supertramp roadie Russel Cope told *The Logical Web* in 2009:

[It was] all of us, including wives, girlfriends and even Dougie and Christine's cat, TC. It was an idyllic winter fantasy with A&M paying all the bills and everyone in a space where anything was possible, and we just knew it was all going to work out and everyone was going to be happy ever after. It was almost fun walking to the pub a mile away in deep snow and stepping on cow turds.

It was a magical time, too, for Davies and Hodgson. They weren't schoolboy chums who had formed a band together. They had been thrown together by circumstance and were very different people – Davies was a working-class blues and jazz fan, while Hodgson was the product of an English private school and loved pop. But they worked well together and, in the beginning, co-wrote all the songs, with Richard Palmer supplying lyrics (as he was to do for King Crimson, as Palmer-James).

Like Lennon and McCartney, their two different voices made the band's sound more distinctive – Hodgson a soft, Jon Anderson-like tenor, Davies a more muscular, raspy baritone – and, like the Fab Two, they tended to sing the songs they had each originated. They also stopped writing together pretty early on in their career – all the songs on *Crime Of The Century* are credited to them both, but, in truth, only 'School' was really jointly authored.

Later, their different personalities and musical styles would cease to complement each other, and they would split with a certain amount of acrimony. But 'getting it together in the country', as bands were wont to do back in those days (Traffic set the trend in 1967), helped focus their songwriting minds and, by the time they were ready to go into the studio, they had no fewer than 42 new compositions, including the ones Margereson had seen them play live before the break-up. Others, with titles including 'Black Cat', 'Chicken Man' and 'Pony Express', were played during BBC sessions, then disappeared without a trace.

Two of the demos were chosen as a stopgap single, released in early 1974. Producer/engineer Ken Scott, who had worked with David Bowie and The Beatles, was brought in to remix 'Land Ho' and its B-side, 'Summer Romance', and he wasn't very impressed, describing the songs as 'half-baked'.

Listening to them now, one can understand his reaction: 'Land Ho' is like a prototype 'Dreamer', with the band's trademark stabbing Wurlitzer piano chords, a tired, bland melody and lots of dreaming in the lyrics, while 'Summer Romance' is a mundane, bluesy stomper packed full of cliched lines about seeing 'the lovelight in her eyes'. But Scott changed his mind after seeing the band live, saying: 'They're incredible!'

With Scott's help, Supertramp whittled down the 42 demos to just eight. Just two were deliberately written with a concept in mind – 'School' and Davies's 'Bloody Well Right'. Hodgson claims that it then became a case of arranging the songs in the order they thought best, but, somehow, everything they wrote seemed to fit the broad story arc of Sad Rudy.

'School' was mostly Hodgson – he was 23 in 1974, so had left posh Stowe School in Buckinghamshire just four years earlier, with memories of the institution's crushing conformity still fresh in his mind. A little unfair, perhaps – The Beatles played there in 1963, and it was a teacher at the school who taught him his first guitar chords. But Hodgson was still trying to break out of his school conditioning and wanted to have a go at it.

The song opens with Davies's ghostly solo harmonica, wailing mournfully like Harmonica Man in Ennio Morricone's soundtrack for *Once Upon A Time In The West*. Hodgson sings, accompanied by a gently fingered electric guitar, before drums and bass pile in at the 80-second mark, the guitar playing funky chords. The backing stops for a lead guitar mimicking the harmonica over keyboards before everything builds up again into an insanely catchy piano melody, played over the chords of Am, Em, G and Dm.

A powerful, rocking middle eight punches home Hodgson's lyrical attack – 'Don't do this and don't do that/What are they trying to do? (Make a good boy of you)/And do they know where it's at?' Then the song drives home with an urgent third verse before ending on Hodgson's solo voice over a single, dramatic minor chord. The song is interspersed with the sound of children playing, and a child's scream that could be laughter or something more sinister, recorded by Scott at his daughter's school.

Davies's love of jazz is displayed in the lengthy intro for 'Bloody Well Right' – he began his musical career as a drummer, heavily influenced by the great Gene Krupa, who played with Benny Goodman before forming his own orchestra in 1938. Davies plays what sounds like a bit of bluesy improvisation over alternating chords of Fm7 and Bb with occasional stabbing chords from the rest of the band. After about 50 seconds of jazziness, the band come in with a slightly more relaxed rhythm, led by wah-wahed lead guitar, before dropping into G for the first verse.

As Hodgson stated earlier, the opening line was written to link thematically with 'School'. But where the latter comes from a first-person perspective, 'Bloody Well Right' seems to be the voice of the Establishment responding dismissively to the complaints. 'You're bloody well right', he says. But 'Me, I don't care anyway' and 'You've had your cry … in the meantime, hush your face'. All this is set to a fun, cheeky stomp laced with humour, a nice antidote to the anguished intensity of 'School'.

'Hide In Your Shell' continues the themes of loneliness and alienation. "Cos the world is out to bleed you for a ride', sings Hodgson, adding 'you've got demons in your closet'. In a Facebook post, Hodgson explained:

I was 23 when I wrote 'Hide In Your Shell'. I was confused about life, and like a lot of people are at that age, I was very shy and tried to hide my insecurities. I've always been able to express my innermost feelings more openly in song, and 'Hide In Your Shell' came to me at a time when I was feeling very lonely – both in life and within the band – with no-one who shared my spiritual yearnings. It's a song that speaks to that place in all of us that feels alone or misunderstood, that place where we just want to hide from the world, that longs for connection yet doesn't feel safe to reach out for help.

For such an emotional song, 'Hide In Your Shell' has a surprisingly sprightly opening, with jaunty, major-key Wurlitzer piano chords and a driving beat.

Hodgson's delicate voice emphasises his fragility and vulnerability, while the choir of backing vocals (including Helliwell's wife Christine, Benberg's missus Vicky and future Thin Lizzy guitarist Scott Gorham) helps punch the messages home: 'Too frightening to listen to a stranger/Too beautiful to put your pride in danger/You're waiting for someone to understand you'. His soul-baring lyrics take on a more positive bent for an irresistibly catchy and uplifting chorus, 'Don't let the tears linger on inside now/'Cos it's sure time you gained control/If I can help you just let me know', as Helliwell provides tasteful saxophone commentary.

At nearly seven minutes, 'Hide In Your Shell' is a lengthy song by Supertramp standards – the verses and pre-choruses take a while to go through before we hit the chorus, and there's a Beatley interlude, during which Hodgson repeats 'I wanna know' over a cycle of three or four chords, before the song fades out on the chorus. 'Hide In Your Shell' wasn't released as a single but has become Hodgson's most requested song – there must be lots of lonely Supertramp fans out there.

Davies continues the damaged personality theme with the closing song on side one, only things have gotten so bad we're now in an 'Asylum'. Sweeping and cinematic, the song is a mini-epic that moves from tinkling solo piano through powerful, string-driven choruses complete with angelic choir and Davies sounding like Roger Waters in full 'deranged singer' mode. It reminds me of early 1970s Elton John in the way it is so cleverly arranged and beautifully played – Davies was a superior pianist to Hodgson, who tended to rely on simple chord shapes.

But while Hodgson was happy to lay all his feelings on the table for inspection, Davies tended to create characters and little dramas in his songs – even when singing in the first person, we know he is playing a part and keeping himself a little detached from the proceedings. So in 'Asylum', we have interaction between the unidentified protagonist and 'Jimmy Cream' – he asks Jimmy to lend him 15p for a smoke.

Davies's character admits he can't keep tabs on his brain but insists unconvincingly, 'I'm just as sane as anyone/It's just a game I play for fun'. He has dialogue, too: 'Look, I said, I'm not the way you're thinking/Just when I'm down, I'll be the clown, I'll play the fool/Please don't arrange to have me sent to no asylum'. In the third verse, he talks about 'Bluesy Monday' when 'they haunt me and they taunt me in my cage', reminding us that London's notorious Bedlam Asylum used to let the public pay to see mentally-ill people in cages in the early 18th century.

The chorus is written from a third-person perspective and asks 'Will he take a sailboat ride?' It's not easy to understand what Davies is saying here, as I'm sure most asylums can be reached without having to cross a body of water. Perhaps it means he is going on a journey over which he has no control. Whatever it means, the chorus holds out little hope for the character's recovery: 'Will he feel good inside? Well, he ain't very likely to'.

After passing through many musical sections and key changes, 'Asylum' ends with Davies screeching and gibbering uncontrollably, while repeating 'Mad, mad, mad, mad, mad … not quite right!' over heavy rock riffs and dramatic strings before fading out on tinkling piano.

Side two opens with the hit single. 'Dreamer' was composed by Hodgson at his mother's house when he was 19. He and Davies had just bought a Wurlitzer electric piano, and it was the first time Hodgson had laid hands on it. The instrument was invented by US radio engineer Benjamin Miessner in 1935, but wasn't put into production until 1954, when the patent was bought by the Rudolph Wurlitzer Company. Its design gave it a unique sound – bright, sharp and punchy – that suited Hodgson's simple, rhythmic playing style. He recorded a demo using cardboard boxes and light shades as percussion, which then sat in a drawer until he brought it out as a possible track for *Crime Of The Century*. He told Redbeard:

I don't know where it came from, but I know it came out in a rush, and I did all kinds of weird things like banging cardboard boxes, banging electric fires, anything that clanged … that demo really pointed the direction the song wanted to go. In fact, when we started doing that song in the studio, it started going in a different direction. For a while, we tried to duplicate the demo by playing to it, but the tempo was so off that we had to scrap it. We actually tried to get as close to the demo as possible, that's why there aren't too many drums in there – I think there are even cardboard boxes on there! There are all kinds of things – there are mouth noises, there are glasses being rubbed around the edge to get that high sound … 'Dreamer' really took off in England. It was a very different song and really attracted the attention of the public.

And no wonder. The song is insanely catchy, based around the repetition of the major chords of D, G and A, with a dive down to C, F and G before returning to the home chord. The bright pop sound of the Wurlitzer is matched by Hodgson's chirpy vocals, high-pitched keyboard flourishes from Davies and admirable restraint from the rest of the band, who have little to do for most of the song. There's a bit of Hammond organ in there, some call and response vocals from Hodgson and Davies, brief glockenspiel from Benberg and, apparently, those glasses being rubbed by Helliwell.

The song slips into A flat for the middle eight, and there is a 90-second interlude in the middle in which the vocalist repeats lines over alternating C and B flat chords. When the band finally go back into D towards the end, it sounds like a key change and has the same uplifting effect, finishing on Benberg's glockenspiel.

The music may be relentlessly upbeat, but the lyrics are dark and cynical – 'Dreamer, you stupid little dreamer' sings Hodgson, demanding that the target of the song do something, anything, with their life instead of dreaming. 'You know you had it coming to you', he adds, 'and now there's not a lot I can do'.

In fact, the words 'dream' and 'dreaming' are mentioned no fewer than 27 times, making this one of the most annoyingly repetitive songs Supertramp ever recorded. But the fans didn't mind – the song reached number 13 in the UK, and a live version later reached number 15 in the US.

Hodgson may have claimed there was no real concept to *Crime Of The Century,* but in other interviews, he revealed there WAS a nebulous character referred to in the songs, and his name was Rudy. In Hodgson's view, Rudy was Rick Davies – he told Redbeard:

It was very much autobiographical in a way, with where Rick was at the time. He's a very eccentric guy anyway and doesn't operate too well in social circumstances, and I think he was pretty lonely; he didn't have a girlfriend at the time. But he was a very interesting guy once you got to know him. He was really very difficult to get to know and kept to himself, in his shell, a lot. And I really think he was writing about himself when he wrote 'Rudy'.

Davies, on the other hand, described Rudy as a composite of people he had met. But he has also admitted he is a 'professional worrier', so there may be some truth in what Hodgson claimed. Whatever the truth about Rudy, it provided Davies with one of his most celebrated songs, a complex, multi-sectioned beast that displays his playing, composing and arranging skills. In fact, I would go so far as saying it is Davies's contributions that make Supertramp a progressive band – without him, it would be just a pop group.

The song opens with ambient noise from London's Paddington Station, recorded by Scott. Then Davies plays some pretty piano figures, followed by a bluesy flourish down the keyboard until he reaches A minor for the start of the verse. 'Rudy's on a train to nowhere', he sings. Rudy's not sophisticated or well-educated (in one of the dodgiest couplets in songwriting history, 'it's not as though he's fat, nah, there's more to it than that'). There's a nice swinging rhythm to the verse, with frequent stops for some thoughtful, introspective minor chords.

Thomson's bass punches in at the one-and-a-half-minute mark for the lines 'He needs time' – the pace starts to pick up as the clock is ticking. Lead guitar riffs burst in, the piano chords pound away and then everything simmers down again before more guitar riffs take over.

Okay, so far, we've had about three and a half minutes of music, and very little of it has repeated itself, and it has ranged from moody reflection to crunchy riffs. There's another reflective section of a gentle piano and keyboard melody overlaid on the sound of train announcements, again from Paddington.

On stage, 'Rudy' would be played to a blown-up video of the London to Brighton train journey, filmed by the BBC in 1953 and sped up to squeeze the then one-hour journey time (it now takes about an hour and a half on average – so much for progress) into just four minutes. The frantic nature of the footage matches the pace of the song as it really picks up speed about halfway through. There's a funky guitar deep in the mix to emulate the sound of wheels clattering along a track as Hodgson sings 'All through your life/All through the years/Nobody loved/Nobody cared'.

As the song builds up steam, Davies references Hodgson's 'Hide In Your Shell' with lines about gaining control of his life – 'it's make or break, give or take' – until dramatic, string-backed chords step up and up until we stop for the sad ending. Over the sound of a milling crowd, the song reprises the opening verse melody with sad lines about Rudy coming out of the movie and getting back on his train, returning to his lonely life.

Like a lot of great prog songs, 'Rudy' consists of several distinct musical sections skilfully stitched together to tell a cohesive story, one that in this case suggests that any attempt to change your life for the better is doomed to failure.

Hodgson channels good old Billy Shakespeare for the penultimate track on the album 'If Everyone Was Listening'. 'All the world's a stage', wrote Will in *As You Like It*, 'and all the men and women merely players'. To sombre minor chords, Hodgson sings: 'The actors and jesters are here/The stage is in darkness and clear/For raising the curtain/And no-one's quite certain whose play it is'. It's a bit of a corny concept, but it works here to emphasise the lack of control we all have over our own destinies – our scripts are written, we have our exits and entrances, and we are all helplessly playing a part.

Musically, the song is a fairly straightforward minor-key sad ballad based on Hodgson's gently pulsing piano keys, occasionally bursting into life for a slow, somewhat ponderous major-key chorus, backed with tasteful strings. Helliwell also provides a slightly bluesy clarinet solo in the middle. It is a pretty song, but pales in comparison to the more superior compositions that surround it.

Finally, we reach the title track, closing the album. Again, this is mostly a ballad with an even gloomier concept – it deals with the follies and foolishness of Mankind, not just one particular character. Rudy's failings become the failings of us all, but on a grander scale – 'men of lust, greed and glory' whose crime is to 'rape the universe'. But who are these people? Rip off the masks and, oh no, 'there's you and me'.

Davies takes the lead vocal, indicating that he is the author of the piece. But Hodgson had some input, too. He told my fellow Sonicbond author Steve Pilkington for his 2024 book on the album:

Well, 'Crime Of The Century' is certainly Rick's song, but until we had nearly finished the album, he still didn't have any words, and time was running out. By then, we knew the running order, and I think he took the cue directly from 'If Everyone Was Listening', and quite brilliantly, I thought. It's a fantastic lyric and quite 'un-Ricklike' in many ways. There was a little bit of collaboration in there; I had some input, though I can't really remember exactly how much. However, my forte was really in arranging the songs – everyone chipped in on that side, of course, but I had the main hand in which way the songs should be arranged, bass parts, vocal arrangements and things like that. So, that gave many of the more complex songs an element of collaboration in itself.

'Crime Of The Century' certainly needed a good arrangement – it contains just 13 lines of lyrics that end a quarter of the way through the song. The rest is instrumental, including some impassioned lead guitar over moody piano backing, followed by a dramatic section with the strings building up over repetitive A minor and F chords, accompanied by a Helliwell sax solo, that slowly fades out at the end.

Now, you would have thought this relentless parade of misery would make *Crime Of The Century* an album to slit your wrists to. But thanks to its catchy melodies and careful balance of light and dark, it became Supertramp's breakthrough LP, peaking in the top five in the UK, Canada and Germany. It led to a lengthy tour across the UK, Europe and North America that resulted in Supertramp finally becoming a headline act that could fill concert venues with adoring fans.

Retrospective reviews made the release one of the 200 greatest albums of all time (*The World Critics List*, edited by Paul Gambaccini), and it was listed in the book *1001 Albums You Must Hear Before You Die* (Universe Publishing). It is now generally regarded as a progressive rock masterpiece. Even *Rolling Stone* magazine, which initially criticised the album's songs for being too long (sometimes you do wonder what planet these reviewers are on), later revised its opinion and dubbed it the 27th best prog album of all time.

Hodgson himself singled out producer Ken Scott's sonic wizardry for its success, but also said there was a definite chemistry at the time between five very different people from diverse backgrounds who somehow clicked in the studio and made musical magic. He told Redbeard:

I think *Crime Of The Century* was a major education; it really made us wake up to what was possible. It was the first time we had the opportunity to flex our musical muscles, our arranging muscles … it really was the start of Supertramp. I really don't consider anything before *Crime…* to be Supertramp – it was like school years somehow. The album, the tour and everything else that followed it suddenly propelled us into the world.

Gentle Giant – *The Power And The Glory*

Key personnel:
Derek Shulman: vocals, tenor saxophone
Gary Green: guitars, backing vocals
Kerry Minnear: piano, electric piano, Hammond organ, Minimoog, Mellotron, marimba, clavinet, vibes, cello, vocals
Ray Shulman: bass, violins, acoustic guitar, backing vocals
John Weathers: drums, tambourine, sleigh bells, cymbals, backing vocals
Recorded between December 1973 and January 1974 at Advision Studios, London
Produced by Gentle Giant
Engineered by Gary Martin
Record label: WWA (UK), Capitol (US)
Release date: 22 September 1974
Chart placings: US: 78, CA: 91
Tracks: 'Proclamation', 'So Sincere', 'Aspirations', 'Playing The Game', 'Cogs In Cogs', 'No God's A Man', 'The Face', 'Valedictory'
All tracks composed by Kerry Minnear, Derek Shulman and Ray Shulman
'The Power And The Glory' single recorded in June 1974 at Advision Studios, London
Produced by Gentle Giant
Record label: WWA
Release date: November 1974
Chart placings: did not chart.
Tracks: 'The Power And The Glory', 'Playing The Game'
All tracks composed by Kerry Minnear, Derek Shulman and Ray Shulman

The Story So Far...

Born the sons of a jazz trumpeter in Glasgow, Scotland, the three Shulman brothers put an R&B band together that eventually became Simon Dupree and the Big Sound (Derek was Simon) and had a psychedelic hit, 'Kites', in

1967. Follow-ups flopped, so, in 1969, the brothers recruited Dorset-born multi-instrumentalist Kerry Churchill Minnear, who had graduated from the Royal Academy of London, London guitarist Gary Green and former Dupree drummer Martin Smith. The new lineup's name was a reference to a fictional 'gentle giant' who happens upon a band of musicians. Signed to Vertigo, their self-titled 1970 debut was challenging but criticised for poor recording quality. Their 1971 follow-up, *Acquiring The Taste,* showed a further experimental approach, after which Smith left and was replaced by Malcolm Mortimore. Their first concept album, *Three Friends*, came out in 1972, after which Mortimore was injured in a motorcycle accident and replaced by John Weathers (born Carmarthen, Wales) for the second album that year, *Octopus*. Phil Shulman left following arguments with his brothers, and the band released *In A Glass House* in 1973.

The Album

'I am not a crook!' spluttered US President Richard Nixon, dark jowls wobbling with faux outrage. He was a crook, of course, and on 8 August 1974, he was forced to resign as the Watergate scandal came to its inevitable conclusion.

This is not the place to explore the labyrinthine intricacies of the scandal because they are long and complicated and, quite frankly, terrifically boring. Let us just say that Watergate provided a prime example of the overweening arrogance of power, the delusion too many leaders possess that they are somehow above the law, that it's not a crime when THEY do it. (Does that sound like anyone else we know in more modern times? Just saying.)

Most progressive rock bands took scant notice of it – after all, there are not many rhymes for Nixon – except one, and, ironically, it was a band that seemed less in touch with contemporary events than most others. Gentle Giant seemed to live in their own unique world in which they channelled the musical genres of the last 600 years (at least), dove deep into earthy French Renaissance literature for their lyrics and employed time signatures that only theoretical physicists could understand. They also seemed to be able to play any musical instrument invented by Humankind.

Yet the Watergate scandal and associated international crises, such as the Cold War, helped provide the inspiration for their sixth album, *The Power And The Glory*. That's not to say there were specific references to those events in the songs because there weren't. Instead, as Derek Shulman told the *Ultimate Classic Rock* website in 2014:

The concept for the album was based on the corruption of power and how people at the bottom are affected by the people on top. Money and power will win no matter what, and the people who are hoping for the best won't usually get the best. The label we were on at that time, WWA, was an imprint of Vertigo. Vertigo was a fully owned company of Phonogram, which is Polygram, which is now Universal, which will probably be GE in a week, which is going to be the government soon enough. So there's the corruption of power right there! The power and the glory! Again! Still to this day!

So far, so cynical. But let us wind back a little bit here to 1973, after Gentle Giant had released their fourth and arguably their finest album, *Octopus*, and toured with Black Sabbath. It seemed the Portsmouth-born band were on the cusp of commercial success – they already had the critical praise but had struggled to translate that into record sales, particularly in the UK.

Then Phil, the oldest of the Shulman brothers, dropped a rather large bombshell by announcing he was quitting. He was fed up with touring and wanted to spend more time with his wife and two children. Unfortunately, Phil played a large part in setting both the musical and moral direction of the band – apart from being a key songwriter, he established such ground rules as 'no extramarital nookie on tour.'

For a brief moment, Gentle Giant considered packing it all in. But the non-brothers were keen to keep going, even though Minnear had to learn even more instrumental parts on his bank of seven keyboards, and the band quickly recorded and released a post-Phil album, *In A Glass House*. In the liner notes for the Blu-ray release of *The Power And The Glory*, Ray Shulman said:

> We were considering our future when Phil left. We had to buy ourselves out of the management company contract and all that stuff; we were like, 'Shall we carry on?' I was even thinking of applying to music college at the time as a way of doing something else. *In A Glass House* was a reaction to all of that and was really quite a frantic record to make.

It was also an important record because it showed the band could make Gentle Giant albums without Phil. So when it was time to record album number six, they were more confident and considerably less frantic. Indeed, *The Power And The Glory* proved to be one of the easiest albums they had made so far.

GG had a set way of working. They would record an album, take it on tour and then, just weeks after the final date, they would start work on the follow-up. The main responsibility for the music rested on the shoulders of Minnear and Ray Shulman, who would both record fragments of ideas in their own home studios before meeting up to pool their efforts.

In the liner notes, Ray explained: 'I'd probably start off improvising on guitar or something, recording a whole load of stuff and just keep going. Then, when listening back, there may have been a certain phrase or a small run that would make you sit up and take notice.' Kerry added: 'You can't collaborate until you've got an idea, but once you had something that worked, we'd phone each other up and arrange to meet after a couple of weeks.'

In the early days of the band, the songs would be true collaborations, with Ray and Minnear fitting together bits and pieces of each other's ideas. By 1974, however, each writer would tend to deliver almost-completed compositions, with a minimum of tweaking required. Derek would then write most of the lyrics, although he would also contribute musical ideas and occasionally complete songs. Then the whole band would meet up for rehearsals in Portsmouth. Drummer John Weathers told Sid Smith in the Blu-ray liner notes:

> It always took a week to ten days. We were very workmanlike, going through the demos that Ray and Kerry had brought, learning them off by heart and arranging them until we were all happy with the end result … The more complex tracks took a lot longer, as you would expect. There were no written parts as such, so we just took them bit by bit using the rough demos I'd been sent earlier in the post, so I had a rough idea of what to expect, as a guide.

Gentle Giant's compositions were demandingly complex (although they became more straightforward as time went on), and songs would frequently stop and start, change direction, change key, change rhythm and change genres. In fact, being 'unique, adventurous and fascinating' was written into their mission statement, included in the liner notes of their second album. They certainly had the musical chops – they played about 46 instruments between them. And they had the ability to craft intricate, complicated compositions drawing on medieval and baroque music forms, as well as folk, jazz and rhythm and blues.

In fact, practically everything went into the melting pot of the typical Gentle Giant creation – it seems too trivial to call them 'songs' – along with an apparent complete and utter disregard for commercial success (although that also changed as time went on). You want progressive? Gentle Giant were way out there, even compared to some of the other prog bands highlighted in this book. Yes, they could rock as hard as anyone else in the genre. But they could also sound like a bunch of minstrels playing at the court of a Tudor monarch.

With five singers in the band, they were capable of the most intricate multi-part harmonies – listen to 'On Reflection' from 1977's *Playing The Game* album and marvel at the sweet and precise vocal blending. And they did it live while playing several instruments each. Amazing.

Their lyrics were as dense and complex as their music and would frequently be drawn from 16th century French literature. Francois Rabelais was a particular favourite. Like the music, the words were simplified as time went on and the band came under pressure from various record labels to be a tad more commercial – and concept albums always demand something a bit more stripped down to carry the story.

In the case of *The Power And The Glory*, the concept was about how power always corrupts – the album's unnamed protagonist, the leader of an equally mysterious state or country, sets out to make life better for his followers but is knocked off course by ambition, greed and hubris. The album opens with 'Proclamation' as the leader addresses his adoring people. Crowd noise gives way to Minnear's sparse keyboard, playing the slightly jazzy melody line, then Derek sings lyrics that will be very familiar to every power-crazed politician: 'You may not have all you want or you need/All that you have has been due to my hand/It can change, it can stay the same'. Even though this was mostly Minnear's song, Derek had a powerful, raspy voice that was more suited to the rockier tracks.

Bass comes in and Minnear plays another jazzy line before going back to the melody under the second verse, the bass playing a bouncy counterpoint melody. 'Hail, hail', cry the people. Verse three continues with themes we are all familiar with from leaders across the world and through the mists of time – 'Unity's strength and all must be as one' – with Weathers providing a steady 4/4 rock beat.

There's a keyboard solo over a fast bass and guitar riff, followed by the band singing 'Hail to power and to glory!' over dramatic church organ chords, then a short silence before tentative keyboard chords take us back for a repeat of verses two and three, and the song fades out on chanting crowd noise again.

It is a powerful and, dare I say it, glorious opener that guitarist Gary Green said was 'tricky to play; you had to wrestle with it so you could get comfortable with it'. Meanwhile, Derek revealed he would psyche himself up to get into character like a method actor before recording his vocal (Blu-ray liner notes, 2014).

It is followed by the even trickier 'So Sincere', in which one of the citizens explains his faith in the leader, who is wise and knowing and always tells the truth. But we also detect a hint of doubt with the juxtaposition of yes and no, lies and truth, full and empty, good and bad, sincere and … sin.

Musically, this exemplifies the gleefully complex nature of some of Gentle Giant's compositions. It opens with Minnear on cello and Ray on violin, the two instruments duelling with short, staccato and apparently random notes. Then Derek starts singing a similarly staccato melody that seems to bear absolutely no relation to what Minnear and Ray are playing. Yet, it somehow manages to fit together, even if it will never be something you'll be humming in the shower.

There is a chorus of sorts that sounds like it's been shoehorned in from a different song, in which Minnear and Derek repeat the title to the sound of discordant guitar and keyboard lines. So weird.

'Aspirations' is a Kerry Minnear song, a mostly gentle (giant) ballad led by his keyboards and sung in his soft, wistful voice. (On stage, Derek would take most of the vocals because Minnear's voice wasn't strong enough.) Lyrically, it's a plea from the people to their leader to 'be our guide, our light and our way of life', and includes the line 'Please make your claims really so sincere', which appears to reference the two preceding tracks.

'Playing The Game' shows us the world through the eyes of the leader as he gains in confidence and arrogance: 'I can view the power of my position, and my eyes can see more than anyone in any place, I'll play the game and never ever lose', sings Derek to a steady rock backing centred on a catchy guitar riff. Halfway through, the song seems to fade out before Minnear croons a sombre middle-eight over some tricksy keyboards, as the leader admits he would never give voice to the delusions of grandeur flitting through his head.

In 'Cogs In Cogs', Derek offers up the metaphor of a wheel turning relentlessly, grinding down everything before it; think of the scene in the 1936 film *Modern Times* when Charlie Chaplin is dragged through the cogs of a huge machine. Once again, the song rocks, but with complicated guitar and keyboard interplay and frequent stops and starts during the verses. There's a middle section in which two voices sing different lines simultaneously – apparently, one voice is in 6/4 and the other in 15/8, which was the sort of thing Gentle Giant used to do for fun.

They do it again on 'No God's A Man', weaving contrapuntal vocal lines together until it is almost impossible to make out the melodies. By GG standards, this is a very pretty song with a more acoustic backing and strummed electric guitar drenched in phasing. The message of the song seems to be the opposite of the title, that no man is a god, no matter how much power he thinks he has, and he will soon fall once the people have turned against him. History shows us that all tyrants eventually fall, although not before they drench their hands in blood, and they are frequently replaced by other tyrants. 'It happens all again', sings Derek.

A frantic violin and popping bass open 'The Face', another song that drives along nicely with frequent instrumental passages. 'The Face' is the mask politicians wear when they have to placate the people with mealy-mouthed apologies and fake concern: 'Use the time, show the face that is sorry … Time to confess, clean up the mess, cast off the mould, buy all you've sold'.

The original LP album ends with 'Valedictory', which reprises the vocal melodies and riffs from 'Proclamation'. However, the message has altered from 'it can change, it can stay the same' to 'things must stay, there can be no change'. In other words, there's nothing we can do to change anything – everything happens over and over again. A cheerful note to end on.

Later CD versions of the album include a single released a month after the album, and confusingly given the same title. In the US music magazine *Trans-Oceanic Trouser Press*, Ray Shulman explained:

[Gentle Giant record company] WWA said, 'Now, boys, you've got to be commercial, you've gotta make singles. Now you run away and write us a single.' So we did three atrocious numbers. This song's the worst – 'You've got it, lads!' – and we went into the studio and handed over the tapes when we came out. They put it out, we yelled at them and they gave it back – took it off the market.

It's not as bad as that. Sure, it romps along in a thoroughly predictable 4/4 rhythm, with a mundane verse-chorus-verse-chorus structure. But there's some great lead guitar, a chopping keyboard backing and lyrics that continue the album's theme of, well, power and glory and how it inevitably corrupts.

Released in an eye-catching cover showing the King of Spades playing card, the album became the band's first top 50 hit in the US, thanks to a hugely successful tour there, including five nights at the famous Whisky A Go Go in Los Angeles. But it flopped in the UK after Gentle Giant fell out with their management. In the CD liner notes, drummer John Weathers said: 'We made a big mistake. We had a tour set up, but because of the management thing, we pulled the tour at the last moment. We stiffed then in England; we were just about to break.' Fifty years later, guitarist Gary Green told *Prog* magazine:

It's always been a mystery to me as to why we never went over as well in the UK as we did elsewhere. We did okay playing big theatres and other large venues, but we largely went unnoticed. The press in Britain love to build you up and tear you down – of course, in our case, we never got built up! They never took a shine to us. There was a sense that we were 'pretentious' and that was the last thing on our mind, honestly.

Gentle Giant were perhaps a little too unconventional, confrontational and idiosyncratic for their own good and probably suffered from the lack of an identifiable frontman like Peter Gabriel or Jon Anderson. Their following is usually described as 'cult', which is another word for 'small'. But over time, they have been recognised as one of the most talented bands to come out of the prog genre.

So far as *The Power And The Glory* is concerned, many fans and critics see it as one of their finest albums in a successful run that goes from, say, *Three Friends* in 1972 to *Freehand* in 1975. They may not have got any glory or power, but they have certainly gained a lot of love and respect.

Gong – *You*

Key personnel:

Daevid Allen ('Dingo Virgin'): glissando guitar, vocals

Gilli Smyth ('Shakti Yoni'): vocals

Didier Malherbe ('Bloomdido Bad de Grasse'): wind instruments and vocals

Tim Blake ('Hi T Moonweed'): Moog, EMS synthesizer, Mellotron

Miquette Giraudy ('Bambaloni Yoni'): vocals

Steve Hillage: lead guitar

Mike Howlett: bass guitar

Pierre Moerlen: drums, percussion

Mireille Bauer: pitched percussion

Benoit Moerlen: pitched percussion

Recorded in the summer of 1974 at The Manor, Oxfordshire

Produced by Gong and Simon Heyworth 'under the universal influence of C.O.I.T., the Compagnie d'Opera Invisible de Thibet'

Engineered by Simon Heyworth

Artwork by Daevid Allen, Tim Blake and Brigitte Blake

Record label: Virgin

Release date: 4 October 1974

Chart placings: did not chart

Tracks: 'Thought For Naught', 'A P.H.P.'s Advice', 'Magick Mother Invocation', 'Master Builder', 'A Sprinkling Of Clouds', 'Perfect Mistery', 'The Isle Of Everywhere', 'You Never Blow Yr Trip Forever'

All tracks by Gong

The Story So Far...

Christopher David 'Daevid' Allen left his home in Melbourne, Australia, to chase jazz and the Beat poets. Arriving in England, he formed The Soft Machine in 1966 with Canterbury Scene alumna Kevin Ayers, Mike Ratledge and Robert Wyatt. Refused entry back into the UK after a European tour, he went to Paris, where he met Londoner Gilli Smyth, who was teaching at the

Sorbonne. Together they formed the Bananamoon Band but had to flee France to Majorca after being caught up in the 1968 student riots. In Majorca, they found Parisian wind instrument player Didier Malherbe living in a cave on the property of writer Robert Graves. Returning to France, Allen was offered a multi-album deal by the Byg Actuel label, so he formed the first proper Gong band with Gilli, Didier and percussionist Rachid Houari. This lineup, with additional musicians, recorded the album *Magick Brother*, released in 1970. After recording solo album *Banana Moon* in the UK, Allen returned to France to create a new Gong lineup, losing Houari but adding Christian Tritsch on bass and Canterbury Scene drummer Pip Pyle. They recorded *Camembert Electrique*, released in 1971, and the soundtrack *Continental Circus*, not set free until 1972. Laurie Allan replaced Pyle on drums, Tritsch moved to guitar, Francis Moze joined on bass and piano and Tim Blake arrived from London to play synthesiser. With Houari back on percussion and Chingford guitarist Steve Hillage arriving too late to provide more than rhythm on a few tracks, they recorded *Flying Teapot* (1973), the first album in the so-called Planet Gong trilogy. Fiji-born Mike Howlett replaced Moze on bass, and Pierre Moerlen replaced Allan on drums, bringing his partner Mireille Bauer on glockenspiel for *Angels Egg* (1973).

The Album

A long time ago in a galaxy far, far away … oops, sorry, wrong cultural myth. But not far off. Because our story does indeed begin in the empty darkness of space – in a black hole, actually, as black as your hat, where there exists a luminous green planet populated by Pot Head Pixies, cheerful little fellows with propellers on their heads. In 1966, they travelled in their space ships – which bear a remarkable resemblance to teapots – to the planet Earth, where they set up camp in the Tibetan Himalayas to broadcast telepathically using Radio Gnome Invisible.

These telepathic messages somehow found their way into the head of one Dacvid Allcn, an Australian department store worker turned beatnik turned guitarist, band leader and potty poet. And what they told him to do was this: write and record a trilogy of albums telling the story of Zero the Hero and his journey to enlightenment. A parable, if you wish, spread across three vinyl LPs and introducing such characters as the Octave Doctors, Fred the Fish, Banana Ananda, the Good Witch Yoni and Captain Capricorn.

The first of the trilogy was *Flying Teapot*, in which we are introduced to the main characters, and Zero leaves his body and the planet Earth. *Angels Egg* dealt with his journey to the Planet Gong, where he is given instructions on how to replicate its peaceful, playful and compassionate society back home. *You* was supposed to complete the story by chronicling his attempts to realise the Gong vision on Earth through a rock festival.

It all sounds very silly – and it is, deliberately so. But there were some serious philosophical and religious ideas behind the tomfoolery. There were certainly influences from Buddhism in the search for enlightenment and the emphasis on optimism and love. The frequent mentions of 'tea' are no doubt a euphemism for cannabis (and had been since the 1940s). And the flying teapots are inspired by philosopher Bertrand Russell's analogy to illustrate that the burden of proof lies on those making unfalsifiable claims, particularly about gods; if he were to assert, without proof, that a tiny teapot, too small to be seen by telescopes, orbits the Sun between Earth and Mars, it would be his responsibility to prove he was right, not others to prove he was wrong.

So far, so weird. But does all this add up to a great progressive rock record? Well, by jingo, it does – the trilogy is revered by all those with musical taste, and *You* is regarded by many as the pinnacle of Daevid Allen's achievement, an irresistible mixture of space-rock and jazz fusion that takes the listener out of the solar system to a galaxy far, far away.

However, it was not without its teething troubles. Allen is frequently depicted as a pixie-like clown, full of merry japes and child-like simplicity, yet he could be a hard-nosed bugger when he wanted to be, particularly when it came to keeping control of the music and the royalties (just ask Tim Blake). Some of the band were unhappy with the occasionally random nature of the composing credits on the *Angels Egg* album – particularly as much of it was composed while Allen and Smyth were on a sabbatical – and began agitating for more equal billing.

Eventually, it was decided to credit all the tracks on *You* to the entire band under the whimsical name of COIT, the Compagnie d'Opéra Invisible de Thibet (although I notice that Wikipedia has separate credits for each song, which makes me think there were some later changes for the Performing Rights Society). And that was fair because the music came from a period of intense collaboration during a gruelling European tour that stretched from October 1973 to May 1974, and then at a rented cottage in Little Bedwyn, Wiltshire. On the *Planet Gong* website, Allen recalled:

We lived there for a week, we saved up some wonderful acid and we took this acid together as a group. And this was one occasion where there was no paranoia; it was just a wonderful, wonderful trip, and we all played and played and played. And we connected so strongly together out of the improvisations, we just improvised and recorded it, and then at the end of the day, we would listen to the recordings and take the pieces out that we wanted to learn.

Some of the tracks they rehearsed slipped into the live setlist from April 1974, including an early version of Steve Hillage's 'Solar Musick Suite' that ended up on his first post-Gong solo album. Songs that were definitely played in that month include 'Perfect Mistery', 'The Isle Of Everywhere' and 'A Sprinkling Of Clouds'. However, few of the new *You* tracks had any lyrics at that stage as Allen didn't write them until May that year. Then in July, Gong went into Manor Studios to make an album that would eventually tear them apart.

You is truly a collaborative effort, with the album dominated by four big beasts – 'Master Builder', 'A Sprinkling Of Clouds', 'The Isle of Everywhere' and 'You Never Blow Yr Trip Forever' – created out of the swirl of musical ideas emanating from every member of the band. The emphasis is on soundscapes and grooves, with fewer vocals and less wacky humour than its predecessors.

That doesn't mean there is nothing here to make you smile. The opener, 'Thought For Naught', is a gentle, Eastern-influenced Didier Malherbe flute tune, just one and a half minutes long. It is a meditation on the meaning of life – Zero has returned from the Planet Gong to find himself tucked up in bed and has to do some serious thinking. Didier does most of the singing in his lugubrious French accent.

'A P.H.P.'s Advice' is another brief ditty, a whimsical, cheeky little tune not unlike a stoned nursery rhyme with tuned percussion, clip-clop and boinging noises, and comedy clarinet licks. Allen's lyrics do what it says on the tin, dispensing advice from a Pot Head Pixie, while Smyth adds child-like interjections.

Two minutes of deep, mystic 'omming' with added space whisper from Gilli and Tim Blake's buzzy synth slip seamlessly into 'Master Builder', a track that has become a Gong classic and one of the few to have been kept in the setlist by the current Gong incarnation. The chunky, Eastern-influenced riff was composed by Hillage – in fact, he woke up one morning in the farm where the band were staying with it in his head. Rushing down to the cottage at Little Bedwyn, he tried it out on guitar, with Mike Howlett on bass.

In the liner notes for the *Love From Planet Gong* boxset (it gathered together the trilogy albums, plus 1976's *Shamal* and associated live recordings), Hillage said: 'We loved it! After a day of jamming around, we had pretty much the whole arrangement, including the melody at the end, to which Daevid later added the 'Master Builder' lyrics. We thought this was one of Gong's finest moments!' So good, in fact, that Steve also recycled it for his 1978 album *Green* as 'The Glorious Om Riff'.

Divided into three sections on the lyric sheet, it opens with the 'Mystic Mister Invocation' – a chant by the band that emerges from the 'oms' of the previous track, rising in volume and intensity. They sing 'iao za-i za-o', representing sexuality; 'ma-i ma-o', representing the mother force; and 'ta-i ta-o now', representing the light force. The melody consists of just two alternating notes, G and G sharp. Pierre's drums build up in intensity until the whole thing explodes into Didier's saxophone solo.

Then, after a few brief key changes, everything suddenly stops, and there is a brief moment of silence apart from the sound of birds twittering before Allen's vocal comes in for section two, in which Zero seeks to bring his vision from Gong down to Earth. 'Maybe you know', says Allen, as the band jump in and out of earshot, punctuated by strange discordant sounds on Hillage's guitar. Then we leap back into the chants, with frantic, piercing lead guitar from Steve.

After about five-and-a-half minutes, we enter section three, in which Zero asks Hiram the Builder how to structure his vision. The answer comes in Allen's 'Master Builder' lyric – 'Master Builder, tell me how you make a temple? Tools and moon stones, you don't really need them you know' – as the song's key rises up ... and up ... before coming to a sudden and unexpected stop.

'A Sprinkling Of Clouds' is another opportunity for Hillage to squeeze cosmic notes out of his guitar. However, it was written mostly by Tim Blake, who composed the twinkling synth part in his room at the farm – Mike Howlett remembers he had a fairly large space above what were originally cowsheds with his synth studio dominating most of the area. He told me:

> It was a beautiful piece built on arpeggios with a very long tape echo, so the harmonies all built on each other and slowly revolved. I thought it took a lot of inspiration from [US minimalist composer] Terry Riley, who was a long-time friend of Daevid and Didier. I brought the two riffs to the piece, the first half being constructed with four bars of 5/8 and one bar of 4/8, adding up to 24 quavers.

Mike plays a nice little bass solo at about three minutes in, there's a warm glissando underneath and the whole thing feels like you are drifting through the clouds. Restrained drums in 4/4 – just some cymbals and rimshots – come in at about the two-minute mark as everything begins to build up in volume and intensity. Blake's keyboard flourishes become more pronounced before, at about five and a half minutes, everything kicks into top gear, with Howlett contributing a tricky, driving bass pattern and Hillage's lead guitar crashing in, playing discordant, apparently random notes before settling into a riff that's reminiscent of section three of 'Master Builder'.

Didier comes in with a sax solo at seven minutes, the drums are now pounding away and the music is almost literally taking the tops of our heads off and sending them into orbit. Finally, we have a slow winding down and the tune ends on Didier's bamboo flute and Blake's synth. In an album packed full of wonderful musical moments, this is almost – but not quite – the high point.

Allen was criticised by some members of the band for having little to offer the *You* recording sessions apart from stuff dating back to 1970. But Steve Hillage said he wanted an old song to link the new material with the earlier Gong sound. 'Perfect Mistery' certainly dates back to at least 5 January 1971, when it was performed for French TV and released on an 'unofficial' CD of *Continental Circus* in Sweden in 2011 under the title 'Excerpt From Camembert Electrique' (although it doesn't actually appear on that album).

It opens with four piercing notes on guitar, followed by a tune Allen had already used a few times in the past – the Irish song 'Oh, Can You Wash Your

Father's Shirt', a pretty nursery rhythm-style piano practice piece using just the black notes. Then comes the first verse, which has the same lyrics as the 1971 version, including the amusing and slightly paranoiac couplet 'Cops at the door! No cops at the door...' A short, gentle interlude of Gilli talking over minor chords picked out on guitar leads us back into the four-note intro again and another rendition of the Irish nursery rhyme.

The second verse has clearly been freshly-written for *You* as it references the track that is about to follow, 'The Isle Of Everywhere', and takes Allen's Zero the Hero story a little further – he has set off for the island in search of illumination. It ends with Gilli intoning: 'What a surprise – she looked around for Zero but he's lost his eyes in a fruitcake'!

If one were to identify the track that most fully represents Gong in all its groovy, space-rock glory, it would probably be 'The Isle Of Everywhere'. It's not the longest recording in the trilogy – that's 'Flying Teapot' from volume one, which originally clocked in at more than 12 minutes – but this is still nearly ten and a half minutes of pounding, funky, glissando-drenched wonderment, with inspired soloing from Steve and Didier, nimble and inventive drumming from Pierre and a funky bassline from Mike that holds everything together.

In fact, one can look at this and 'You Never Blow Yr Trip Forever' as one continuous 22-minute track, if you like, as it was recorded in a single live take, solos included, with only a few minor overdubs and Allen's vocals added later. Bearing in mind the many changes of chords, timings and pace involved, that is an astonishing feat and could only be achieved by a group of musicians who were at the very top of their game.

According to the original lyric sheet included with the first pressing of the album, there are three sections to 'The Isle Of Everywhere'. The first, called 'The Melting Feast Of Freaks', was devised by Mike Howlett, who came up with the bouncing bass riff and the continuous cycle of three semi-tone key changes, similar to the verse chords in 'Oily Way' on *Angels Egg*. He told me: 'My intention was to create a structure for improvisation that would allow us to roam freely wherever the music took us, but to have a base to return to so that it was not aimless.' The band discovered the bass riff worked in a number of different timings, including 7/8 and 3/4. Didier and Steve both solo over the cycle of chords, Daevid adds glissando guitar and Tim supports with warm synth pads.

Section two, entitled 'Get It Inner', was written mostly by Didier and consists of the sax player making mischievous pixie sounds before engaging in a bizarre, barely audible little dialogue with Zero over Pierre's steady, no-frills drumming and various squeaks and pops of musical sound from Tim. Finally, section three, called 'Peace Of Mind Or Piece Of Cake Or Zero Goofs Again', is Tim's synth wash under Allen singing 'Zero ... where are you...' as the band begin to play the chords for the following track, and Didier provides swooping flute. Howlett told me:

Everyone brought something to the piece because of the improvised solos – Gilli's magical space whisper on the intro, Didier's beautiful solo cycle and, of course, Steve really kicking it up a level for his final cycle. Daevid's glissando guitar creates wonderful and strange harmonic frameworks that shift the tonal sense around, as well as being a big part of the illusion of constantly rising throughout. I think that combination of ingredients, including Tim's special synth bubbling and swoops, was just about the most perfect instance of Gong's unique sound.

The last of the four big pieces on the album, 'You Never Blow Yr Trip Forever', is, once again, a multi-sectioned beast with riffs and musical ideas both old and new. Most of it came from Steve and Daevid; some of it originated during the rehearsals in Little Bedwyn, and one part dates back to 1969. The track starts slowly but quickly bursts into life with Hillage playing the powerful, disturbing riff, accompanied by some apparently random time signatures between Allen's lyrics. 'Maybe you're here for the giggle, maybe you're into the puzzle', Allen sings, addressing the listener as much as any of the characters in his story.

There's a chorus of sorts in the 'more you know the more you know you don't know' stanza that ends with a statement of the song title, although this particular musical sequence is repeated twice more without the title making another appearance. Then we enter the oldest section of the song, the 'hole in the morning', originally part of a composition called 'Mana Maya Mantram' from 1969 – a short snippet appeared on a limited-edition tape from the Gong Appreciation Society.

We are now about halfway through, with Allen scatting along to Hillage's lead guitar as the band play a steady, pulsing three-quarter time rhythm that builds up in volume and power before seemingly falling apart into the final sequence of 'Why don't you try?' and 'You are I and I am you'. Didier's flute, Gilli's space whisper and Daevid's ghostly chanting take us into the final few minutes that, live, would be a chance for the entire audience to join in the final lines and express their 'oneness' with the band, winning over even the most cynical listener. The sound fades ... slowly ... to silence.

Released at a time when Virgin Records were in dispute with Allen's original label, Byg, the album probably didn't get the promotional push it really deserved. At one point, all Gong records were pulled off the shelves after Byg obtained an injunction against Richard Branson's company. There were also the inevitable lineup changes – and some of them would completely alter the nature of Gong. On 10 April 1975, Daevid Allen left the band he had created five years previously. As usual, he had a somewhat whimsical explanation for his departure during a gig in Cheltenham:

I couldn't actually get on stage. It was as though there was an invisible curtain of force that was stopping me from going through the door. I threw myself at the open door and bounced back off – nothing. And this blew my mind so thoroughly that I just ran out of the theatre into the rain and started hitch-hiking on the road with all my clothes, my stage clothes, my costume and face painted with fluorescent colours. And then a woman looked at me so strangely that I started thinking I was a murderer and I was hiding in the bushes. Finally, I got picked up by somebody who had left the concert, was taken home, and then I had to realise that I had to leave Gong, so that's the way it all ended.

In hindsight, however, it's clear Allen's dissatisfaction went way back to *Flying Teapot* and the difficulties he had with record companies and drummers, and keeping control of the monster he had created. Hillage accepted that Allen was feeling frustrated at not being at the creative core of so much of the music on *You*, while Pierre Moerlen said Allen believed the music was becoming too complex and virtuosic. Allen also had two young children to bring up, who had decamped to Deya with their mother, Gilli. He had simply had enough.

It would be another 18 years before an Allen-led Gong album would re-emerge. But he had certainly left on a high – the album was named one of *Rolling Stone* magazine's 50 Greatest Prog Rock Albums Of All Time, and its influence in the five decades since its release has stretched beyond progressive rock into the worlds of ambient, techno and trance music. In 1997, it was released as a double album remixed by the likes of The Orb, The Shamen, Astralasia, Youth and System 7. For many fans, it is the pinnacle of Gong's art – it is certainly a big, bold album that has lost none of its impact.

Sadly, Allen died in 2015, but the band he created and led for the preceding five decades is still going strong, releasing new albums and touring across the world – despite the fact that some of the current members weren't even alive when the first Gong album came out! These days, Gong's setlist consists mostly of new material recorded and released in the last decade, but one track – 'Master Builder' – always makes a welcome appearance.

It's a reminder that, with *You*, Daevid Allen and Gong created a masterpiece that still thrills and enthrals some 50 years later.

Jethro Tull – *War Child*

Key personnel:

Ian Anderson: vocals, flute, acoustic guitar, alto, soprano and sopranino saxophones

Martin Barre: electric guitar, Spanish guitar

John Evan: piano, organ, synthesisers, accordion

Jeffrey Hammond: lead vocals and spoken word (on 'Sealion II'), bass guitar, string bass

Barriemore Barlow: drums, percussion, glockenspiel, marimba

Recorded between 7 December 1973 and 24 February 1974 at Morgan Studios, London, except track 6 on 10 September 1972, and track 8 on 15 September 1972 at the Château d'Hérouville, France

Produced by Ian Anderson & Terry Ellis

Engineered by Robin Black

Record label: Chrysalis

Release date: 14 October 1974

Chart placings: US: 2, CA: 3, IT: 7, NO: 8, DK and AU: 9, UK: 14

Tracks: 'War Child', 'Queen And Country', 'Ladies', 'Back-Door Angels', 'Sealion', 'Skating Away On The Thin Ice Of A New Day', 'Bungle In The Jungle', 'Only Solitaire', 'The Third Hoorah', 'Two Fingers'

All tracks by Ian Anderson

The Story So Far...

Originally called the John Evan Band/Smash, formed by Blackpool schoolmates Ian Anderson, Jeffrey Hammond and John Evans (the 's' came and went) in 1964. They recruited drummer Barriemore Barlow and guitarist Chris Riley, playing blue-eyed soul. Hammond was replaced on bass by Glenn Cornick and Riley by Mick Abrahams. By 1967, they were a four-piece blues band with Clive Bunker on drums. The new name, Jethro Tull, came from a booking agent's staff member, who was a history buff (Mr Tull invented the horse-drawn seed drill in 1700), and the first single, 'Aeroplane' – originally recorded by the John Evan Smash – was released in 1968 on MGM Records (and famously mistakenly credited to 'Jethro Toe'). Signed to Island Records, the band recorded a blues album heavily influenced by Abrahams, who left soon after (or was pushed). The title, *This Was*, suggested changes to come. Recruiting new guitarist Martin Barre, leader Anderson took Jethro Tull in the direction of progressive blues and folk, releasing the UK number-one album *Stand Up* in 1968 and the number-three single 'Living In The Past'. The follow-up, *Benefit*, in 1970 fared less well despite the return of John Evan(s) on keyboards, but 1971's *Aqualung* was a million-seller, cracking the US top ten. Bunker left in May 1971 and was replaced by Barrie Barlow. 1972's single-track opus, *Thick As A Brick*, was a number-one record in many countries, while the denser *A Passion Play* (1973) received such hostile reviews from some quarters that it was announced the band had split up.

The Album

'Jethro Retire Hurt!' screamed the headline in *Melody Maker*. 'Jethro Tull, high in the world's charts with *A Passion Play*, amazed the music world this week by announcing their retirement because of 'the abuse heaped upon the show by the critics", the article continued.

It was, of course, total bunkum, a publicity stunt engineered by the band's manager, Terry Ellis. But it was true that Tull had been mauled by the critics over their 1973 album *A Passion Play* and subsequent tour, with Chris Welch of *Melody Maker* saying it 'rattles with emptiness', and the *New Musical Express* predicting the band's 'fall'.

Ian Anderson was certainly hurt by the criticism – in the liner notes for the 2014 boxset he admitted:

> We felt a bit betrayed ... and a bit bemused, really, as to why they didn't like it. We didn't feel it was that bad, y'know. I guess I had the feeling that it was a bit ponderous, a little too pompous and a bit overly-complex, but I didn't expect to get hammered ... It was a salutary experience in accepting that not everything you do is going to be appreciated, or tolerated even. So, ultimately, a good lesson – just like being caned at school.

With their backsides smarting, Anderson and his crew kept their heads down for a while before bursting back into the music press with grandiose plans for their next project. Not only was there going to be a new album, they said, but there was going to be a feature-length film and a soundtrack release.

It was the sort of ambitious guff that bands used to come up with back in the 1970s, and, unsurprisingly, things didn't quite work out the way they intended. However, there WAS a synopsis for the movie, written by Anderson in mid-1973 and inspired by the quasi-religious concept that underpinned *A Passion Play*. It would be a musical fantasy about a young girl who dies and goes to heaven, only to find that it looks just like a small English town. There then follows a series of 'hilarious' misadventures during which the powers of

Good and Evil – represented by the rulers of heaven, G. Oddie & Sons, and the devilish Peter du Jour – battle for her soul. There would be jokes by John Cleese of *Monty Python* fame.

Anderson even went so far as to attach some big names to the project. He offered the role of Peter du Jour to Donald Pleasence, star of such films as *The Great Escape* and *You Only Live Twice*. But Pleasence wanted to get away from being typecast as the villain and asked to play God, which Anderson thought would be 'a fun twist'.

He also approached Dame Margot Fonteyn for a ballet dancing role, and signed up Jane Colthorpe, who was the loose-limbed ballerina on the cover of *A Passion Play*. Then he went hunting for a director. Lindsay Anderson (no relation), who had made *If...* and *O Lucky Man!*, was, apparently, rude and dismissive; Bryan Forbes (*Seance On A Wet Afternoon, The Colditz Story, An Inspector Calls*) was interested but wanted to set the film in an underground railway station during World War II.

The next problem was money. Basically, the UK didn't have any, certainly not for a rock star trying to make a dark, arty film. So Anderson (the Tull one) looked to America, only to face demands for US stars and a director before anyone would consider investing a cent. Anderson said: 'So at that point I ran out of steam … I thought, sod it, this is going to take such a long time and lots of work. It's not the moment, move on.'

He did get something out of the project, and that was plenty of music. Usually, a film is shot first and the score is written to an early cut. But Anderson had already sketched out some rough ideas for the soundtrack, and, with the help of the band's arranger David (now Dee) Palmer, had recorded 30 minutes of music with a full orchestra at London's Conway Hall in February 1974, as well as contributions from the rest of Tull at Morgan Studios.

The results were hidden away in a vault for 40 years until their release in the 2014 boxset – and they make fascinating listening for any rabid Tull fan. 'The Orchestral War Child' is, as the title suggests, an orchestral version of the eventual group album's title track, a swelling, emotional piece of music that could have come from the combined pens of John Barry and Elgar (Palmer liked it so much he recreated it for Tull's 1985 classical crossover album *A Classic Case*).

'The Third Hoorah' is like a Scottish jig, again recorded with an orchestra, that could have come from the Broadway show *Brigadoon* – you can almost see the cast dancing across the stage, kilts a-flying. There's even bagpipes towards the end. Och-aye! 'Mime Sequence' is another folk-influenced tune in jig rhythm, with the orchestra tooting over Martin Barre's acoustic guitar, breaking off for a contemplative central section, while 'Field Dance' is in a similar vein but with less of a rhythmic pulse, although it reprises 'The Third Hoorah' at the end. Think Ralph Vaughan-Williams crossed with Delius.

'Waltz Of The Angels', which Palmer compared to Tchaikovsky, is a pretty tune led by the flute, with lovely orchestral flourishes and some pretty violin work. It was the only one of these tracks to be officially issued before the box set, as 'War Child Waltz' on a 2002 release of the *War Child* album. 'The Beach Parts I & II' are more sombre pieces led by piano and featuring what sounds like a smaller orchestral ensemble than the previous tracks – they were intended for an opening sequence set, unsurprisingly, on a beach.

So there was plenty of crossover between the 'soundtrack album' Anderson planned and the eventual group LP – indeed, most of the songs appear to have been written and recorded at the same time. The exceptions are two songs that came from 1972 sessions at Chateau d'Herouville (where Elton John recorded his album *Honky Chateau*) that were supposed to be the follow-up to *Thick As A Brick* but were scrapped because of technical problems (and dubbed Chateau d'Isaster by Anderson). Meanwhile, a third track was a reworking of an aborted single from 1971. In the box set liner notes, Anderson says:

I think after the pressures of the Chateau d'Isaster and *A Passion Play* album, this was a more relaxed record to make. It was mostly recorded at Studio 2 in Morgan, which was the smaller one and was really quite cosy, and was my preference. The studio equipment worked; the sound in the studio was very workable, and what you heard was what you got on tape. So the atmosphere within the band was very settled and very productive. And it helped that everyone was able to stay in their own homes and commute to work.

Anderson also recalls that guitarist Martin Barre had bought a Bentley car and had to check beneath it every night just in case the IRA had decided to blow it up. As to his comments about productivity, the band managed to record more than 20 tracks, some of which didn't reach fans' ears until the aforementioned 2014 box set, although a few came out as singles.

By the time *War Child* was being put together for release, it was clear there was going to be no film and no soundtrack album. Instead, it is a return to the song-based albums before *Thick As A Brick*, with ten tracks, the longest clocking in at a mere five and a half minutes. Like *A Passion Play*, however, it showcases more saxophone than flute, even though most people's idea of Anderson was of a one-legged flute warbler. He was a good sax player, but, in his own words, 'it was an instrument I was never ultimately to enjoy having in my life, and especially in a practical sense of having another lump of plumbing to carry around.'

The album opens with the title track, a rock band version of the orchestral piece arranged by Palmer. But the intro caused a certain amount of consternation for unwitting listeners, as it contains the sound of air raid sirens and exploding bombs. I remember playing it when I was living at home, and my father thinking World War III had started. It also includes a woman's voice saying: 'Would you like another cup of tea, dear?' That was Jackie, the tea lady at Morgan studios.

Lyrically, 'War Child' is about the good and evil that lies within us all, our ability to be both destructive and constructive, and also refers to the central character in the aborted film. 'War Child, dance the days and nights away', sings Anderson before a sax solo over pounding piano chords. 'Queen And Country' is a jaunty tune led by an accordion that refers back to the Elizabethan swashbucklers such as Sir Walter Raleigh and Sir Francis Drake, with a great Barre guitar solo in the middle. 'Ladies' is an idealised vision of prostitution, depicting high-class hookers with a 'Florence Nightingale vibe'. Anderson said in the liner notes:

> Like many people, I was brought up to believe that prostitutes were dirty creatures who were unclean and smelly and awful. So I had in mind when writing this song to put the veneer of respect on what was historically a sordid profession. But it was something that was largely a romantic notion on my part because at that time I'd never actually met anyone who I knew to be a prostitute.

Well, that's his story, and he's sticking to it. The, er, ladies of negotiable affection also turn up on 'Back-door Angels', which has a darker vibe compared to 'Ladies' and shows off Martin Barre's guitar skills in two extended instrumental sections. The lyrics in 'Sealion' suggest a performing pinniped in a circus, but the song, according to Anderson, is 'an allegory for the pressures of modern life, but in the context of a looming ecological disaster scenario.'

We forget that even 50 years ago, scientists were warning about climate change, although they were predicting a new Ice Age caused by global cooling, a scenario given greater prominence on Jethro Tull's 1979 album *Stormwatch*. It wasn't until the 1980s that samples from the north and south poles suggested the threat would be from increasing temperatures, not decreasing.

Tull were one of the few bands writing about the impending ecological mayhem at the time, although Anderson's messages were mixed up with ideas about using animals as a metaphor for human behaviour. These ideas fuelled the abortive Chateau d'Isaster sessions that were eventually scrapped in favour of *A Passion Play*, but Anderson resurrected some of the concepts for *War Child*.

Indeed, the side two opener, 'Skating Away On The Thin Ice Of A New Day', was one of the chateau recordings, with accordion and flutes added later. A bright, upbeat ditty driven by Anderson's acoustic guitar, it offers an optimistic assessment of climate change – 'we've been here before, we can cope', explained Anderson. It has become a much-loved Tull classic and was the second single released from the album.

The first single, the catchy 'Bungle In The Jungle', was another reworked Chateau d'Isaster concept – the ideas first surfaced in abandoned tracks including 'Law Of The Bungle' and 'Tiger Toon'. Human beings are nothing more than monkeys trampling on each other in their fight to get to the top of the tree and grab most of the coconuts. An intro complete with jungle animal sounds drives the message home. A catchy chorus helped take the song to number 12 on the US *Billboard* chart, but Anderson admitted, 'it kind of gets on your tits after a while.'

Another song that survived from the chateau sessions was 'Only Solitaire', a short, solo acoustic piece that served as Anderson's response to a critical review of *Thick As A Brick* by *Sounds* journalist Steve Peacock, who complained: 'Ian Anderson has borrowed and created his own cliches, and stays with them – even on this new album.'

Anderson parodies critics' complaints by describing himself as a 'weary, winsome actor spewing spineless chilling lines … and really not an awful lot of fun', ending by addressing Peacock directly to describe his music-making activities as 'only solitaire'. Anderson adds in the liner notes: 'I'm basically saying, don't worry about it because I'm not doing it for you, I'm doing it for me.' The song was even more apt by the time it was released, with many fans thinking it was a riposte to the biting criticism directed at *A Passion Play*.

'The Third Hoorah' we've met before, as a Scottish-sounding jig tune initially intended for the film soundtrack, complete with bagpipes by an unknown musician who played outside a shop near the Chrysalis offices. Anderson adds lyrics that take the almighty mickey out of his school song at Blackpool Grammar, a version of 'When The Foeman Bares His Steel' from Gilbert & Sullivan's *The Pirates Of Penzance* that depicts going into battle as a gloriously romantic pursuit rather than being the bloody butchery it usually is. The title is a reference to the 'hip, hip, hoorah' chant that, for some reason, always comes in threes.

Finally, Anderson goes back to 1971 for the closing track on the album, one that also references the themes in *A Passion Play* and the movie synopsis. 'Two Fingers' was originally recorded as 'Lick Your Fingers Clean' during the *Aqualung* sessions, and narrowly avoided being a single. For the *War Child* album, Anderson wrote an acoustic guitar strum that alternates between A and D, then B and E. The lyrics are about facing judgment in the afterlife – 'I'll see you at the weighing-in, when your life's sum-total's made/And you set your wealth in goodly deeds against the sins you've laid'. But Anderson says it wasn't chosen for the album because of its lyrical content, but simply because he had run out of songs.

Actually, that doesn't really ring true because, as I've already pointed out, some 20 songs were written and recorded as possible album contenders, including two that didn't appear until the band's *Ring Out Solstice Bells* EP in 1977. One of them was a flute-led instrumental called 'Pan Dance' that was written for Pan's People – an all-girl dance troupe from BBC TV's *Top Of The Pops* – to cavort along to on stage during Tull's *War Child* tour.

The album was released with a cover showing a negative image of Anderson holding a Roman war standard, superimposed over the Australian city of Melbourne, and a picture on the back of various members of the band, crew, record label bosses and various wives and girlfriends dressed to depict songs from the album.

As predicted in 'Only Solitaire', the critics fell over to tell themselves that *War Child* was boring. *Rolling Stone* magazine said every track was 'chock-full of schmaltz', adding: 'Remember: Tull rhymes with dull.' Later reviews suggested *War Child* suffered in comparison to its predecessors because it was a step back to shorter, separate songs, although it is hard to see what else Anderson could have done after the bruising experience of *A Passion Play*.

The fans, however, liked it enough to give it a good top 20 showing across most of the globe, including a number two hit in the US, and there are enough good ideas on it to make *War Child* a middle-tier Jethro Tull album. And in my totally unbiased opinion, even an average Tull album is better than most bands' bangers.

Jethro Tull posed in a typically eccentric fashion around the time of *War Child*'s release.

Christian Vander & Magma – *Tristan Et Iseult (Wurdah Itah)* & *Kohntarkosz*

Key personnel:
Klaus Blasquiz: vocals, percussion
Stella Vander: vocals
Gerard Bikialo: pianos, Yamaha organ
Michel Graillier: pianos, clavinet
Brian Godding: guitar
Jannick 'Janik' Top: bass, cello, vocals, piano
Christian Vander: drums, vocals, piano, percussion
Tristan Et Iseult (Wurdah Itah) recorded between 4 and 8 April 1974 at Studio de Milan, Paris
Produced by Laurent Thibault
Engineered by Jean-Pierre Bameulle
Record label: Barclay (1974), Egg (1978), Seventh Records (1989)
Release date: 15 June 1974 (as Tristan Et Iseult), 1978 (as Wurdah Itah)
Chart placings: did not chart
Tracks. 'Malawëlëkaahm', 'Bradïa Da Zïmehn Iëgah', 'Manëh Fur Da Zëss', 'Fur Dï hël Kobaïa', 'Blüm Tendiwa', 'Wohldünt Mëm Dëwëlëss', 'Waïnsaht!!!', 'Wlasïk Steuhn Kobaïa', 'Sëhnntëht Dros Wurdah Süms', 'C'est La Vie Qui Les A Menés Là!', 'Ëk Sün Da Zëss', 'De Zeuhl Ündazïr'
Additional track on 2017 release: 'Wurdah Itah' (Prima Materia)
All tracks by Christian Vander
Kohntarkosz recorded some time in 1974 at Bastide de Pierrefeu, Valbonne, with the Manor Mobile
Produced by Giorgio Gomelsky
Engineered by Simon Heyworth
Record labels: Vertigo, A&M, Seventh Day
Release date: 10 September 1974
Chart placings: did not chart
Tracks: 'Kohntarkosz Part 1', 'Ork Alarm' (Jannick Top), 'Kohntarkosz Part 2',

'Coltrane Sundia'
All tracks by Christian Vander unless stated

The Story So Far...

Inspired by the death of John Coltrane, rhythm and blues band drummer Christian Vander (born Nogent-sur-Marne, Val-de-Marne, France) formed Uniweria Zekt Magma Composedra Arguezdra with saxophonist René Garber, bassist Laurent Thibault, singer Lucien Zabuski and organist Francis Moze to play his own compositions.

The name was soon mercifully shortened to Magma. After their first tour, Zabuski was replaced by Parisian Klaus Blasquiz, pianist Eddie Rabin joined and left, replaced by Francois Cahen, and Thibault left, with Moze moving to bass. With the addition of Claude Engel on guitar, Ted Lasry on sax and clarinet, Richard Raux on sax and flute, and Paco Charkery on trumpet, the band signed to Phillips Records and released their self-titled debut album in 1970. Engel left, Jeff Seffer replaced Raux and Louis Toesca replaced Charlery for the second album, *1001 Centigrade* (1971). There was a mass exodus in 1972 as Cahen, Toesca, Seffer, Moze and Lasry quit. In 1973, Vander added his Paris-born wife Stella as second vocalist, Claude Olmos on guitar, Jannick Top (born Marseille, France) on bass, Rene Garber on sax and clarinet and Jean-Luc Manderlier on keyboards. This lineup, with additional vocalists, released the band's most acclaimed album, *Mekanik Destruktiw Kommandoh*.

The Albums

Christian Vander and Jannick Top had fallen out. So much so that when classically-trained drummer Vander moved into a hilltop castle in Spain, bassist Top bought another castle in a nearby valley just to annoy him. Then things got a bit weird...

The band's management sent Martin Cole to patch things up between them so they could get back to work recording their strange but compelling music. But when Cole arrived at Top's castle, he found him with serious chest wounds, as if he had been attacked by a wild animal.

Top's explanation was almost – perhaps entirely – unbelievable. He claimed that he and Vander had been locked in a 'magic war', with the pair hurling spells at each other from their respective castles like something out of Harry Potter, and Vander had magically forced Jannick to attempt to rip out his own heart...

Welcome to the disturbing world of Magma.

In many ways, Magma were the polar opposites of Gong, the dark to their light, the yang to their yin. Like Gong, they were formed in France in the late 1960s by a visionary maverick. And just like Gong, the maverick invented an entire mythology centred on a made-up planet, claiming the music was somehow beamed into his head.

But where Planet Gong was a benign green sphere populated by friendly pixies with propellers on their heads, travelling around in flying teapots, the Magma planet Kobaia was a refuge for humans fleeing their polluted Earth, sparking a cosmic conflict. And the music that accompanied it wasn't hippy and trippy like Gong, but dark, menacing, repetitive and drenched in doom.

Oh, and there was another important difference between Gong and Magma. The former sang, mostly, in recognisable English with an Australian twang. Magma sang in Kobaian, an aggressive, Germanic-sounding language wholly invented by Vander. It was the language from hell. In a 2017 interview with website *Musoscribe*, Vander explained:

The main purpose of the lyrics is to allow the music to be as expressive as possible. I'm always giving the example of John Coltrane, who was playing an instrument; any people who are playing an instrument are expressing something that people can understand, even if there are no words. So, the lyrics are the closest possible thing to the music to make it *sound* right, because I never wanted to write in French (except for a few words in French – and a few in English). Because the idea is to have a novel of sounds that expresses the most from the music, and that's why I invented the language: because I couldn't do it with any existing language. The sound of the vocal is very important in Magma's music. It has to not [distract] from the expression felt by the people listening to it.

The fact that it sounds somewhat Germanic is, perhaps, not an accident. Vander clearly wanted the vocals to come across as aggressive, militaristic and threatening. Langue francais, the language of love, simply wouldn't have worked. Vander said the sounds came naturally to him as he sat composing on a piano – 50 years later, you can find an entire Kobaian dictionary online if that is your idea of a good time. Here's a sample: Kobaia means Eternal Land; Zimehn, The Initiated; Kreun Kohrmahn, Kobaia's Supreme Being; Hur!, Hello; Hoi Hamtai Sim Rim Hamtai, a formal Welcome; Wlasik, Sorry! I apologise!

Imagine every Magma singer from 1970 to the present day – because the band is still going, still led from the drum kit by Vander and still releasing powerful albums – having to learn the language. Oh, and imagine all those words smothered in umlauts. The band's militaristic approach was echoed in their stage persona – black outfits, frowning faces – and Vander's metal drum kit with spikes sticking out of it.

As I mentioned above, the Magma mythology has an ecological bent – the polluted Earth is doomed, so a group of people flee to settle on Kobaia. When descendants of the colonists return to our planet, they spark conflict with the humans. Vander may seem ahead of his time – here we are, 50 years later, suffering the effects of climate change and fearing for the future of our existence – but it wasn't so much the ecological message that he wanted to communicate, but the stupidity of Mankind. It was mean and selfish men who were the problem, and Kobaia was a planet that was mercifully free of them.

This brings us to some worrying aspects of Vander's mythology. There have been claims from fans and a former Magma keyboard player, Emmanuel Borghi, that Vander's beliefs slip into what most people would define as fascism. Some of the assertions include album credits thanking 'our Uncle' – an alleged reference to Hitler – the lyric 'Fuhl mehn Fuhl ehndoh litaah' in *Mekanik Destruktiw Kommandoh* that is supposed to translate as 'fur mein Fuhrer Adolf Hitler', and a vocal section on the 2019 album *Zess* that is said to be phonetic excerpts from one of the Nazi leader's speeches.

There are more claims about overheard statements and incidents of alleged racism, but it is only fair to point out that Vander has never made any public statement supporting Nazi ideology, and the claims seem to rest on interpreting – or misinterpreting – coded messages in a language only Vander truly understands. It has also been pointed out that he married a Jewish woman, Stella Zelcer, the daughter of Polish immigrants, who still performs with him in the band despite the fact that they divorced in the 1980s.

Musically, we know Vander was heavily influenced by John Coltrane – in an undated online interview with *The Rocktologist*, he said he was inspired by Coltrane's 'energy, the fury of playing, construction, the 'sound', the long-term vision … I always hear his music differently, I rediscover him every time, and it always fascinates me.'

Magma's music reminds me of *Carmina Burana* by Carl Orff, the 20th-century German composer who set medieval monks' chants about sex, drinking, gluttony and gambling (well, they were monks after all) to heavily rhythmic, harmonically simple melodies. So was Vander; he says he first heard Orff's work in 1972 and found surprising similarities to his own music. He said to himself: 'This is exactly the orchestration and formation I would like to have in Magma.'

By 1974, Magma were riding a relative commercial high after the release of their most acclaimed album, *Mekanik Destructiw Kommandoh*, which had taken two difficult years to record. It was with this album, the band's third, that Vander solidified his musical style, which came to be dubbed Zeuhl, defined as a hybrid of jazz fusion, symphonic rock and neoclassical music.

What does Zeuhl sound like? Pumping bass, jazzy drums, two or more voices weaving melodic chants around each other, and plenty of hypnotic repetition that slowly builds into a climax. Or, as Vander told Dominique Leone for *Pitchfork* magazine in 2000:

L'esprit au travers de la matière [Mind over matter]. That is Zeuhl. Zeuhl is also the sound that you can feel vibrating in your belly. Pronounce the word Zeuhl very slowly, and stress the letter 'z' at the beginning, and you will feel your body vibrating. That is exactly what our music is all about: the kind of sound that comes from way down.

It is a tribute to Vander that there have been more than 20 bands that have since defined themselves as Zeuhl, including Art Zoyd and Zao from France, Happy Family and Koenji Hyakkei from Japan, Univers Zero and Present from Belgium, Guapo from the UK, Universal Totem Orchestra from Italy and Zamla Mammaz Manna from Sweden. By the way, it has nothing to do with Zuul, the totally invented 'Terror Dog' in the first *Ghostbusters* movie.

So in 1974, Magma's record company was champing at the bit for another *Mekanik Destruktiw Kommandoh*. What it got was, first, a Christian Vander solo album. This was his score for *Tristan Et Iseult*, an avant-garde film by Yvan Lagrange that retold the medieval tale of the doomed love affair between Tristan, a Cornish knight, and an Irish princess, Iseult, during the days of King Arthur. The music for the film (used without Vander's permission, according to some sources) was originally recorded in 1972 as a 25-minute suite with just bass, piano, vocals and percussion.

Two years later, Vander gathered together another small group consisting of himself on keyboards, drums and vocals, Jannick Top on bass, Stella on vocals and Klaus Blasquiz on vocals and percussion to record 12 short pieces drawn from his original 1972 musical sketch. The result is sparser than the usual Magma output but no less powerful – chanting voices on the edge of hysteria shout away repeatedly over pounding piano, bass and drums.

The original recording pretty much overpowers the film (which could easily have been the blueprint for *Monty Python And The Holy Grail* – it is ludicrous nonsense) every time it appears. The remake has more light and shade to it, with the music swelling and fading like waves pounding a Cornish beach. What it lacks in orchestral density, it certainly makes up for in energy, melody and menace.

It was released in 1974 as a film soundtrack under Vander's name, but was later re-released as a bona fide Magma album with the title *Wurdah Itah*. Furthermore, it was divorced from the movie by the claim that it was actually part two of a three-part musical fresco called *Theusz Hamtaahk* (part three was *Mekanik Destruktiw Kommandoh*, part one was a live track not released until 1981. Never let it be said that Magma do things in a logical manner.)

If *Wurdah Itah* became known as the band's fourth album, then *Kohntarkosz* is the fifth, recorded just a month later. It, too, is now known to be the second part of a trilogy, with the first, *KA (Kohntarkosz Anteria)*, released in 2004, and the last, *Emehntehtt-Re*, coming out in 2009. Liner notes in the 2023 re-release provide the links: Kohntarkosz is an explorer who finds the tomb of a great master of ancient Egypt, Emehntehtt-Re. He was an assassin before achieving his supreme goal: to achieve magical immortality. As he descends into the tomb, Kohntarkosz hears haunting chants from deep inside. He slides off the heavy slab covering Emmentehtt-Re's sarcophagus and then falls into a trance, receiving all the magician's research and wisdom. When he awakes, he decides to devote his time to finding the Formula of Life.

Anyone expecting *MDK* Part 2 would have been disappointed – or delighted, depending on their viewpoint. On *MDK,* the approach was Wagnerian – gritty and relentless, filled with pounding, repetitive musical phrases and walls of guttural vocals. It was like being mown down by a musical tank. Yet, on the original studio version released in 1973, the 38 minutes of music were sliced into seven easily-digestible pieces.

Kohntarkosz, on the other hand, consists of two 16-minute slabs that, on the original LP, were placed on each side of the vinyl and separated by another track because of time restraints – CD versions placed the two tracks together to create parts one and two of a 31-minute monster. Despite that, the music is a bit more restrained and varied. It opens not with a barrage of sound but with an overture of single organ chords, a Bbm, then a Db, then an Eb, a Dbm7, another Eb, then back to Bbm, then Ab. No wonder it confused some fans who expected the same four notes repeated for nine minutes.

The drums are a little looser – instead of pounding away like a demonic jackhammer, they roll and ebb and flow with jazzy intent, the sound warmer and spacier. When the guitar comes in to repeat some solid descending notes, they are slow and steady, not picking up the pace until a good two and a half minutes into the track. As for the vocals, they wait for a minute and a half before making an appearance.

That's not to say *Kohntarkosz* is all sweetness and light – this is Magma after all – but there are moments of relative peace and beauty within the madness, dominated by a slightly buzzy Yamaha organ. At times, Vander's drums are so laidback and echoey, you wonder if he's nodded off in the studio toilets.

MDK was lyric-heavy. But on *Kohntarkosz,* the vocals take a backseat to the instruments – there are long passages without any singing at all, just organ, piano, bass and drums battling it out. What vocals there are frequently consist of ooohs and aaahs – they are there for atmosphere rather than meaning.

Part 1 ends with a long organ and then high-pitched vocals set against a solo piano, with some gorgeous little notes tinkling away. Part 2 also opens with solo piano in delightful major keys with a single voice crooning melodically deep in the mix. Top supplies some evocative, fretless bass, and the drums are notable for their absence. When they do come in, it is as a jazz-influenced accompaniment, not as the driving force as heard on *MDK.* As a result, the music is mysterious and pregnant with possibilities rather than awe-inspiring and crushing.

In fact, it takes about six minutes before we reach something that sounds like classic Magma, but even then, the drums and bass seem to be playing off each other rather than locked together in unison. A four-note riff is repeated almost viciously, fierce organ licks sound like a demonic saxophone, vocals come in with sharp oohs and aahs, gaining in volume, and Vander's drumming gets busier, hitting everything in sight.

There's a key change, and some fast vocal gibberish, furious piano 'dyads' (two notes played simultaneously, creating harmony or dissonance), and the vocals get even more hysterical. Finally, we fade out on slow piano chords and what I guess is the Kobaian equivalent of 'Ommmmm....', sung low enough to rattle your fillings.

There were two further pieces on the original album, one of them Jannick Top's composition for the band. 'Ork Alarm' is a truly disturbing piece of music, with groaning cello introducing deep, guttural vocals set against rasping and staccato string-led chords. Apart from a few brief pauses for breath, it powers along for five-and-a-half minutes as the vocals get wilder and more animalistic, with apparently random, high-pitched, squeaking guitar notes and Vander hitting sheet metal. It cuts out abruptly on metal percussion and demonic laughter.

Finally, Vander's 'Coltrane Sundia' is a low-key (in both definitions of the phrase), piano-led tribute to his muse, John Coltrane, who died in 1967. The title translates from Kobaian as 'Coltrane Rest In Peace'. It's mostly meandering in the key of F major, with cello providing a low drone throughout.

Enthralling, atmospheric and unpredictable, *Kohntarkosz* was a detour for Magma – inspired, allegedly, by Vander's fear that other artists were stealing his ideas (including Mike Oldfield, who visited the studio during the making of *MDK*). It received few reviews when it was released (in fact, I can't find any, which suggests the music papers at the time were not that interested in Zeuhl), but many modern-day critics have hailed it as a masterpiece.

Allmusic gives it four and a half stars, stating: 'Although the definitive version of the title suite is found on 1975's *Magma Live*, this record stands alongside the best Magma studio releases.' Julian Cope – yes, the chappie from The Teardrop Explodes – adds on his website: 'A huge and epic mantra, a heathen movie score for an unfilmed religious epic.'

In fact, let us give Julian Cope the last word, with some excellent advice:

Buy and listen to *Köntarkösz* and *Mekanik Destruktiw Kommandoh*, then go to an oldies record shop and check out the sleeves of the other LPs. You don't need ALL these records, but you sure as hell gotta grab the two classics. Then the genius of Christian Vander will slowly become subsumed into your consciousness, and you'll want to own the others just because of what he symbolises.

Hatfield And The North – *Hatfield And The North*

Key personnel:

Phil Miller: electric and acoustic guitars

Dave Stewart: Fender Rhodes electric piano, Hammond organ, Hohner Pianet, piano, tone generator, Minimoog

Richard Sinclair: bass guitar, vocals

Pip Pyle: drums, percussion, sound effects

With:

Robert Wyatt: vocals

The Northettes: Barbara Gaskin, Amanda Parsons, Ann Rosenthal

Geoff Leigh: tenor saxophone

Didier Malherbe: tenor saxophone

Jeremy Baines: pixiephone, flute

Sam Ellidge & Cyrille Ayers: vocals

Recorded between October 1973 and January 1974 at the Manor Studios, Oxfordshire

Engineered & produced by Tom Newman and The Hatfields

Cover design & photography by Laurie Lewis

Record label: Virgin

Release date: February 1974

Chart placings: did not chart

Tracks: 'The Stubbs Effect' (Pip Pyle), 'Big Jobs (Poo Poo Extract)' (Richard Sinclair, Pyle), 'Going Up To People And Tinkling' (Dave Stewart), 'Calyx' (Phil Miller), 'Son Of 'There's No Place Like Homerton'' (Stewart), 'Aigrette' (Miller), 'Rifferama' (Sinclair), 'Fol De Rol' (Sinclair, Robert Wyatt), 'Shaving Is Boring' (Pyle), 'Licks For The Ladies' (Sinclair, Pyle), 'Bossa Nochance' (Sinclair), 'Big Jobs No2 (By Poo And The Wee Wees)' (Sinclair, Pyle), 'Lobster In Cleavage Probe' (Stewart), 'Gigantic Land Crabs In Earth Takeover Bid' (Stewart), 'The Other Stubbs Effect' (Pyle)

The Story So Far…

Guitarist Phil Miller and drummer Phillip 'Pip' Pyle first met at nursery school in Sawbridgeworth, Hertfordshire, when they were four. In 1966, they formed

Bruno's Blues Band with Miller's pianist brother Steve and bassist Jack Monck. Saxophonist Lol Coxhill joined, and the name was changed to Steve Miller's Delivery in 1968. Singer Carol Grimes arrived, and Roy Babbington from the Keith Tippett Group and jazzers Nucleus replaced Monck on bass. This lineup released the album *Fool's Meeting* in 1970 under the name Carol Grimes and Delivery. Pyle left in 1971 to join Gong, and the band folded soon after. Phil Miller formed Matching Mole with Robert Wyatt (ex-Soft Machine) and Dave Sinclair (ex-Caravan), but the band ended after two albums when Wyatt was paralysed in a fall from a window during a party. Steve Miller replaced Dave Sinclair in Caravan, appearing on the album *Waterloo Lily* (1972). In early 1972, Phil Miller revived Delivery – Pyle joined from Gong, Steve from Caravan, Babbington and Coxhill returned, and Canterbury-born Caravan bassist Richard Sinclair came along as a vocalist. Soon, Babbington and Coxhill left, and Sinclair took over on bass. Steve Miller became unhappy with the direction of Delivery's music and quit, replaced briefly by Dave Sinclair before he, too, decided he didn't like the musical direction. The band was renamed Hatfield and the North and replaced Dave with Londoner Dave Stewart from Egg.

The Album

There aren't many bands named after road signs. Sure, there are plenty of groups called after towns, cities, countries and even continents – Boston, Chicago, Japan, Asia, to name a few. But, to my knowledge, only one band appears on a road sign on the A1 out of London, and that's Hatfield and the North.

In many ways, it was a stroke of genius – how else would you get such valuable free publicity alongside a busy main road? Unfortunately, it didn't help sell any records – the band released two albums before breaking up in 1975, and neither of them charted anywhere in the known universe, not even in Hatfield (20 miles north of London, in Hertfordshire). Too few passing motorists were able to make the connection between a useful traffic direction and four British musicians playing quirky jazz-prog.

We have already made a brief visit to Canterbury in the chapter on Robert Wyatt's Rock Bottom album, so we already know that the city in Kent spawned a number of idiosyncratic bands and artists that, collectively, tend to go under the name of the Canterbury Scene. The big three, the ones that are usually mentioned as prime practitioners of the Canterbury sound, are Soft Machine, Caravan and Hatfield and the North.

But we shouldn't ignore the many other bands who hailed from the city or were linked to it stylistically, including Egg, National Health, Khan, Gilgamesh, Isotope, Mashu, Mirage, Centipede, The Polite Force, Rapid Eye Movement and the multi-national beast that was Gong. Getting into Canterbury music is like falling through a brightly-coloured hole into a surreal, Alice-in-Wonderland world of jazzy-prog, quirky (sometimes saucy) lyrics, very British accents and silly song titles.

The grand-daddy of them all was The Wilde Flowers, who operated between 1964 and 1968, providing many of the musicians that splintered off into the various bands listed above and moved between groups like participants in a city-wide game of musical chairs. So Miller knew Pyle, who knew Richard Sinclair, who played with his cousin Dave and knew Robert Wyatt, who knew Daevid Allen, who knew Pyle … and so on.

So it is no surprise that the early days of Hatfield and the North are marked by a revolving door of personnel that didn't settle down until the arrival of keyboard player Dave Stewart. He is not to be confused with the Dave Stewart of The Eurythmics – our Stewart was a Londoner who formed a band called Uriel with Steve Hillage (Khan, Gong) and Mont Campbell (Egg, Gilgamesh, National Health) when the three were at City of London School in 1968.

Hillage left, and the remaining members, including Clive Brooks on drums, changed their name to Egg (because Uriel sounded too much like 'urinal') and recorded two albums of classically-inspired, experimental keyboard-dominated prog (a third came during a one-off reunion in 1974). When their record label gave up on them in 1972, Stewart was jobless and living with a bunch of unsuitable housemates in South London. In the liner notes for compilation album *Hatwise Choice*, Stewart recalled:

> Then the phone rang – it was a bad line, but somewhere beneath the crackling and spluttering, I could dimly discern a voice mumbling something about 'band … tape … Dave Sinclair…' This turned out to be Pip enquiring about my musical availability … Some time later, a cassette arrived in the post containing a muffled noise which bore a passing resemblance to music but lacked the usual distinguishing features. Apparently, it was a tape of an early Hatfield gig with Dave Sinclair on keyboards, but the sound was so bad I couldn't hear what they were doing.

An audition was arranged at Phil Miller's flat, and God knows what the neighbours thought. There was Miller on guitar, Pyle on drums and Sinclair on bass playing a thunderous, demonic tune called 'Nan True's Hole', originally recorded by Matching Mole and named after Radio One DJ John Peel's Suffolk home. Then Stewart added his fuzzed-up organ sound, which probably shook the building to its foundations. At the song's conclusion, as the dust settled all around them, Pyle said: 'Well, Dave, I think it's fair to say you're in the group now.'

In the beginning, Hatfield and the North played Miller's compositions for Matching Mole, but new tunes started to appear. Pyle said:

> Phil's tunes often had a jazzy tinge, but his quirky, eccentric sense of harmony and melody avoided all the jazz cliches. Richard wrote all these lovely lyrical songs with nice chords. Dave wrote more challenging material, which, while hell to play, sounded pretty impressive sometimes, even live. I

wrote, well, whatever it was … ('extended, riff-based instrumental blowing pieces, the occasional song and lyrics for some of Richard's songs', interjects Dave Stewart). Either way, we certainly covered a lot of ground. Differ we certainly did, but, for a while at least, we were in full agreement (albeit occasionally).

Like Soft Machine and Matching Mole, the Hatfields used to play hour-long sets at gigs with no breaks between the tracks. That way, said Pyle, you only had to confront the audience's apathy twice – once when you walked on and then when you walked off. Live, the band would include copious amounts of improvisation over a bassline in 13/8, an approach that seemed to go down better in the rest of Europe than it did in the UK.

They realised that, for some people, listening to an hour of dense jazz-rock was their idea of hell, so they leavened their serious musical approach with on-stage antics, saucy lyrics and silly song titles. How could you not warm to a band that would introduce its next number as 'Finesse Is For Fairies', or 'Lobster In Cleavage Probe'?

Then, in the spring of 1973, there were talks between the Hatfields and Simon Draper of Virgin Records – no-one can remember who called whom (although it could have been Sinclair). Virgin were fresh off the success of Mike Oldfield's *Tubular Bells,* so they were keen to find other bands who could play intricate instrumental music that went on forever, or at least across two sides of vinyl. They even gave the Hatfields the same engineer who had recorded Oldfield's opus, Tom Newman (on the album sleeve, he is credited as Tom 'Bulk Erase' Newman for accidentally wiping Pip Pyle's best playing on one of the tracks).

What Virgin DIDN'T give the band was the publishing rights to their songs – they lost those to Richard Branson in a game of skittles in a local pub. Pyle said: 'The financial consequences for the band were disastrous.'

Another disaster was narrowly averted when the band were invited by Gong to live and rehearse at their studio in Sens, south-west of Paris, while the latter (then led by Steve Hillage) were on tour. The studio had poor electrics with a loud mains hum. So the band ran a cable out of the window to an iron spike stuck beneath an oak tree in the garden.

That worked fine until there was a violent storm and lightning struck the tree before leaping onto the iron spike and travelling all the way up the cable to whoever was at the other end, which proved to be Sinclair. He said: 'There was a loud bang and a spark came off the end of my Fender bass and went PLIMP onto Phil's guitar. Amazing. We were electrically mated by God … The lightning made the tree all black, and there was a black line right across the grass where it had burned the cable out.' Luckily, all Sinclair suffered was a nasty shock.

In August 1973, the band went into the Manor Studios in August 1973, bringing with them three female singers they dubbed The Northettes in tribute to the cheesy names of 1960s girl groups, such as The Ronettes. They consisted of Barbara Gaskin, who was Steve Hillage's girlfriend at the time and later became Stewart's musical and romantic partner (she was actually born in Hatfield and recalled Pyle saying 'I've always wanted to call a group Hatfield and the North'), Amanda Parsons and Ann Rosenthal.

They had sung together in 1971 in a short-lived project called the Ottawa Music Company, led by Stewart and Chris Cutler of Henry Cow, and they added angelic wordless vocals to some of Hatfield and the North's instrumental pieces. However, they were never in the studio at the same time – they learned and recorded their pieces separately.

The music on Hatfield and the North's debut album is fun, unpredictable and technically brilliant. There are exquisite melodies, powerful riffs, complex time signatures and sudden musical changes. Miller's guitar soars and screeches, Stewart's fuzzy keyboards growl like a pissed-off grizzly, Pyle's drums are a masterclass in tasteful busyness and Sinclair's oh-so-English vocals croon banal yet strangely affecting lyrics.

Some of the tracks on the album date back to 1972 and were played live during the last dying days of Delivery. 'Fol De Rol' was written by Sinclair as a 'geometric finger exercise' – in the *Hatfield Choice* liner notes, he explained:

You start on low F#, go up a fifth, take it down a semitone, go up a fifth, down a semitone, play another fifth, go up, repeat it and come back down. I came across it by chance, and as I was playing it, I thought, hang on, that's rather nice, this actually makes 11 beats. So I carried on playing it and got sort of hypnotised by it, and then, of course, I was forced into making it a tune by Phil, who always tries to make my simple little things into major productions!

Miller came up with chords, and Robert Wyatt, who had been invited into the studio to add guest vocals, wrote some lyrics with his partner Alfie Benge. Not that they required a great deal of thought. 'Fol de rol de ra diddy da day', sings Sinclair, mournfully and mysteriously, 'a rum de pum de da de da da ya do'.

Sinclair also came up with the melody for 'Licks For The Ladies', a pretty guitar-based tune with lyrics by Pyle in which, characteristically, he muses on the nature of the music the band was playing. 'Just in case you think it's a waste,' sings Sinclair, 'in the end, choosing notes to see if they make friends/A D# minor flattened 5th will go to C/Dotted crotchets usually divide by three/ We don't really know now exactly what we mean/Still we had the gist of it till the chords changed unexpectedly'.

Another early Sinclair/Pyle composition is the childishly-named 'Big Jobs', which is split into two pieces on opposite sides of the original vinyl. Again, it's a wistful ballad, this time in a minor key, and, again, the lyrics are an observation on the music-making process: 'Here's a song to begin the beginning/A few notes which are arbitrary/We try our best to make it sound nice/And hope that the music turns you on to our latest LP/Should be a laugh certainly'. Sinclair provides strange vocal noises by wobbling his finger in his mouth, a little affectation he used to employ with Caravan, while Stewart contributes a playful organ solo over the end.

Yet another early Sinclair offering is 'Rifferama', a very fast and unpredictable bass riff over which both Miller and Stewart take turns in providing equally fast and unpredictable solos, with uncredited saxophone from Didier Malherbe of Gong. The tune is punctuated by babbling voices, featuring Robert Wyatt's son Sam, and ends on a sudden burst of surprised laughter from a crowd. The recorded track also absorbs another early Hatfield composition, a tribute to Wyatt called 'For Robert'.

Another track played shortly before Delivery became Hatfield and the North was Pyle's contribution, 'Shaving Is Boring', a nearly nine-minute tune with a funky guitar riff in 5/8, a driving, repetitive, three-note bass run and a cheeky synth solo from Stewart that gets steadily dirtier as he switches on his fuzz pedal. Eventually, all semblance of a melody is abandoned as Miller and Stewart just play random noises over the bass and drums with added sound effects.

There's a short break about two-thirds in, when, with the sound of running footsteps, someone opens various doors to let in snippets of other tracks before settling on a fuzz organ riff, followed by a Miller guitar solo over more riffing bass and driving drums. The title is a bit of French wordplay – 'Raser est rasant' – but Pyle simply thought shaving WAS boring.

By early 1973, when they were officially Hatfields, they had a Miller-penned tune initially called 'For Cyrille' – in the studio, Wyatt contributed some tuneful, wordless cries and the track was renamed 'Calyx'. Later in 1974, Wyatt would pen lyrics about his partner Alfie and sing them live at the Theatre Royal, Drury Lane – 'Poetry in motion is what you've become/From the front and from behind you're a star/Sideways, on the top and underneath/Close inspection reveals that you're in perfect nick/You'll perform like a dream'.

Stewart was a later contributor to the Hatfield musical catalogue, but once he started, he composed four substantial tracks for the album, including the ten-minute centrepiece, 'Son Of 'There's No Place Like Homerton''. Homerton is a London suburb situated north of the Tudor city and about 26 miles from Hatfield – more importantly, it is just six miles from Stewart's birthplace in Waterloo.

Other Stewart tunes include the delicate 'Lobster In Cleavage Probe', which features The Northettes singing gentle but surprisingly complicated melodies over soft electric piano. 'Time is only dust, when it's done we will fly.../Like a tea-tray in the sky', they sing. There is a mention of a lobster, but, sadly, no cleavage. The track speeds up a bit and merges into 'Gigantic Land Crabs In Earth Takeover Bid', which Stewart described in the liner notes for another compilation album, *Hattitude*, as 'based on a riff with alternating bars of 11/8 and 19/8. The group turned this into a rampaging, riotous piece of rock 'n' roll – when soloing on it, Phil got right out there and discovered several theoretically impossible notes and facial expressions.'

One final Stewart composition to mention is 'Going Up To People And Tinkling', which begins as quietly and delicately as 'Lobster...' but then picks up pace, with Miller doubling up Stewart's melody lines and Sinclair providing bubbling bass notes.

With *Tubular Bells* no doubt in his mind, Tom Newman programmed the tracks so they would merge effortlessly into each other, with the help of a few short and sweet melodic links, including the opening keyboard flourish of 'The Stubbs Effect' (reprised at the end of side two) and the 40-second long (or short) song fragment 'Bossa Nochance', written and sung by Sinclair.

The result is two brilliant 20-minute slices of superbly crafted jazz-prog that bounce deliriously from quirky ballads to furious keyboard onslaughts, showcasing the band's astonishing musical dexterity and sense of fun. Their mixture of the mundane and the marvellous is captured in the record sleeve, which shows a panoramic view of Iceland's capital Reykjavik (for some reason) merging into a 16th century fresco called 'The Damned' – all tormented naked bodies – painted by Luca Signorelli.

Sadly, neither the cover nor the musical delights contained inside were enough to propel the album into the musical charts anywhere in the world. But over time, it has built up a loyal cult following and is seen as one of the cornerstones of Canterbury music.

Hatfield And The North in 1974. Dave Stewart (far right) also recorded *The Civil Service* with Egg in the same year.

Kraftwerk – *Autobahn*

Key personnel:
Ralf Hutter: vocals, electronics
Florian Schneider: vocals, electronics
Wolfgang Flur: percussion
Klaus Roder: violin, guitar
Recorded sometime in 1974 at Kling Klang studio, Düsseldorf, and Conny's
Studio, Cologne
Produced by Ralf Hutter and Florian Schneider
Engineered by Konrad Plank
Record label: Philips
Release date: 1 November 1974
Chart placings: UK: 4, CA and US: 5, DE and NZ: 7, AU: 9, NL: 11
Tracks: 'Autobahn', 'Kometenmelodie 1', 'Kometenmelodie 2', 'Mitternacht',
'Morgenspaziergang'
All tracks written by Ralf Hutter & Florian Schneider, with additional lyrics on
'Autobahn' by Emil Schult

The Story So Far...

Florian Schneider and Ralf Hutter met while students at a music school in
Düsseldorf in the late 1960s and formed Kraftwerk after releasing an album
as part of a short-lived experimental band, Organisation zur Verwirklichung
gemeinsamer Musikkonzepte.

Inspired by visual artists Gilbert and George, they wore suits and ties and
tried to bring 'everyday life into art'. Signed to Philips records, their early
albums *Kraftwerk* (1970) and *Kraftwerk 2* (1972) – engineered by pivotal
Krautrock figure Konrad 'Conny' Plank – showed Schneider and Rutter
improvising with traditional rock band instruments (the first album actually
used real human drummers, Klaus Dinger, who later formed Neu!, and Peter
Schmidt. Other members at one time or another included drummers Andreas
Hohmann, Thomas Lohmann and Hans-Gunther Weiss; bassists Eberhard

Kranemann and Plato Kostic; and guitarists Michael Rother – another Neu! man – Houschang Nejadepour and Emil Schult.) The third album, *Ralf & Florian* (1973), introduced more electronic instruments, moving towards the signature Kraftwerk sound.

The Album

In many ways, Kraftwerk were Germany's Beach Boys. The California group encapsulated what it meant to be young and American – basically surfing, cars and girls. In fact, they released more songs about cars than surfing – all those Little Deuce Coupes, Hondas and 409s and the girl having fun, fun, fun until her daddy takes her T Bird away.

But what did it mean to be young and German in the decades after World War II? As percussionist Wolfgang Flur told *Uncut* magazine in 2016: 'Germany also needed something like The Beach Boys. Something with self-understanding and immaculate presence, after the ugly wars that our parents inflicted on the world. Something positive and youthful that freed us from the stench of the past.'

And what was more modern than the autobahns that stretched into the horizon across Germany, offering freedom, escape and endless mobility? These were roads without limits – almost literally. About half of Germany's motorway system has no mandatory speed restrictions whatsoever (a limit of 130kph is advisory, and driving faster than that is not illegal), except in urban areas or where roads are under construction or prone to accidents.

Germany also produces great cars. BMW, Mercedes-Benz, Audi, Porsche – these are vehicles in which to go fast in luxury, to switch on the cruise control and feel the hypnotic thrum of the asphalt beneath the wheels, creating a strange, almost musical drone. Pedestrians couldn't have created *Autobahn,* the album. It had to come from musicians who had travelled those long, lonely roads between gigs or to and from the studio, who thought more in terms of machines than instruments (although Hutter had a Volkswagen Beetle – not exactly designed for comfortable long-distance driving).

But we're racing ahead of ourselves. Brake!!! Let us reverse and talk about Krautrock – a derogatory name, actually, coined by the sniffy British musical press. But it is a label that has stuck and describes the experimental rock that emerged in the old West Germany in the late 1960s and early 1970s. It was partly inspired by rebellion – young Germans rejected the cultural dominance of American pop and rock, but hated the sickly sentimentality of so-called 'schlager' easy listening music their parents grooved to.

What floated their boat was the more mechanical, minimalist music of Terry Riley, the experimentation and genre-blending of Frank Zappa, the deliberately home-made approach of The Velvet Underground and, of course, the inventive genius of The Beatles, particularly the 'proto-krautrock' of 'Tomorrow Never Knows'. They also wanted music that was more essentially German when most rock bands had British names and sang in English.

Central to the development of 'krautrock' – or 'Kosmische (Cosmic) Musik', as some artists preferred to label themselves – was Konrad 'Conny' Plank, a German musician who built his own studio and produced albums for Berlin's underground scene. One of the first recordings he engineered was *Tone Float*, the first and only release by Rutter and Schneider's first band, Organisation, followed by *Klopheizhen*, the 1970 debut for experimental music group Kluster. When Rutter and Schneider formed Kraftwerk, Plank was virtually a third member of the group. He went on to work with Neu!, Ash Ra Tempel, Brian Eno and Ultravox – all big names in the world of experimental electronic music.

At the same time, technological developments around the use of sequencers, synthesisers and tape collages inspired artists who preferred twisting knobs to stroking strings, leading to the formation of bands such as Tangerine Dream and Faust. But most of these groups were influential rather than commercially successful until they began to break through in the 1970s.

For Kraftwerk, it took three albums to hone the sound that eventually gave them chart success in 1974. Indeed, the band considered the first two LPs to be 'archaeology' and believed the real story started with number three. *Ralf & Florian* introduced the vocoder, which transforms the human voice into something inhuman and mechanical, and made more use of synthesisers, electric piano and preset rhythm machines.

But those earlier years were important, particularly in their exposure to the drumming of Klaus Dinger and what was dubbed the 'motorik' beat – a powerful, relentless, driving 4/4 rhythm with minimal changes, a sound that was more robotic than human. It was, claimed Brian Eno, one of the three most important beats of the 1970s, along with Fela Kuti's Afrobeat and James Brown's funk. The 'motorik' beat would, appropriately enough, become the basis for a song about motoring.

By 1973, Rutter and Schneider were looking for new musicians to augment their live sound – apart from the two core members, the Kraftwerk lineup seemed to change with head-spinning rapidity. They approached percussionist Wolfgang Flur, who had played in several bands, including one with future Neu! guitarist Michael Rother, but by 1973 had given up music in favour of being an architect. Rutter and Schneider turned up at his office and begged him to join their band.

Eventually, Flur relented and was introduced to Kraftwerk's ramshackle Düsseldorf studio, named Kling Klang after a track on *Kraftwerk 2*. Disgusted by the unprofessional kit he was expected to use, he created the world's first electronic drum pads using the rhythm unit from a Farfisa organ, operated while standing up with what looked like a conductor's baton. In David Buckley's 2015 book *Kraftwerk: Publikation*, Hutter says:

Wolfgang Flür had joined us to play a custom-built drum system and was our first percussion player to accept electronically produced drums. Electronic music was quite new as a musical medium in the early 1970s, of course, and many people were just starting, like the Can group in Cologne. I think we were one of the first groups to have an electric drummer, with Wolfgang Flür. As well as the custom drum console, we now have two sets of drums that consist of six metal pads triggered by metal sticks on contact. These are not touch-sensitive, so accents and dynamics come from separate volume foot pedals. Sometimes we link one or more pedals to change other parameters, such as tone or pitch.

Another new addition to the lineup was Klaus Roder (sometimes spelt Roeder) on violin and guitar. Born in Stuttgart when it was part of the US occupation zone just after WW2, he first met an impressed Hutter in 1971. Three years later, he received a telegram asking him to get in touch with a view to joining Kraftwerk. His was a short stint with the group – he quit or was fired (depending on which story you believe) about a year later and, he claims, has never profited from the success of *Autobahn*.

With a fresh lineup and a desire to push the band further into the realms of electronic music, Kraftwerk bought a Minimoog synthesiser – it cost as much as Hutter's Beetle – and began experimenting with new ideas for the next album. One of them was inspired by the road from Düsseldorf to Hamburg, which passes through the industrialised Ruhr valley to the rural peace of Munster (or it could have been the A555 from Cologne to Bonn – memories differ).

In David Buckley's book, Schneider says: 'Several years ago, we were on tour, and it happened that we just came off the autobahn after a long ride, and when we came in to play, we had this speed in our music. Our hearts were still beating fast, so the whole rhythm became very fast.' And Hutter told *Uncut* in 2016:

The white stripes on the road – I noticed them when driving home every day from the studio. Then the car sounds, the radio – it's like a loop, a continuum, part of the endless music of Kraftwerk. In *Autobahn*, we put car sounds, horn, basic melodies and tuning motors. Adjusting the suspension and tyre pressure, rolling on the asphalt, that gliding sound – pffft pffft – when the wheels go onto those painted stripes. It's sound poetry … It was an exciting experience that makes you run through a huge variety of feelings. We tried to convey through music what it felt like.

The band attempted to recreate the journey through electronic sound, synthesising the growl of motors, the parp of car horns and the rumble of tyres on the road. Indeed, the 23-minute title track that fills side one opens with the real sound of a car door slamming and a motor starting up before moving off. The first synthesised noise is a car horn – it's practically an Eb7 – then a low, robotic voice chants 'Autobahn' through a Robovox voice changer before an insistent, rhythmic Moog bass note in F major takes over.

The main melodic element of 'Autobahn' – and the tune everyone knows from the later edited single release – is a simple four-chord pattern on an organ of F, Bb, C and back to F again. This moves up to G, C, D and G, then into the key of D, with pretty little descending notes over the top, ending with the chords of Bb, C and D before everything goes back to F.

The pattern is repeated frequently as the band sing what sounds like 'fun, fun, fun on the autobahn'. More echoes of The Beach Boys? Well, almost. What they are actually singing is 'Wir fahren, fahren, fahren auf der autobahn' – 'fahren' being German for 'drive'. It really is as simple as that. The vocals are accompanied by random synthesised wooshes as cars whizz past at crazy speeds. There are hardly any drums – the rhythm comes from the bass and gentle 'tishes' from the electronic drum pads ('our drummers don't sweat', Hutter told reporters).

At the three-and-a-half-minute mark, the song introduces a poppy little bass riff in A major, with simple, pretty melodies over the top, including from Schneider's flute – he is not listed as playing it, but it is definitely there. The flute is meant to represent the countryside in rural Munster, and the bright, optimistic nature of the song certainly does suggest the manicured fields and gardens, a sort of synthesised countryside rather than something wild and untamed.

At the seven-minute mark, the track reprises the 'fahren, fahren, fahren auf der autobahn' section before a soft but insistent 'motorik' beat takes over, accompanied by the sound of cars whooshing by, occasionally blasting their horn at Hutter's slow-moving VW. As more keyboards are applied, we return once again to the original four-chord motif, then … a moment of peace, a low hum with just the briefest hint of a melody as more natural male voices slowly sing 'fahren auf der autobahn' with a rising melody. The track picks up a bit of speed but ends undramatically with a short burst of synthy noise.

Clinical and mechanical yet surprisingly warm, with touches of self-deprecating humour, the 23-minute 'Autobahn' doesn't really have enough in it to keep your attention – at times, I found my mind wandering and my eyes looking at guitar websites online – and it certainly doesn't challenge Yes or Jethro Tull in the classic prog epic stakes. But it is a brave attempt to do something interesting with the electronic technology Kraftwerk had embraced, and I think it is more successful than a lot of material pushed out by their contemporaries (yes, Tangerine Dream, I'm looking at you).

Side two of the album contains four tracks, two of which are linked. 'Kometenmelodie' 1 and 2 were inspired by the Kahoutek comet – the title translates as 'Comet Melody' – which passed close to the sun in March 1973. It was predicted to be spectacularly bright but, in the end, was barely visible to the naked eye and a bit of a damp squib.

Nevertheless, Kraftwerk give the comet a sense of grandeur and mystery with, firstly, a six-and-a-half-minute atmospheric piece that sounds like washes of electronic noise in the vastness of space, with a pretty, repetitive piano melody set against whistles, whooshes and hums. Part 2 follows the comet on its journey through the cosmos with a surprisingly cheery tune, interspersed with starry tinkles, like the scattering of ice crystals across the velvet blackness.

'Mitternacht' is a slow, moody piece full of gloomy and ominous bass notes, echoey drips and bangs, and what sounds like seagulls in pain. The title translates as 'Midnight' – but this is the witching hour in a cemetery. Finally, 'Morgenspaziergang' – or 'Morning Walk' – suggests birdsong, bubbling waters and chuckling insects, with the occasional short tunes played on recorder and flute, with harp strums in the background.

Autobahn was released to mostly general indifference, even hostility, from the critics, some of it verging on xenophobia and unacceptable tastelessness. The band invited journalists to join them on a car journey and played the album through the vehicle's speakers – the response, said Schult, was 'So what?'. *Rolling Stone* magazine dismissed it as not as good as Wendy Carlos, whose 1968 album *Switched-On Bach* was produced using a Moog synthesiser, and *Village Voice* critic Robert Christgau claimed it was for 'unmitigated simpletons.'

In Britain, writer Barry Miles headlined a review of a live gig with 'This is what your fathers fought to save you from', while a US music journalist asked in the *New Musical Express* if Kraftwerk were the 'final solution' for music, the band pictured over an image of a Nuremberg rally. Unbelievable.

Then the title track, edited down to a catchy three and a bit minutes, was released in February 1975 and charted all over the world. Critics suddenly realised that, far from being the 'final solution', Kraftwerk were the future of modern music, a 'landmark in avant-garde pop minimalism', said Stephen Dalton in the book *1001 Albums You Must Hear Before You Die*. *NME* said, in a 180-degree U-turn, the album is of 'enormous historical significance.'

Even the original cover by Emil Schult, a strangely banal painting of German cars on a wide, open motorway stretching towards sunlit green hills, has become something of a style icon. Meanwhile, the British release sported something more streamlined and futuristic – stark, simple converging white lines on a blue background, an instantly recognisable Kraftwerk logo.

Fifty years on, Autobahn is still seen as a startlingly new direction in modern music, one that followed its own aural road map. Even today, the image of black-clad, expressionless musicians standing motionless in front of clinical keyboards while producing relentlessly pounding electronic sounds is synonymous with Germany's most innovative and successful band.

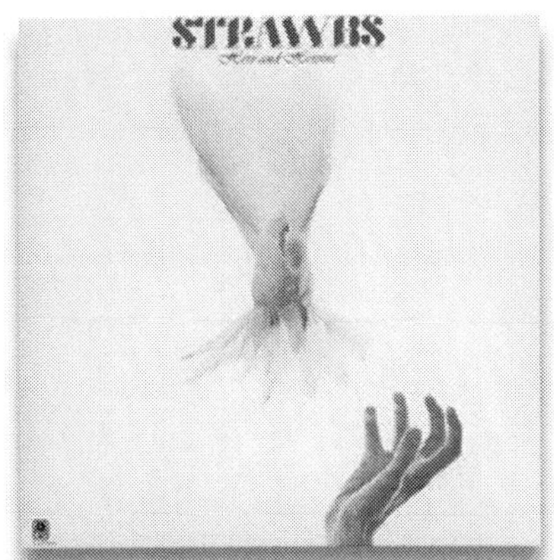

The Strawbs – *Hero And Heroine*

Key personnel:
Rod Coombes: backing vocals, drums, percussion
Dave Cousins: lead vocals, backing vocals, acoustic guitar, electric guitar
Chas Cronk: backing vocals, bass guitar, synthesiser
John Hawken: organ, piano, electric piano, Mellotron, synthesiser
Dave Lambert: lead vocals, backing vocals, acoustic guitar, electric guitar
Recorded in November 1973 at Rosenberg Studios, Copenhagen
Produced by Dave Cousins and Tom Allom
Engineered by Tom Allom and Freddy Hansson
Record Label: A&M
Release date: March 1974
Chart placings: NO: 20, UK: 35, CA: 70, US: 94
Tracks: 'Autumn – i) Heroine's Theme ii) Deep Summer Sleep iii) The Winter Long' (John Hawken, Dave Cousins), 'Sad Young Man' (Rod Coombes), 'Just Love' (Dave Lambert), 'Shine On Silver Sun', 'Hero And Heroine', 'Midnight Sun' (Chas Cronk, Cousins), 'Out In The Cold', 'Round And Round', 'Lay A Little Light One Mc', 'Hero's Theme' (Lambert)
All tracks by Dave Cousins unless stated otherwise

The Story So Far...

The band was formed in 1964 by Dave Cousins, Tony Hooper and mandolin player Arthur Phillips as The Strawberry Hill Boys, named after the area of Twickenham, London, where they rehearsed, playing folk and bluegrass. Having lost Phillips, they recruited double bass player Ron Chesterman, and were persuaded to shorten their name to The Strawbs because it fitted better on posters. They hooked up with young female folk singer Sandy Denny, recording the first version of her folk-rock classic 'Who Knows Where The Time Goes' in Cousins' front room. Demo tapes clinched them a deal with Denmark's Sonet Records, and they recorded an album on a cinema stage in Copenhagen during the day while playing locally at night. But Denny left, so the album remained in the vaults for five years before being released as *All Our Own Work*. Meanwhile, the Copenhagen tapes persuaded A&M to offer a new contract and the band released their first single, 'Oh How She Changed', in 1968. For the debut album, The Strawbs recorded with Elton John producer Gus Dudgeon (who was then Hooper's flatmate). Both the single and the album failed to chart. Second album *Dragonfly*, released in 1970, featured short-lived new member cellist Clare Deniz, and session musician Rick 'One-Take' Wakeman on one track, 'Vision Of The Lady Of The Lake'. Wakeman joined, Chesterman left, cellist/bassist Lindsay Cooper came and went, bass player John Ford and drummer Richard Hudson – both Londoners – were recruited. A concert at Queen Elizabeth Hall in London gave the band their first charting album in 1970, *Just A Collection Of Antiques And Curios*, thanks to the performance of pianist Wakeman, dubbed 'Tomorrow's Superstar'. Their follow-up, *From The Witchwood*, was recorded in early 1971, but issues arose with Wakeman, who was in a dire financial situation and needed to do session work to make ends meet. He may – or may not – have started working with Yes. Wakeman's departure occurred just a few months later. Despite that, 1972's *Grave New World*, with new keyboard player Blue Weaver, was a triumph and is regarded as the quintessential Strawbs album. Hooper left, replaced by guitarist Dave Lambert from Hounslow, Middlesex, and pop success was achieved in 1973 with the single 'Part Of The Union', which reached number 12 in UK chart, from the harder-edged *Bursting At The Seams* album, which was a UK number-two hit.

The Album

In February 1974, the Conservative government in the UK, under the leadership of Edward Heath, called a general election on the issue of 'Who governs Britain?'. The answer was 'Not you, Mr Heath' as voters turfed out the Tories.

It was an ill-judged gamble that came after nearly 18 months of industrial unrest following a wage and price freeze introduced in November 1972 in a bid to dampen soaring inflation. The trade unions in Britain were at the height of their powers in the early 1970s, and they reacted to the freeze with crippling industrial action.

The 1973 energy crisis boosted the power of the National Union of Mineworkers, who launched pay strikes in November of that year, plunging Britain into chilly darkness. The government declared a national emergency and imposed a three-day working week to save energy. The election resulted in a minority Labour government that struggled but failed to curb union power, which continued to grow until it was brutally handbagged by Margaret Thatcher.

In the midst of all the unrest came a single that seemed to encapsulate the confidence and power – or some might say the arrogance and selfishness – of the trade union movement. 'You don't get me, I'm part of the union', proclaimed the song. With its oompah rhythm, pub piano instrumental and singalong chorus, it sounded like something you would have expected from, say, a Germanic Chas 'n' Dave.

But it was actually by The Strawbs, a band that started life as a folk group before embracing tuneful prog, and once counted among its ranks the quintessential prog keyboard player, Rick Wakeman. 'Part Of The Union' was written by two of its members, Richard Hudson and John Ford, and it would tear the band apart in much the same way as the union movement was fracturing Britain.

The problem was that it sounded nothing like The Strawbs and was certainly miles away from what Dave Cousins, the only remaining founding member and the de facto leader of the band, wanted to do. It was originally recorded without any input from him at all and initially intended to be released under the pseudonym of The Brothers. Cousins added vocals and guitars, but his distinctive, warbly voice was buried in the chorus.

'Part Of The Union' didn't sound like anything else on the album *Bursting At The Seams* – even the other Hudson and Ford song on the LP, 'Lady Fuschia', was more in keeping with Cousins' wistful prog-folk, and their contribution to 'Tears And Pavan' helped make it a mini-prog epic. But its success encouraged Hudson and Ford to demand more control of the group's repertoire – a demand Cousins refused to meet. In the liner notes of the 1998 reissue of *Hero And Heroine*, he said:

> We spent a lot of time making *Bursting At The Seams*, and the band had become very big, touring everywhere, but already there were great differences of opinion on what songs we were going to do between Hud and John and me. They'd written the big hit record, I'd written the epics, so the band was split between being a college band, if you like, which was where I came from, and the pop tradition, which was where they wanted to go. We were both right and both wrong.

When the split hit the fan, Cousins was taken to one side by the manager, who said, 'The band have decided to fire you. We're going to keep you on as a solo artist and they're going to carry on as Strawbs.' Cousins said, 'Over my dead body.' Instead, Hudson and Ford departed, forming a short-lived but successful group called, with a brave lack of imagination, Hudson Ford. Blue Weaver also quit, eventually joining The Bee Gees and playing on the *Saturday Night Fever* soundtrack.

That left Cousins and Lambert having to piece together a new lineup. The first fresh recruit was pianist John Hawken from Bournemouth, whom Cousins had heard playing on the 1969 debut album of Renaissance. Hawken had left full-time music to become an estate agent, but the two Daves went to see him playing in Ealing, London, with a 'pick-up band' and invited him for a jam. In a 2006 interview for the website *Secret Records Limited*, Hawken said:

> The first thing Dave [Cousins] did was to introduce me to the Mellotron, which I'd never played. He said, 'We're going to be using two of these, so why don't you give it a shot?' It felt like nothing I had ever played – you get this tremendous lag from the time you hit the keys to the time you get the sound. I thought, 'Oh Jeez, I'm in deep doo-doo here.' Then he mentioned we were going to use a synthesiser, another thing I'd never used. But it worked out well.

The next step was to find a new bass player and drummer. The original plan was to bring in Ric Lee and Leo Lyons, the rhythm section of the recently disbanded Ten Years After. But Lambert disagreed, saying it wasn't the right feel for The Strawbs. Instead, Rick Wakeman recommended his friend Chas Cronk on bass (Cronk and Cousins's mums used to work together for the London Borough of Hounslow council), while Rod Coombes from labelmate Stealer's Wheel, who had also just broken up, was available to play drums.

The new lineup decamped to Devon, where Cousins was living, to 'get the band together' and work on musical ideas. With their equipment set up in a village hall, The Strawbs began to shape the tracks that would make up their seventh studio album. In the Secret Records Limited interview, Cousins recalled:

> It was a really rural location, farmers coming in and watching us play, the mothers-in-law were coming along, people walking in with prams, watching us rehearse, this very long-haired heavy rock band starting out, learning what to play and working songs out. 'Hero And Heroine' started out as a country jig, but in that hall was the foundation of the rock sound of The Strawbs.

Indeed, it is surprising that in those peaceful rural surroundings, the band managed to produce possibly the bleakest album of their career. Certainly, the second side of the original vinyl, which runs from 'Hero And Heroine' to 'Hero's Theme', offers a continuously cynical view of life, mostly from the pen of Cousins. Perhaps he was still smarting from the break-up, although it's hard to see how that would have inspired some of his lyrics that touch on isolation and even suicide.

But first the A-side, and a multipart opening song that stretches for nearly eight and a half minutes. 'Autumn' is split into three sections, beginning with the menacing, pounding lead guitar and Mellotron riff of 'Heroine's Theme', written by Hawken. This merges into some minor key acoustic guitar fingering in a slightly Spanish style for part two, 'Deep Summer's Sleep' – autumn is coming, and there are lots of greens, browns and 'the sun sinking red and deep/The fires burning in the fields/As late summer falls asleep'.

Another blast of Mellotron leads us into the gentle, pastoral melody of part three, 'The Winter Long', sung by Lambert. The chorus – 'Hold on to me/I'll hold on to you/The winter long/I will always be with you' – gave the song another title, 'Hold On To Me', when it was released as a single. For a while, it became a popular song to get married to in the US.

'Sad Young Man' is, apparently, about a lonely Brummie who has travelled south and is a 'stranger to a strange new town' who has created his own isolation. Written by drummer Coombes, it was one of three songs he penned for The Strawbs, and is actually a very clever keyboard-based power ballad with some unexpected chord changes and plenty of dynamics throughout.

We shall gloss over 'Just Love' – a fairly forgettable Lambert pub rocker – and alight upon the minor hit single, 'Shine On Silver Sun', a straightforward up-tempo ballad with a simple, singalong chorus that managed to reach number 34 in the UK when it was released in 1973.

The title track may well have started as a jig, but its lyrical themes are as far from a folkie dance tune as you can get. Cousins originally demonstrated it on the banjo while singing lines that depict the deadly appeal of drugs as some sort of Greek romantic tragedy.

Heroine is an 'irresistible white fleece' that beckons 'shipwrecked sailors in the night' – she 'took Hero by the arm, told him that she meant no harm'. But she does, of course, leaving Hero 'crushed and broken in the end'. The banjo influence still exists in the fast picking that appears to take place under the driving verses (although it's actually Hawken's piano played at double speed), but what lifts the song into another realm entirely are the powerful and dramatic minor-key Mellotron chords in a medieval style (think Gaudete by Steeleye Span) that open and punctuate the song.

'Midnight Sun', written by Cousins and bass-player Cronk, ruminates on lost love and life after death to a pretty acoustic guitar backing and Latin bongos, while 'Out In The Cold' sounds like a bona-fide folk song, with fingerpicked guitar and harmonica, and lyrics about loneliness. It includes the rather saucy lines 'I sucked on your breasts, your legs opened wide/I could scarcely believe all the pleasure inside/But now I know how it feels to be old/Out in the cold'. You can get tablets for it, Dave.

'Round And Round' has a pounding bassline and a twisty little keyboard riff that makes the song sound like it's in a tricky-dicky time signature (although most of it is in straight 4/4). Driven by Lambert's heavy guitar chords, it depicts Mankind as trapped on a 'spinning wheel' – there is no freewill here, just the endless cycle of fate. 'Round and round we go', sings Cousins. Round and round we go... There's a spoken-word coda in which he says: 'After all it's just the revolution I despise/The dawn of revelations and the flower power prize/And I pity those poor children with no sunshine in their eyes'. It also contains some of the most chilling opening lines on any album – 'I drew the blade across my wrist/To see how it would feel'. Ouch.

'Lay A Little Light On Me' could well be a plea to a higher power from the desperate man in the previous song – Cousins was baptised a Catholic but went to an Episcopal church as a child because his stepfather was antagonistic to the Roman faith. Cousins was confirmed as a Catholic when he was 16, and several of his songs contain vivid religious imagery. He told journalist Dan Wooding of the *Middlesex County Times*: 'I do not regard myself as deeply religious, but I have very strong spiritual leanings and love biblical imagery. I always visit churches when I am away from home and feel comforted in the presence that I feel.'

Kicking off as a gentle ballad led by electric piano, Cousins blasts 'superfakes offering their empty creeds/That have no faith or substance/That change to suit the doubter/To satisfy his needs'. The entire band kick in for the powerful chorus, followed by a doom-laden, heavy riff that leads the listener into the closing track 'Hero's Theme', which reprises lines from the earlier 'Shine On Silver Sun'.

The new lineup released a second album in the UK at the very end of 1974 – although the rest of the world had to wait until 1975. *Ghosts* is a fine rock LP, but for many Strawbs fans, *Hero And Heroine* is the pinnacle of their achievement, an album that bursts at the seams with bittersweet emotion, beautiful melodies and moments of sublime progginess, mostly thanks to that difficult-to-play, time-lagging Mellotron.

In fact, it may well be fair to say that The Strawbs never quite reached these heights again – it ranks at number 44 in *Rolling Stone* magazine's 50 Greatest Prog Rock Albums of all Time. Tellingly, no other Strawbs album makes the list. And, equally tellingly, it is the only Strawbs album to be re-recorded 17 years later as *Hero And Heroine – In Ascencia*.

As I write this, Strawbs founder, leader and main songwriter Dave Cousins has passed away at the age of 85. He leaves behind him a fine body of work stretching from 1967 to 2023 – many of the albums he and his band recorded have become rock classics, none more so than *Hero And Heroine*. The Strawbs would never be as proggy again.

A 1974 promo shot of The Strawbs, looking very dapper in white tuxedos.

Focus – *Hamburger Concerto*

Key personnel:
Thijs van Leer: vocals, organ, piano & electric piano, flute & alto-flute, ARP synthesiser, harpsichord, recorder, Mellotron, vibes, accordion, handclaps & whistling
Jan Akkerman: guitars, lute, timpani, handclaps
Bert Ruiter: bass, autoharp, triangles, Chinese finger cymbals, Swiss bells
Colin Allen: drums, congas, tambourine, castanets, cabasa, woodblock, Chinese gong, timpani, flexatone, cuica
Recorded between January and March 1974 at Olympic Sound Studios, London
Produced by Mike Vernon
Engineered by Bob Hall with Rod Thear and David Hamilton-Smith
Record label: Polydor (UK), Atco (US)
Release date: May 1974
Chart placings: NL: 5, AU: 14, NO: 16, UK: 20, US: 66
Tracks: 'Delitiae Musicae' (Trad, arranged by Jan Akkerman), 'Harem Scarem' (Thijs Van Leer), 'La Cathedrale De Strasbourg' (Van Leer), 'Birth' (Akkerman), 'Hamburger Concerto – i) Starter (Trad, arranged by Van Leer) ii) Rare (Akkerman) iii) Medium I (Can Leer, Akkerman) iv) Medium II (Akkerman) v) Well Done (Van Leer) vi) One For The Road' (Akkerman)

The Story So Far...

The band was formed in 1969 by Amsterdam-born keyboard player, flautist and singer Thijs van Leer, who recruited Martijn Dresden on bass and Hans Cleuver on drums after meeting them at radio sessions in Hilversum, Netherlands. Guitarist Jan Akkerman, also from Amsterdam, was invited to join the trio.

They became the pit band for the Dutch touring production of the hippie musical *Hair* (and are on a cast album recorded in 1970) while building a live reputation. Their first album was recorded in London, funded by Dutch record producer Hubert Terheggan, but the band couldn't find anyone willing to release it. They then recorded 'House Of The King', written by Akkerman, which secured them a deal with Imperial Records. Their debut album, *Focus Plays Focus* (later retitled *In And Out Of Focus*), was released in September 1970, and 'House Of The King' reached number ten in the Dutch charts. Akkerman, unhappy with Dresden and Cleuver, threatened to quit unless they were sacked. Cleuver was replaced by Akkerman's pal Pierre van der Linden, also from Amsterdam, and Dresden was replaced by Cyril Havermans. The new lineup recorded *Focus II* (better known as *Moving Waves*), which was an international hit in 1971, along with the single 'Hocus Pocus'. Havermans quit because he wanted to do more singing and was replaced by Bert Ruiter from Hilversum, who played in various local bands and once auditioned alongside van der Linden. This lineup released *Focus III*, with the second hit single 'Sylvia' released in 1972.

The Album

Plenty of songs have been written about food. 'Custard Pie' by Led Zeppelin is one. 'Savoy Truffle' by The Beatles is another. *Double Egg, Chips & Beans* is a great EP by the Antique Seeking Nuns. And Frank Zappa was seemingly obsessed with cheese.

But very few foodstuffs have inspired a 20-minute progressive rock suite. True, Genesis said 'Supper's Ready', but any correlation between the title and an actual supper of any description, even a light snack, is hard to find.

No, I'm going to stick my neck out and say that 'Hamburger Concerto', by Dutch band Focus, is the ONLY prog epic that is all about food. I mean, look at the titles of the various 'movements' in the piece: 'Starter', 'Well Done', 'Medium'. All that's missing is 'Do You Want Fries With That?' Perhaps they ran out of space. Or fries.

The story goes that Focus guitarist Jan Akkerman had his first encounter with a hamburger as the band was touring the US in 1973 – he ate it while watching cartoons in his hotel room. Now, I find that a little difficult to swallow, for the simple reason that Holland was the first country in Europe to have a McDonald's outlet. In 1971, to be exact, in Zaandam, north of Amsterdam. I'm sure there was a massive queue of Dutch people when it opened, and I would be very surprised if Jan wasn't one of them.

Nevertheless, here is the 'Hamburger Concerto' on the album of the same name. Now, it is true that Focus reached their peak, their progtastic pinnacle, with *Focus III* in 1972, and I wouldn't suggest that this meat-monikered disc would topple that album off its perch. But plenty of Focus fans rate *Hamburger Concerto* very highly, and it's pretty much downhill from then on (although *Focus 12*, released in 2024, is a triumphant return to form). As for the concerto itself, there is a large body of opinion stating that it is superior to 'Eruption' on *Moving Waves* and 'Anonymus II' on *Focus III*. I'm listening to it now as I write, and I think it's bloody good!

It's an interesting album in another way because it signals the beginning of the end of the musical relationship between Thijs van Leer and Jan

Akkerman – not to mention the departure of drummer Pierre van der Linden (although he came back later). What happened to cause Focus to, well, lose focus?

Neither Akkerman nor van Leer has spoken at any length about why they fell out. Van Leer has touched on 'creative tension' between them that was sometimes constructive and sometimes not, and that's not unusual between talented musicians itching to do their own thing. Van Leer released *Introspection* in 1972, and Akkerman recorded *Tabernakel* a year later. Perhaps that's when each thought they didn't need the other fella.

Then there was the pressure of playing live – in 1973 alone, they did two tours of the UK and THREE in the US supporting more established bands, including Frank Zappa, Yes and Gentle Giant. Four guys trapped in a van together on interminable journeys across America, playing the same songs over and over and over again … it would drive even the most tolerant and saintly individuals totally bonkers.

By the time they got together to work on their fourth album, they were physically and mentally exhausted, and the relationship between Akkerman and van Leer had deteriorated to such a point that they refused to be in the studio together. Nevertheless, they managed to record about 40 minutes of music in the delightful rural setting of Chipping Norton in Oxfordshire before abandoning the sessions – the tracks eventually saw the light of day on a 1976 album of bits and bobs, *Ship Of Memories*.

They show a band experimenting with a range of styles but struggling to create much that justified the time and effort. The folky tune 'P's March' was briefly considered as a single but dumped in favour of the live album *At The Rainbow*, while 'Focus V' is a pleasant, slow instrumental with Akkerman playing high up his fretboard. (Whatever happened to Focus IV? That turned up on *Mother Focus* in 1975.)

The first to crack was, surprisingly, drummer van der Linden. Returning from the second US tour at the end of 1973, he simply failed to turn up for rehearsals, leaving the band just a few weeks to find a replacement before their next live commitments. Van Leer later claimed the drummer wanted to pursue jazz rather than rock, although he immediately joined prog-rock band Trace.

According to Stephen Lambe, author of *Focus In The 1970s*, van der Linden also felt ignored by audiences, who tended to 'focus' their attention on Akkerman and van Leer. Ah, the plight of the poor overlooked drummer.

It was producer Mike Vernon who recommended Colin Allen from Bournemouth, who was at a loose end after the breakup of Stone The Crows. He arrived just eight days before the start of the tour. In a 1974 interview with Chris Welch of *Melody Maker*, van Leer said about the new arrival:

He has changed us. He was really the one we were looking for. We had a difficult time with Pierre … [he] didn't want to go with us to a heavier, clearer style. Not so many fugues and flute! We needed a tighter drum sound, and we wanted to play more major music than before. It was all minors. Colin gives much more space, especially to Bert [Ruiter], who is playing like no-one else now. He always had it in him, but Pierre was always filling too much.

A year later, Akkerman would decide Allen WASN'T the one they were looking for and gave him his marching orders. The drummer told Willem Hoos of *Veronica* magazine in 1975: 'Jan Akkerman didn't want me around anymore, and if Jan doesn't want something, there's no point in talking. He's a very dominant, not to say dictatorial, figure, and what he thinks needs to happen, happens. There's nothing you can do about that. It's a shame.' In response, Akkerman's spokesperson told me: 'Jan thinks highly of Allen, and he's a nice person and a great drummer.'

Dominant and dictatorial … was Akkerman the problem when the band went back into the studio in early 1974 to restart the recording sessions for album number four? According to Peet Johnson in his book *Hocus Pocus: The Life & Journey Of Rock's Dutch Masters*, van Leer, Ruiter and Allen worked together during the day, and Akkerman recorded his parts in the evening, so it seems he fell out with everyone else in the band. Akkerman and van der Linden were also close friends from their days together in Brainbox in 1968, so the guitarist may have thought he had lost an ally in the drummer.

Thankfully, the fallout did not affect the quality of the music that was produced. After the abandoned sessions the previous year, the band seemed to be firing on all cylinders – indeed, Akkerman had recently been voted 'Best Guitarist in the World' by *Melody Maker*, and he certainly doesn't disappoint on *Hamburger Concerto*.

One of his strengths was his sheer musical eclecticism – he was as much at home with, say, 17th-century lute music as he was with six-string electric guitar heroics. The opening track on *Hamburger Concerto*, 'Delitae Musicae', is based on a dance tune published in 1612 by Flemish composer Joachim van den Hove. It is a pretty lute melody that hovers between minor and major chords – think of Henry VIII leading one of his many unfortunate wives through a stately dance – accompanied by van Leer on recorder.

Van Leer offered up 'Harem Scarem' as an obvious attempt to repeat the successes of earlier Focus hits 'Hocus Pocus' and 'Sylvia'. Like those tunes, it has a pounding rhythm and frantic organ and piano, and some non-lyrical vocals, although this time they are more groans than yodels. Akkerman is a bit muted on this, confining himself to background riffs until he plays slower, melodic lines in the middle and towards the end, plus a short bit of restrained improvised lead. Released as a single in April 1974, it failed to repeat its predecessors' chart performances anywhere outside the Netherlands.

The album was recorded at Olympic Sound Studios in London – specifically a district called Barnes in the borough of Richmond in the south-west of the capital. On the very same road as the studio was St Mary's Church, where van

Leer recorded the pipe organ for his composition 'La Cathedrale De Strasbourg'. Opening with dramatic, minor-key piano chords that sound as if they, too, were recorded in the nave of a church, the organ joins in at around the 50-second mark. After two minutes of slow, stately, dramatic music, bass and drums join for a vocal section in which van Leer is double-tracked singing 'La cathedral de Strasbourg, ding dong, ding dong, la nostalgie se reveille' (or 'nostalgia awakens'). There's some nostalgic-sounding whistling, repeated guitar phrases from Akkerman and finally a stately melody with wordless vocal accompaniment.

Side one ends with 'Birth', an Akkerman composition that opens with van Leer on classical-sounding harpsichord. Someone shouts 'Here we go', and thumping drums usher in low bass notes, slashes of Hammond organ and a lead melody on flute. Then Akkerman enters with a slow, melodic trademark Focus solo. The track chugs along for nearly eight minutes, swapping between flute and electric guitar as the lead instrument. Later CD issues of the album include an earlier version that probably benefits from being a good five minutes shorter. As it is, the full-length version illustrates why Focus were frequently compared to Jethro Tull.

So we come to the title track, the 20-minute concerto itself, split into six sections mostly written individually by van Leer and Akkerman – only on part III, 'Medium I', do they collaborate.

Focus always had one foot in the classical world and were inspired by the works of long-dead orchestral composers. The concerto is partly based on 'Variations On A Theme By Haydn', composed by Johannes Brahms in 1873. At least, he thought it was by Joseph Haydn. The theme, 'Chorale St Antoni', had Haydn's name on it, but it was common back in the day to attribute works to well-known composers in an attempt to boost sales. So misinformation was alive and well even in the 19th century.

It is difficult, if not impossible, to spot where the various parts of the 'Hamburger Concerto' begin and end – they are so skilfully woven together. We can say that van Leer opens proceedings on the pipe organ at St Mary's Church, with three powerful major chords, and then plays a variation on 'Chorale St Antoni'. Allen (or Akkerman, they are both credited) is let loose on timpani, while Ruiter plays very fast little bass notes. Akkerman uses his volume pedal to make his guitar notes sound almost like a high trumpet as he matches melody lines with van Leer's keyboards, giving the impression of an opening fanfare.

Allen's drums usher in a repeated 13-note guitar phrase from Akkerman, reminiscent of the guitar coda to The Beatles' 'You Never Give Me Your Money', interspersed with van Leer's classical keyboard phrases. For part III, van Leer provides some clownish vocal noises and the first yodelling on the album, a technique that came about during the recording of 'Hocus Pocus' in 1971, when he was trying to make himself heard over the rest of the band. On 'Hamburger Concerto', it ranges from deep, guttural muttering to falsetto screams.

Van Leer changes to Hammond organ for a slower section of fast, improvised notes alternating between the chords of A major and G minor. He also adds flute to a sparse guitar and bass backing before Akkerman takes over on an extended improvisation over the organ.

The only proper lyrics in the concerto appear in part V, 'Well Done' – they are the first two verses of the Dutch Christmas carol 'O Kerstnacht, Schoner Dan De Dagen' ('O Christmas Night, More Beautiful Than Day'). Van Leer is the only one credited with vocals on the album, so his voice must be double – and sometimes triple – tracked with simple organ backing.

This leads into the final part, a series of doom-laden power chords with piano followed by lead guitar over bass, drums and organ, plus what sounds like chorale 'aaahs' (although no choir is credited). The tune slips into a major key for a triumphal, bombastic climax, a repeat of the 13-note guitar motif and a slow-down ending. We hear keyboards and tuned percussion playing the Third Quarter chimes from the Palace of Westminster in the last dying seconds.

Despite the animosity between Akkerman and van Leer, 'Hamburger Concerto' fits together like, well, a perfectly-constructed hamburger – if the various sections had not been credited, it would be a struggle to work out who composed what. Its success as a cohesive piece of classical prog-rock is illustrated by the fact that it seems to go by much more swiftly than its 20-minute running time would lead you to expect. If we pretend that 1975's *Mother Focus* – which mostly sounds to me like bland elevator music – didn't happen, then it could be seen as a most appropriate ending to the partnership.

Hamburger Concerto is generally viewed as the last great album from Focus, despite their resurgence in the 21st century, and its relatively poor showing in most album charts across the world did it no justice. My view is that it doesn't quite have the sense of wild abandon that accompanied the band's first three albums, but it is nevertheless stuffed full of great musical moments – and in the title track, Focus almost created a solid gold symphonic prog masterpiece.

Utopia – *Todd Rundgren's Utopia*

Key personnel:
Todd Rundgren: electric guitar, vocals
Mark Klingman: keyboards
Ralph Schuckett: keyboards
Jean-Yves Labat: synthesizer
John Siegler: bass, cello
Kevin Ellman: percussion
Recorded in early 1974 at The Secret Sound studio, New York. Track 1 recorded live at Fox Theater, Atlanta, Georgia, on 25 April 1974
Produced by Todd Rundgren
Engineered by Todd Rundgren and David La Sage
Record label: Bearsville
Release date: 4 October 1974
Chart placings: US: 34
Tracks: 'Utopia' (David Mason, Todd Rundgren), 'Freak Parade' (Mark Klingman, Rundgren, John Siegler), 'Freedom Fighters' (Rundgren), 'The Ikon' (Klingman, Rundgren, Ralph Schuckett, Siegler)

The Story So Far...

Philadelphia-born Todd Harry Rundgren taught himself guitar and started playing in bands at age 17. In 1967, he formed Nazz, who were signed by Atlantic Records subsidiary Screen Gems Columbia the following year. Eponymous album *Nazz* (which Rundgren remixed after the producer had left the studio) reached number 118 in the US. Follow-up *Nazz Nazz* (1969) did a little better, but the band broke up, with *Nazz III* (1971) being a collection of outtakes. Rundgren became a producer for Ampex Records, which built Bearsville Studios near Woodstock. Bearsville also became a record label. At the same time, Rundgren recorded his first solo album, *Runt*, released under the same band name in 1970. The single 'We Gotta Get You A Woman' reached number 20 in the US. The second album, *Runt. The Ballad*

Of Todd Rundgren, was released in 1971. The first album officially under his name was *Something/Anything* in 1972, recorded under the influence of Ritalin. Successful singles included 'Hello It's Me', hitting number five. Psychedelic drugs influenced his more experimental fourth album, *A Wizard, A True Star*, released in 1973, while the release of synth-heavy double album *Todd* was delayed to February 1974 because of the vinyl shortage.

The Album

In my opinion, Frank Zappa was a musical genius, along with Duke Ellington, George Gershwin, The Beatles and Joni Mitchell. But Todd Rundgren comes very close. In fact, he said in his autobiography *The Individualist*: 'If bearing a reputation as a weirdo is all it takes to be a genius, I'm a shoo-in. Come to think of it, half the people I know are geniuses – the other half, peculiarly enough, idiots.'

Like Zappa, Rundgren was – and probably still is – more than just a musician. As a celebrated record producer, he has helped birth classic albums including Meat Loaf's *Bat Out Of Hell*, the New York Dolls' debut and XTC's *Skylarking*. He also produced the debut album of a band called Halfnelson, who would later become Sparks.

As a musician, he released a string of hit singles in the early 1970s, along with albums described by music critic Colin Larkin as 'rightly regarded as one of the landmark releases of the early 1970s' (*Something/Anything*) and by journalist Barney Hoskyns as 'the greatest album of all time … a dizzying, intoxicating rollercoaster ride of emotions and genre mutations' (*A Wizard, A True Star*).

Yet, Rundgren is rarely spoken of in the same hushed tones as Yes, Genesis, King Crimson and the rest. Perhaps it was because his work was too eclectic – he leapt about from genre to genre instead of staying within progressive rock. There was also a feeling that he didn't take any genre seriously – that his albums were there to show he could do it all better than anyone else, and after that, he lost interest. Despite that, his 1974 album, *Todd Rundgren's Utopia*, is a superb slice of prog that can hold its head up high. So strap yourself in for a wild ride.

First, let's look at the man's musical influences. He taught himself guitar and grew up loving his parents' records, mostly show tunes and Gilbert and Sullivan operettas. Later, he became infatuated with The Rolling Stones and The Yardbirds from the UK, along with US acts The Delfonics and The O'Jays. But, like many musicians who were in their teens during the early 1960s, The Beatles were his touchstone, his inspiration, and he wanted to create music that matched the artistry of the Fab Four. He was also hugely influenced by New York singer-songwriter Lauro Nyro.

His early solo albums depicted him as a sort of male Carole King – he played piano and sang ridiculously catchy little pop songs. After a while, he got bored with the pop format and began to stretch out on his albums. So

Somebody/Anything offered four sides of vinyl, each with its own stylistic theme and most played entirely by Rundgren.

A Wizard, A True Star combined psychedelic rock, Philly soul, bubble-gum pop, jazz, funk and show tunes, with many of the tracks clocking in at little more than a minute and segueing into each other. It was also notable for containing nearly 30 minutes of music on each side, stretching the possibilities of vinyl to its limit. Rundgren later claimed the album was generally regarded as professional suicide.

In April 1973, Rundgren wanted to tour the album with an ambitious stage show that included a huge silver dome, and put together a band using some of the musicians he had previously recorded with, including the Sales brothers, Hunt and Tony, who later formed Tin Machine with David Bowie, synth player Jean-Yves 'M. Frog' Labat (a would-be French monk), organist David Mason (no, not the guy from Traffic; a different one) and another keyboard player, Mark 'Moogy' Klingman. Their name came from a line from 'International Feel', the opening track on *A Wizard...* – 'Wait another year, Utopia is here'.

But they weren't here for long. The tour was cancelled after just two weeks because of technical difficulties and the lack of an album to show that it was a real lineup and not just Rundgren's backing band. But they did get a chance to rehearse and play a new song that later became known as the 'Utopia Theme'.

Rundgren went back to his production duties before recording his fifth album, *Todd*, heavily influenced by his experiences with psychedelic drugs. Once again, the material was a mix of pop, rock, soul and show tunes with a proggy bent, most of it drenched in synths, with random backwards voices and 'found sounds'.

With most of the album in the can, Rundgren assembled a band to record what became the final track, 'Sons Of 1984'. Inspired by George Orwell's 1949 novel, it asked whether coming generations would be able to resist authoritarianism (I'll leave you to decide if current events suggest the answer is yes or no).

Rundgren wanted to record it live, with a real crowd singing along, so once again, he called upon Klingman, along with LA-born keyboardist and composer Ralph Schuckett, who had done session work for Carole King, among others, plus New York bassist John Siegler and former Bette Midler drummer Kevin Ellman, also from the Big Apple. Together, they called themselves Moogy & The Rhythm Kingz. And why not? Also present were jazzy brothers Randy and Michael Brecker, plus Daryl Hall and John Oates.

The band played at the skating rink in New York's Central Park, where microphones were hung from the trees to capture the audience. Then they went to Golden Gate Park in San Francisco and did it all over again. On the completed track, the SF audience was placed on the left channel of the mix and the Central Park crowd on the right, so the listener was effectively hearing from the west and the east of the US. The collective crowd was dubbed The First United Church Of The Cosmic Smorgasbord.

It was during the rehearsals that Rundgren realised he had the makings of a new Utopia and, with M. Frog retained from the original lineup to twiddle knobs on synthesisers, this new ensemble was officially unveiled for a new tour in November 1973, with Rundgren supporting his own band by playing a solo set before they came on.

The new Utopia was keyboard-heavy, leaving Rundgren to focus on his guitar – he had been playing so much piano, he felt he was losing his chops. In the liner notes for the 1999 reissue of *Todd Rundgren's Utopia*, he said:

> From my standpoint, the only justification for having a band was for me to play more guitar than I would in a solo context. In other words, I made my success at that point as a songwriter and singer, but not principally as a guitar player, whilst when I was in The Nazz, all I had to do was play guitar and sing some background vocals. So I wanted a band principally as an opportunity to play guitar in one form or another, and the fusion music thing also presented challenges, so that you had to be in very good performance shape to approach that music. Generally, it toughened you up for everything you were doing.

Also significant in the development of Utopia was the fact that practically everyone in the band was an established or budding songwriter. Klingman wrote 'Dust In The Wind' for Rundgren's *Something/Anything* album and later released several solo LPs. He also had song credits on Bette Midler's debut album. Schuckett co-wrote songs with Kim Fowley and Rena Sinakin, and later penned one of the most performed country songs of 1988, 'Another World', while Siegler became a prolific film and TV composer.

On tour, the majority of the setlist was drawn from *A Wizard...* and *Todd* – including 'Lord Chancellor's Nightmare Song' by Gilbert and Sullivan! – which was eventually released in February 1974 after being delayed by the vinyl shortage caused by the oil crisis.

It came as a shock to those who were expecting more of the same from the male Carole King, although there was still a fair smattering of poppy, catchy tunes. The slow ballad 'I Think You Know' could have been written by Laura Nyro, and the King-like 'A Dream Goes On Forever' was deemed commercial enough to be released as a single. But tracks such as 'The Spark Of Life', with its whooshing and buzzy synths, the strange, treated piano on 'Drunken Blue Rooster' and the almost-unlistenable sound collages of 'In And Out The Chakras We Go' tested critics' patience to breaking point.

Robert Christgau of *Creem* called the album 'self-deluded', adding: 'The useful moments are buried in a mess of electronic studio junk.' The *New Musical Express* was equally damning, saying: 'On first hearing, the album is the most annoying creation I've encountered in an age.' Even hindsight has not been kind, although former XTC guitarist Dave Gregory was a big fan.

But by the time of *Todd*'s release, Rundgren had already moved on. He was having too much fun with Utopia to worry about what the critics thought of something he had recorded mostly six months before. He and the band were in and out of The Secret Sound in the early months of 1974 – it was co-owned by Rundgren and Klingman, so they could use it whenever they liked, in between producing other people's albums.

It wasn't just The Todd Rundgren Show – there was a lot of jamming and the trying out of ideas from various members of the band, and a noticeable move towards the jazz-fusion being explored by John McLaughlin's Mahavishnu Orchestra and Chick Corea's Return To Forever. In a 2020 *Prog* magazine interview, he revealed the inspirations for the new band:

> The Mahavishnu Orchestra were a big part of our musical lexicon at the time, as were Return To Forever and Weather Report … We weren't ELP fans particularly, and we didn't mix in the same circles, but we were big Yes fans. ELP's music was something else – it was about highlighting an instrumentalist, Keith Emerson, whereas Yes were more of a band … The difference was that those English prog rock bands like Yes and ELP, most of their influences were in the classics, whereas ours were in jazz and R&B, and we were more inclined to do something from a funk standpoint. That didn't necessarily stop us from attempting to play fast, but I don't think anyone in the band had the desire or the chops to play that way.

The band's composing chops are reflected in the credits for two of the four tracks on *Todd Rundgren's Utopia*, including the 30-minute epic that takes up side two, 'The Ikon'. The shortest track, the four-minute 'Freedom Fighters', bore just Rundgren's name, while 'Utopia Theme' – a 14-and-a-half-minute mini-epic – was also credited to David Mason from the first lineup. The version that opens the album was recorded live on 25 April 1974, in Atlanta, Georgia. Drummer Ellman told the website Steve Hoffman Music Forums:

> The night we actually finally recorded 'Utopia', the band was on, everything was working, and it was the best we ever played it. We really captured the greatest version of 'Utopia'. The first two nights it wasn't right, but I remember the last night when we hit the last note, we turned around and said was everybody alright? Did you make a mistake? Everybody played great, so we were all very happy with how that went.

It's not as if it's a straightforward song to play. Fading in on keyboards and drums, it features Rundgren playing dramatic, spikey notes on guitar, doubled up on synth, before settling into a doom-laden chug powered by rolling drums and pounding bass. There's a double-speed section with soaring synth improv and slashing guitar chords, and a short vocal section at the seven-minute mark when Rundgren sings 'City in my head, Utopia/Heaven in my body, Utopia/It's time for me to go'.

Then he lets rip with a magnificent guitar solo over Hillage-like swirling synth before a catchy guitar riff drives the track along, accompanied by quite funky drums and bass – Ellman compared the way he and Siegler locked instrumentals to a soul rhythm. We then return to the doomy introductory section before ending fast and furiously, with Rundgren in full guitar god mode, fingers fretting furiously.

It was Klingman and Siegler who initially came up with the music for the ten-minute 'Freak Parade' – Klingman said in Paul Myers' book *A Wizard, A True Star: Todd Rundgren In The Studio*: 'He had encouraged us to write some weird, wild music. So I had some musical ideas, and John wrote the middle section, which is the funky section that has the vocals over it.'

Opening with a few organ notes, the track flies up through an assortment of chords that are almost impossible to follow, then settles into a lyrical slide guitar solo over gentle, jazzy keyboard and bass backing. Then the music returns to, well, forever as it jumps through several different chords before a funky section of popping bass and jazzy keyboards. Rundgren sings about being a freak, urging other freaks to join the parade. 'Get off the sidewalk!' he cries.

It is an oblique reference to Frank Zappa, who always drew a clear distinction between the 'peace and love' of the hippies and the aggressive, antisocial freaks. Slow, atmospheric keyboards and strange synth-produced noises lead into a fast and furious jazz-fusion sequence that crashes along until it slowly winds down, the track ending on solo bass guitar.

'Freedom Fighters' was Rundgren's concession to record company demands for a single, although it was never released on 45. It's a quirky slice of tuneful psychedelia with occasional stops and starts – it reminds me of Jefferson Airplane circa 1968 – and the lyrics insist that we are all 'soldiers of the mind' who have no choice but to fight for freedom (although who we are fighting against is never stated).

Finally, we come to 'The Ikon', which occupies the whole of side two. In the liner notes for the 1999 reissue, Rundgren explained how the track came about:

> We had a lot of musical ideas when we first started out, many of which were just fragments that guys in the band had been doodling around with … We somehow figured out how to make all these things flow together, just sitting there practising. Nobody sat down like Beethoven and wrote it all out. Eventually, I think an order came out of it, but I'm not sure if it was the exact order that appeared on the record. In other words, we probably recorded several passages having no idea where they would fit in the larger scheme of things.

Klingman had a piece called 'The Conquering Of The West', then Schuckett and Siegler added more – in total, some five or six separate tracks were recorded and then painstakingly stitched together at the mixing stage. It wasn't until much later that the band actually heard the finished track and then had to learn it to play it live, when it would stretch out for up to an hour and a half, with everyone taking turns in providing seemingly never-ending solos.

On record, it has a thrilling, exciting opening with dramatic Mahavishnu flourishes and a driving beat, featuring great keyboard solos from Klingman and Schuckett, before a vocal section that some issues of the album label as 'Movement II: On A Day Like No Other' – Rundgren sings: 'On a day like no other/In a time unique, in a place divine/Keep your eye on The Ikon/Shining in the light of eternal mind'. Pretty damn cosmic, man.

This leads into a slightly more subdued section, mostly alternating between Dm and Eb, with Rundgren playing long, sliding notes over the top. This builds up in instrumentation and volume, getting quite funky, with spacey keyboard solos. Slowing down to a complete stop, we reach 'Movement IV: Still Be Still', another lyric section with cheerful, high-pitched vocals which pretty much repeat the title in various formats.

There's another instrumental section, again pretty fast and furious with great keyboard solos and some fuzzy, dirty guitar from Rundgren, along with short bass and drum solos. A final vocal movement, entitled 'The Question Comes To Mind', opens with some gentle, spacey keyboards before Rundgren sings 'So you never have to be afraid/Never fear, for you are living in eternal mind' over a poppy, melodic backing.

The track ends with nine minutes of instrumental, featuring crunchy guitar riffs and more keyboard solos, a strange section that sounds almost like country rock, some pretty solo piano, eventually joined by melodic lead guitar, before a final Mahavishnu-style flourish of notes brings the track to an abrupt end.

'The Ikon' is not 'Close To The Edge' or 'The Gates Of Delirium', but it is still a thoroughly entertaining epic that hangs together well, with a variety of dynamics and moods and, most of all, some virtuosic playing from all concerned. I'm not sure I really want to hear the live 90-minute version, but, at 'just' half an hour, it holds your attention all the way through, even if Rundgren's lyrics are a little bit trite and cliched.

Released with a suitably swirling, psychedelic cover, *Todd Rundgren's Utopia* divided fans and critics, and still does to this day – his work always had what we call in Britain a 'Marmite' quality (you either love it or hate it, for those of you unfamiliar with the beefy spread). Some see it as ponderous and overblown – Allmusic describes it as 'a little tedious' – while others have called it a tremendous piece of jazz-influenced prog played with faultless precision (again on Allmusic, one fan describes it as 'Idiosyncratic, experimental, non-formulaic, progressive, multi-thematic, with melodic pop sensibilities').

There were further Utopia albums, but, typically, Rundgren refused to stand still, heading in a more commercial direction with shorter songs until it wasn't really prog anymore. I mean, they even had a top 40 US hit in 1980 with 'Set Me Free', while in 1980 they followed The Rutles in creating an entire album of Beatles pastiches.

As for Rundgren himself, he also continued to release his own idiosyncratic solo albums. But rarely was he as progressive as he was on that first Utopia album. In fact, whisper it: he may never again have produced an album as good as this.

Todd Rundgren, the mercurial pop mastermind behind the progressive rock band Utopia, in 1974..

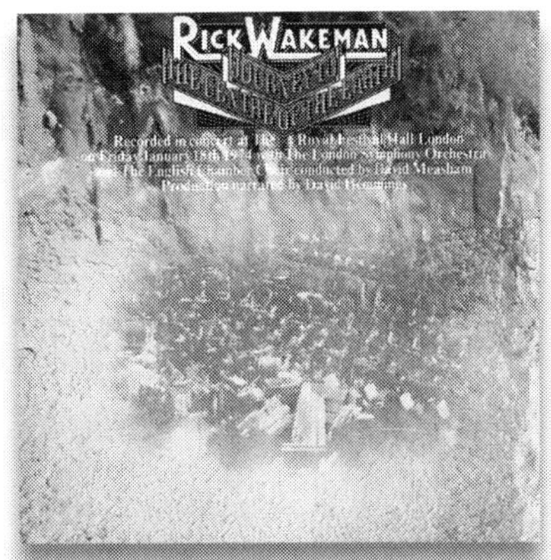

Rick Wakeman – *Journey To The Centre Of The Earth*

Key personnel:
Rick Wakeman: 3 Mellotrons, 2 Minimoog synthesisers, 2 grand pianos,
Hammond organ, Fender electric piano, RMI electric piano, Hohner Pianet,
Honky-tonk piano
Gary Pickford-Hopkins: vocals
Ashley Holt: vocals
Mike Egan: electric guitar
Roger Newell: bass guitar
Barney James: drums
London Symphony Orchestra
English Chamber Choir
David Measham: conductor
David Hemmings: narrator
Recorded on 18 January 1974 at the Royal Festival Hall, London, with Ronnie
Lane's Lyn Mobile Studio
Produced by Rick Wakeman
Production co-ordinator: Lou Reizner
Engineers: Keith Grant, Paul Tregartha, Pete Flanagan
Orchestra and choir arrangements: Danny Beckerman, Will Malone
Record label: A&M
Release date: 3 May 1974
Chart placings: UK: 1, AU & CA: 2, US: 3, NZ: 17, IT: 18, FI: 20
Tracks (original 1974 LP): 'The Journey/Recollection', 'The Battle/The Forest'
All tracks composed by Rick Wakeman except 'The Forest', which includes an
excerpt of 'In The Hall Of The Mountain King' by Edvard Grieg

The Story So Far...
Born in West London, Richard Christopher Wakeman was the son of a pianist
in British musician Ted Heath's big band. He took piano lessons from age
seven, winning a scholarship to the Royal College of Music in London. But he

dropped out to concentrate on a career as a session musician, playing on recordings by, among others, David Bowie, Brotherhood of Man and Marc Bolan. A session for The Strawbs' second released album, *Dragonfly*, led to him joining the band for their third album, *Just A Collection Of Antiques And Curios* (1970), and recognition in the music press as 'tomorrow's superstar'. Their third studio album, *From The Witchwood* (1971), showed a growing split in the band as Wakeman continued to prioritise lucrative sessions, including on David Bowie's *Hunky Dory*, Elton John's *Madman Across The Water* and the Cat Stevens single 'Morning Has Broken'. While in The Strawbs, he recorded an album of covers with John Schroeder and his orchestra and a singer known only as Chris. *Piano Vibrations* is seen as his debut solo album, even though it didn't have his name (or anyone else's) on the cover. Bowie asked him to join his backing band, the Spiders From Mars, on the same day that Yes invited him to replace Tony Kaye. He chose Yes, playing on *Fragile* (1971), *Close To The Edge* (1972) and *Tales From Topographic Oceans* (1973). While in Yes, he recorded his second solo album, *The Six Wives Of Henry VIII* (1973), which reached number seven in the UK and number 20 in the US.

The Album

Rick Wakeman was in despair. He had borrowed to the hilt, mortgaged his house and piled up massive debts to fund his third album. Even the milkman was suing him for not paying his bills. And now A&M Records in London was refusing to release it. 'No-one's going to play it', they said.

It's no wonder that Wakeman later had a heart attack. In many ways, it would have been easier, and probably cheaper, to journey to the centre of the Earth than to make the record. But there was – and probably still is – a stubborn streak in Wakeman, a refusal to bow down to pesky reality. He's a man who doesn't do things by halves, or even two-thirds – it's all or nothing.

There were several albums vying for the coveted 'last chapter' spot in this book. In the end, I was swayed by sheer commercial success. You can't argue with sales of 650,000 in the UK, US and Canada, and an Ivor Novello Award nomination. All hail the keyboard wizard and Grumpy Old Man, Rick Wakeman.

The journey to, er, *Journey* … began way back when he was just eight. His father took him to see a performance of *Peter And The Wolf* by Sergei Prokofiev, and from that moment on, he was obsessed with the idea of telling stories through music. Fast-forward to age 12, when he found a Jules Verne compendium in the school library that contained *Journey To The Centre Of The Earth*, and he was hooked. In a 2013 *Classic Rock* magazine interview with Phillip Wilding, he recalled:

The thing about *Journey...* was that, for a very simple story, it was quite hard reading in parts. I remember doing a little bit of research into Jules Verne because there were things I couldn't quite understand: someone trod on a rock, and then he'd spend the next 17 pages explaining what that rock was made up from. Of course, you then discover he was a scientist, a geologist, and that's where it all came from. So I learned very much to skim over parts. But I thought it was great. And that was the moment, really, when I knew that I wanted to adapt it in some way.

Jules Verne was a 19th-century French novelist whose work embraced and riffed on the scientific and technological knowledge of the time, and, like his British contemporary HG Wells, has been described as 'the father of science fiction'. *Journey To The Centre Of The Earth*, written in 1864, was inspired by seeing volcanic features in Scotland and his friendship with French geologist Charles Deville. The story has Professor Otto Lidenbrock and his team travelling into a strange, prehistoric subterranean world by lowering themselves through an inactive volcano in Iceland. During their travels, they encounter dinosaurs, an underground ocean, cave-ins, tornadoes and volcanic eruptions.

Clearly, this was a tale of geographic notions that demanded to be set to music, preferably using a massive and massively expensive orchestra. But when Wakeman was given his second opportunity to make a solo album while a member of Yes, it swiftly became clear that A&M were not prepared to spew out the substantial amounts of money required for the project. Instead, Wakeman recorded *The Six Wives Of Henry VIII* – inspired by a book on the private life of the notorious axe enthusiast – and planned to use the profits to fulfil his dream. He told *Classic Rock*:

I had a fortuitous thing that year, which was 1973, because The Who had made an orchestral version of *Tommy*, which was produced by Lou Reizner … I was asked to go along and play the keyboards as part of the band, as The Who weren't playing … I met Lou, and he'd heard that I wanted to do *Journey*.… I didn't really know what I was doing; he was the only person I knew who had done anything quite like it successfully. And he said, 'I'd love to be involved because this will be a work specifically done for band, orchestra, choir, as opposed to something that already exists that's going to be adapted.' He introduced me to David Measham, who was the conductor of the London Symphony Orchestra – he was great. Then I met Guy Protheroe, who was young then – weren't we all – and then I met Wil Malone and Danny Beckerman, who had done the orchestration for *Tommy*.

It was clear that the scale of the project meant the only way to make the album was to record live performances rather than trying to cram everyone into a studio. So, after a writing session at his then-home in Devon, Wakeman set about finding a band. He recoiled at the idea of using members of Yes or The Strawbs, as he had on *Six Wives*.… He wanted people to come and listen to the music, not to see star musicians.

Instead, he used a band he had met in a Hertfordshire pub and, on the advice of Yes manager Brian Lane, didn't tell them until the last possible moment that they would be playing two performances, at 6 pm and 8.30 pm, at the Royal Festival Hall. The early show would also be the very first time Rick and the band would play with the orchestra and choir – there was no money or time for a rehearsal.

As seems to frequently happen with a Wakeman project, things didn't quite go to plan. His first choice for narrator, Irish actor Richard Harris, pulled out about a month before the shows because he was getting married. By chance, Wakeman met English actor David Hemmings and asked if he could think of a replacement. Hemmings responded: 'So have you not thought of asking me, for fuck's sake?!'

With Hemmings on board, plans progressed – until they hit another snag. The original idea was to record both shows and edit together the best bits, but that turned out to be too expensive. Instead, only the late show would be taped – warts and all. In another interview with *Classic Rock* magazine, this time in 2023 (check out both interviews; they are a fascinating read), bassist Roger Newell revealed:

I remember Rick coming into our dressing room at the Royal Festival Hall. And he was obviously nervous, bless him, because this was the first thing completely under his name … Then we went out onstage, and there's Steve Howe in the audience, John Lennon and Yoko Ono, Ringo, McCartney with Linda, politicians, Peter Sellers with Britt Ekland and God knows who else. Just faces everywhere. That was when we all went, 'Blimey, this is serious'. I think it's only then that it really hit us.

Across the two gigs on the night of 18 January 1974, more than 3,000 people saw Wakeman, his band, the London Symphony Orchestra and the English Chamber Choir perform *Journey To The Centre Of The Earth* for the very first time. It was undoubtedly nerve-wracking for all the performers and, inevitably, mistakes were made. The recording took three weeks to mix because there were some dodgy timings and bum notes – all edited by slicing pieces of tape with a razor blade.

Finally, the recording was delivered to A&M Records in London, who then dropped the bombshell. In the 2013 interview, Wakeman said the then-boss told him, 'I don't like it, not going to release it. No-one's going to play one track, an orchestra and choir … No, not going to put it out.' But Brian Lane had a brainwave – Wakeman had been signed by A&M in America, so it was their decision, not London's. And A&M in America loved it.

Listening to the original recording more than 50 years later, it is difficult to understand the London office's timidity. It's not as if rock bands had never worked with orchestras and choirs before. And it wasn't the first time someone wanted to put out an album with two side-long pieces of music. It had worked very well for Jethro Tull and Mike Oldfield. And then there was *Tales From Topographic Oceans* – FOUR side-long slabs of sound.

Journey... is also a fairly easy listen, full of rousing fanfares, pretty ballads and lovely keyboard solos all over the place. The pub band perform well, particularly Newell's bass, which is solid and prominent. Hemmings provides commanding commentary that benefits from being performed live in a hall – the ambience gives his voice a hollow, echoey quality that perfectly matches the story of the descent into underground caverns.

There are plenty of standout moments, particularly when Wakeman and the band let rip on rockier segments that were later called 'The Hansbach', 'The Reunion' and 'The Battle'. Sometimes there is too much talking and not enough music. Sometimes the lead singers' voices are not quite as in tune as they would have been if they had been allowed a few more attempts in a studio. But the choir and orchestra sound wonderful – powerful, stirring and well-recorded. And you would be hard-pressed to spot the mistakes.

The fact that it doesn't really hang together as a narrative, despite Hemmings' help, is probably due to Wakeman having to hack 18 minutes out of his score to fit the music on two sides of vinyl – in 2012, he would re-record the longer version for a more spacious CD. But that didn't bother record buyers, who sent it soaring up the charts in many countries across the world. It also cemented the image of the celebrity prog keyboard player in his shimmering silver cape, as depicted on the cover.

The critics were mostly positive, calling it 'entertaining, fresh and disarmingly unpretentious' (*Melody Maker*), 'a striking work' (*The Sunday Times*) with 'no embarrassing excesses' (*New Musical Express*). Allmusic lauds it as 'one of progressive rock's crowning achievements' – although it soon became ammunition for the anti-prog brigade seeking to damn the genre for pretention and excess.

Indeed, Wakeman seemed to play into their hands when he toured the album across the world later in 1974. For one show, at the Crystal Palace Bowl in London, he had giant inflatable dinosaurs fighting each other in a lake. In true Spinal Tap style, the dinosaurs started deflating and sinking. Some of the audience dived in to rescue them.

After the show, Wakeman suffered a heart attack, possibly three, and was advised to recuperate in hospital and even consider retirement. Instead, he checked himself out and went on tour, starting in North America – he had to pass a heart monitor test before each show.

Despite the toll the album and tour took on his health and finances – those were the days when artists made money on selling albums, not on playing live – Wakeman followed up *Journey...* with an even more ambitious, one could say overblown, work: *The Myths And Legends Of King Arthur And The Knights Of The Round Table*. On ice!

It's a miracle that both Rick Wakeman and progressive rock survived.

The Best Of The Rest

We live in an increasingly contrary world, so I will not be surprised if your particular 1974 prog rock favourite managed to slip through the net, and you feel the irresistible urge to express your displeasure on social media. With that in mind, I include this short and sweet mention in dispatches for those bands and LPs that you probably think I should have included but didn't. Oh, and the opinions are all mine, for what they are worth. And, yes, I have listened to them all.

Aera – *Humanum Est*

Delightful jazzy prog from German band Aera, often compared to the likes of Nucleus and Soft Machine. Spirited sax and floaty flute bounce around over bass, drums and guitar. Not to be confused with Area.

Ange – *Au Dela Du Delire*

From France, a band formed in 1969, influenced by medieval themes. They combine pastoral acoustic moments with rock riffs and heavy keyboards. This was voted the 73rd greatest French rock album, and it deserves the accolade.

Aquelarre – *Brumas*

The best of the four albums this Argentine band produced offers a pleasing blend of acoustic and electric guitars, harmony vocals and Hammond organ. Their name translates as 'Witches' Sabbath'.

Arco Iris – *Agitor Lucens V*

Still in Argentina for a prolific band inspired by a female guru called Dana (no, not that Dana). They channel Pink Floyd and Andean folk in this conceptual double album about aliens visiting South America. Originally released in 1974 on cassette, the LP came out the following year.

Area – *Caution Radiation Area*

An Italian band playing loud, keyboard-led jazzy prog with Mahavishnu-style energy. Beware Demetrio Stratos's weird operatic vocals! Not to be confused with Aera.

Arti E Mestieri – *Tilt*

The debut album from Italian band Arti E Mestieri, sporting violin, saxophones and vibraphone. It's very Canterbury in its blend of jazz and prog, with particularly fine drumming from the aptly-named Furio Chirico. If this were a book on Great Prog Albums You've Never Heard, then Tilt would be a shoo-in.

Kevin Ayers – *The Confessions Of Dr Dream And Other Stories*
Probably his last great album – there's a distressing pop element, but the
multi-part title track is an absolute prog classic.

Can – *Soon Over Babaluma*
A surprisingly soulful release from the pioneering krautrockers – Japanese
singer Damo Suzuki had gone, and guitarist Michael Karoli provides diffident
vocals. Musically, they seem to embrace reggae, Cajun and bossa nova. The
album is less uncompromising than its predecessors and that helps make this
one of my favourite Can albums.

Carmen – *Dancing On A Cold Wind*
This UK/US band ambitiously progged up Spanish folk and flamenco
(complete with castanets). 1973's *Fandangos In Space* should be your first
port of call, but this second album is worth a listen. Bass player John
Glascock later joined Jethro Tull. Bizarre, bold and strangely brilliant.

Cos – *Postelian Train Robbery*
'Welcome to the cosy world of Cos', cries this Belgian band over deliberately
ham-fisted piano. Led by a female singer, Pascale Son, this debut combines
soft Zeuhl with Canterbury jazz to create something quirky, melodic and
extremely entertaining. Give it a listen.

The Cosmic Jokers – *The Cosmic Jokers*
A Krautrock supergroup featuring Manuel Gottsching from Ash Ra Tempel
and Klaus Schulze, formerly of Tangerine Dream. This was originally released
as two side-long pieces of hypnotic, almost one-key music featuring electric
guitar whiffling over a soft, steady beat.

Egg – *The Civil Surface*
Before Hatfield and the North, there was Egg, a three-piece featuring Dave
Stewart on organ, Mont Campbell on bass, occasional vocals and French
horn and Clive Brooks on drums. Their tightly-composed, densely played
music was more classical than rock. They split after two albums but came
back for this, their third. It's a bit more playful and laidback, with
contributions from loads of Canterbury and related people. Essential
listening for any Canterbury fan.

Eloy – *Floating*
The third album by prolific German proggers Eloy combines guitar and
Hammond organ for a heavy, almost frantic ELP approach to their usually
spacey rock. A little hilariously bombastic in places but undeniably full of
urgency and fine musicianship.

Brian Eno – *Here Come The Warm Jets & Taking Tiger Mountain (By Strategy)*

The first two albums by the former Roxy Music synth player blend glam and quirky pop with an avant-garde approach that justifies a prog label. He's helped by prog stalwarts such as Robert Fripp, John Wetton, Simon King, Robert Wyatt and Phil Collins.

Esperanto – *Danse Macabre*

Named after the language invented by Ludwig Zamenhof in 1887, this multinational band is notable for the dominance of slightly squeaky violin on tracks that range from frantic and jittery to mellow and spacey.

Far East Family Band – *The Cave Down To The Earth*

Founded initially as Far Out, this much-loved Japanese band included respected synth player Kitaro, alias Masanori Takahashi. The music is Floydian space rock – airy, mysterious and psychedelic, with languid guitar solos – and this is generally regarded as their best album.

Faust – *Faust IV*

Dense, angry, ear-bashing sounds from challenging German innovators, who are generally regarded as the founders of Industrial Rock. It's more accessible than most of their other albums. Opening track 'Krautrock' is an 11-minute roar, but 'The Sad Skinhead' is a deranged pop song with slashing guitars and screams.

Fruupp – *Seven Secrets & The Price Of Heaven's Eyes*

We travel to Northern Ireland this time for a band that never really made much of a mark despite their obvious high standard of musicianship. Perhaps their guitar-driven symphonic prog was a bit too derivative. The band's debut album *Future Legends* is the best – these two are not quite as well-regarded.

Fusioon – *Fusioon 2*

ELP meet Gentle Giant, with Hammond organ and Moog well to the fore, along with harmony vocals like something from Carl Orff's *Carmina Burana* and occasional lead guitar, all set to strange time signatures. Really rather interesting. They are Spanish, by the way, so olé to them.

Greenslade – *Spyglass Guest*

Keyboard player Dave Greenslade's self-named band reached their commercial and artistic peak on this, their third album. Heavily keyboard-driven – the band had two ivory ticklers – the tracks are, in the main, fun, sprightly and accessible.

Gryphon – *Midnight Mushrumps & Red Queen To Gryphon Three*

Another double dose, this time from an English band inspired by Tudor and Renaissance music, so there are plenty of crumhorns, mandolins and recorders. But it's not all 'Greensleeves' – most of the tracks are self-penned and *Midnight Mushrumps* contains an 18-minute epic by multi-instrumentalist Richard Harvey, while *Red Queen...* has four long pieces.

Guru Guru – *Dance Of The Flames*

Krautrock meets Jimi Hendrix. This German trio usually offered trippy, acid-drenched sound collages, but this album injects more rock and jazz, with shorter tracks. The result is their most satisfying record.

Peter Hammill – *The Silent Corner And The Empty Stage & In Camera*

Try as I might, I cannot listen to Peter Hammill. But some people rate these two 1974 releases very highly, particularly the first one, which is almost a Van Der Graaf Generator album. If you love him, you'll probably love them. If, like me, you don't, then you won't.

Hawkwind – *Hall Of The Mountain Grill*

I blow hot and cold on Hawkwind. You have to respect a band that is still going after 55 years, but strip the music of the swirling Mellotron and pseudo-cosmic lyrics, and it seems to me like a simple two- or three-chord thrash. *Hall...* is rock solid but a little repetitive.

Henry Cow – *Unrest*

An album that almost made it into the main section of this book, Henry Cow were part of the British 'Rock In Opposition' movement – they were opposed to simplistic commercial music, and the record industry that perpetuated it. Musically dense and challenging, with a strident left-wing approach, *Unrest* is probably their best album – by which I mean it will only take you about 100 listens to start to understand it.

Il Volo – *Il Volo*

The punchy symphonic prog debut from short-lived Italian supergroup, heavy on keyboards, busy bass and high-pitched guitar. The musicianship here is excellent, with a touch of jazz-rock as well as acoustic folksiness. Like PFM but on uppers.

Invisible – *Invisible*

The debut offering from this short-lived (that word appears a lot in conjunction with progressive rock) Argentine trio, heavily influenced by

Hendrix and Led Zeppelin, but with a pleasing psychedelic bent and gentle acoustic moments.

Isotope – *Isotope & Illusion*

Two albums from a British quartet based on the intricate, mind-boggling guitar work of Gary Boyle and flashy keyboards. The first album is more straightforward jazz-fusion, but the second is dominated by new arrival Hugh Hopper from Soft Machine, so it's almost Canterbury. This is very good music indeed if you enjoy a bit of Mahavishnu and Return to Forever.

Jade Warrior – *Floating World*

There are two tracks here called 'Clouds', and that's how I think of Jade Warrior – as small, wistful clouds drifting slowly through a blue sky over a Japanese Shinto temple. The album is ostly gentle, atmospheric background music.

Jazz Q – *Symbiosis*

To the Czech Republic now for an excellent band with a substantial discography for you to explore. As the title suggests, this is prog on the jazzy side but tightly composed, mostly based on crunchy guitar riffs with electric piano and organ accompaniment. Some of the singing is a bit annoying, though.

Kayak – *Kayak*

The second offering from Dutch band Kayak is made up of punchy but accessible melodic prog songs dominated by guitar. Their first three albums are the best – after that, they go a bit, bluerrgh, commercial.

Kraan – *Andy Nogger*

This German band were more jazz-rock than Krautrock – in fact, their albums remind me more of later jam bands such as Phish and Umphrey's McGee. Andy Nogger is probably their best blend of outstanding musical dexterity, infectious melodies and distinctive, characterful vocals.

Le Orme – *Contrapunti*

Long-lived (and we don't say that every often) French quartet with a definite Emerson, Lake & Palmer bent – fast, heavy keyboards, pounding drums, busy bass, but with occasional dreamy moments.

Lucifer's Friend – *Banquet*

Opener 'Spanish Galleon' is Latin prog with Santana-like guitar! So this band must be from … Germany. This is their fourth and best album, full of energy and aggression.

Missus Beastly – *Missus Beastly*

Not to be confused with their 1970 album of the same name! Missus Beastly broke up for a few years before coming back with, confusingly, an album with the very same title. This German band contained TWO flute players, so the Focus influence is strong here. Slightly abrasive jazz-prog.

Modry Efekt – *Nova Synteza 2 & A Benefit Of Radim Hladik*

Called Blue Effect until the Czech government forced them to change their English name, this is one of my favourite bands, producing mostly instrumental music based on the mind-boggling guitar work of Radim Hladik, with Tull-like flute and occasional violin, brass and even the Czechoslovak Radio Jazz Orchestra. Wonderful stuff!

Moose Loose – *Elgen Er Los*

This Norwegian band's debut offers very Canterbury jazz prog with a funky tinge, right down to the wah-wahed keyboards.

Perigeo – *Genealogia*

Very pleasant and accessible jazz-prog from Italy, sort of like late 1970s Soft Machine.

Pekka Pohjola – *Harakka Bialoipokku*

I'm a big Pohjola fan, and this album hits the spot for me. Classical-style piano followed by jazzy, almost big band instrumentals, tranquil tunes that suddenly burst into life, dramatic sax riffs and virtuoso bass playing. What more could you want?

Pork Pie – *Transitory*

This amusingly-named German band are notable for having future Focus guitarist Philip Catherine in the lineup. This debut is very jazzy, with saxophone as the lead instrument, plus a range of percussion, including pandeiro (Brazilian hand drum) and agogo (a bell).

Procession – *Fiaba*

Some excellent guitar work on the second album from this little-known Italian band. Saxophones and flutes dominate exciting tracks driven by frantic drumming.

Quella Vecchi Locanda – *Il Temp Della Gioia*

The second and last album of quite varied music from Quella Vecchi Locanda – some classically-inspired piano, wistful violin and fingerpicked acoustic guitar with occasional excursions into stomping King Crimson territory, complete with explosive sound effects.

Refugee – *Refugee*

When Keith Emerson left The Nice (he went on to form some band or other), the remaining members recruited Patrick Moraz to produce something that sounds as if Emerson never went! Fast and furious keyboard solos, driven by powerful bass and drums – what a shame they only lasted one album.

Release Music Orchestra – *Life*

A German band with a distinct Canterbury bent – jazzy prog with a light touch and the rare addition of a clarinet. Yes, it's a live album, but all the tracks are new.

Renaissance – *Turn Of The Cards*

This is the one that might inspire strongly-worded letters to *The Times*: one of Renaissance's (try saying that with your teeth out) best albums, relegated to the also-rans? How dare you! But (flak helmet on), it's not one of their best. I mean, it sounds lovely, all classically-inspired piano, lush orchestrations and Annie Haslam's beautiful voice. But the songs, even the epic 'Mother Russia', do nothing for me. In my view, their best work was still to come.

Roxy Music – *Country Life*

Roxy were always more glam than prog, and in *Country Life*, they drop the mask and become a pop group. Ten short, snappy, catchy songs graced with some great violin from Eddie Jobson and two near-naked women on the cover. As if that would help sales.

Rush – *Rush*

The debut album from Canadian three-piece Rush, channelling Led Zeppelin. It's bold, confident and rocks like the devil. Not very prog, but give them time …

Samla Mammas Manna – *Klossa Knapitatet*

Part of the 'Rock In Opposition' movement that included Henry Cow, this Swedish band offers endearingly quirky instrumental music that incorporates folk and jazz, along with a fun sense of humour.

Satin Whale – *Desert Places*

From Germany again, but this time we have a band who have definitely been listening to Jethro Tull and Cream, all flute and heavy lead guitar. It's a bit derivative, but they do it well, with some excellent musical ideas.

Sensations' Fix – *Sensations' Fix, Fragments Of Light & Portable Madness*

No fewer than THREE albums from this Italian band, led by guitarist Franco Falsini. It's all mostly instrumentals, lead guitar over spacey keyboards, a bit

Tangerine Dream, but, er, interesting. *Portable Madness* is generally regarded as the best of the three.

Soft Machine – *Seven*

These Canterbury Scene stalwarts went through a number of stylistic changes, from psychedelia to jazzy prog to straight-ahead jazz fusion. By *Seven*, they were down to the last remaining founder member in keyboard player Mike Ratledge, who left soon after. The music is nice but not terribly inspired, based mostly on repetitive keyboard patterns with added sax.

Spektakel – *Spektakel*

This German trio play lengthy tunes that grow mostly out of improvisation. Sometimes jazzy, sometimes rocking, they have a definite Canterbury feel to them. They only made one album, but it's worth tracking down if you can.

Tasavallan Presidentii – *Milky Way Moses*

One of the earliest Scandinavian prog bands, by 1974, they would become a bit too funky and commercial. Nice guitar from the fellow just below.

Jukka Tolonen – *The Hook*

Regarded as a bit of a guitar legend in Finland (he played with Wigwam and Tasavallan Presidentti), Tolonen's third solo album is a very enjoyable mix of six-string pyrotechnics and horns. Think Jan Akkerman, but slightly softer and funkier.

Tortilla Flat – *Für Ein 3/4 Stündchen*

Tishy tishy jazz drumming, flute, wishy-washy guitars and electric piano combine for the only release by German sextet named after the John Steinbeck novel – not the preferred way to serve Mesoamerican bread.

Trace – *Trace*

Dutch group Trace clearly listened to lots of Focus during the making of their debut album. Furious Hammond organ? Check. Classical pretensions? Check. Someone with the surname van der Linden? Check. In fact, two of them, including Focus drummer Pierre. No flute or yodelling, but in virtually every other respect, it's like listening to a lost Focus album. Quite good actually!

Trettioariga Kriget – *Trettioariga Kriget*

Woah! A blast of sound to the ears! This is heavy prog, man – deep, dark, rumbling bass, wild guitar and drums that sound as if they are pounding on the very gates of hell, with time signatures that change more frequently than the middle aisle in Lidl. Vocals are gentler than you might expect. All in all, very entertaining.

Triumvirat – *Illusions On A Double Dimple*
Generally regarded as the best album by this German trio, who were
sometimes accused of being Emerson, Lake & Palmer clones. This is much
more restrained and with softer edges, thanks to the addition of an entire
brass section and orchestra, and features two side-long suites. A Double
Dimple was a brand of whisky, by the way.

Wigwam – *Being*
Pekka Pohjola's last album with pioneering Finnish band is also their best,
full of twisting, turning melodies a la Gentle Giant and Van der Graaf
Generator. Heavily keyboard-based, it is full of mostly short, quirky tracks
with sometimes bizarrely dramatic vocals. I'm not sure I understand it, but I
do like it.

Supertramp in 1974, around the time of the release of *Crime Of The Century*, arguably
their finest album.

Where Prog Went Next...

When you are at the top, the only way is down. After 1974, some prog bands struggled to maintain their mojo as changing musical tastes took a toll on their confidence and commercial viability. For King Crimson, it was a time for hibernation – a live album was posthumously released in 1975, then silence until the surprise appearance of a new-look and new-sound KC in the 1980s.

Focus had the fall-out that *Hamburger Concerto* foreshadowed, with Akkerman quitting after *Mother Focus* in 1975, and the band entered a 24-year hiatus (apart from a best-forgotten collaboration with singer PJ Proby). Gentle Giant struggled to find an identity that could survive in a more commercial age and pulled the plug after *Civilian* in 1980. And Hatfield and the North proved to be a dead end for the Canterbury crew.

Other artists had their ups and downs, but managed to struggle on. Yes took a three-year break before another personnel change resulted in the chart success of *Going For The One*. After that, it all got a bit patchy, despite a surprise 1983 hit single with 'Owner Of A Lonely Heart'. But, as I write, they are still touring and releasing new albums. As is Rick Wakeman, whose ambitious *King Arthur* on ice lost him so much money that he was forced back into the arms of his former bandmates.

PFM maintained the quality with 1975's *Chocolate Kings*, but after that, only a rabid fan would deny that they have been living on past glories. Jethro Tull produced a better album in 1975's *Minstrel In The Gallery*, but the following year's *Too Old To Rock 'N' Roll, Too Young To Die!* was a bit of a stinker. Thankfully, Ian Anderson pulled his tartan socks up for 1977's *Songs From The Wood*.

But some bands actually flourished – although not necessarily in prog. Genesis recovered quickly from Peter Gabriel's departures with the excellent *A Trick Of The Tail* and good-but-not-quite-as-good *Wind And Wuthering* (both 1976). But when Steve Hackett left, the remaining trio ditched prog and became a very, very successful pop band. Traitors.

Supertramp also took the commercial route – 1975's *Crisis? What Crisis?* was a disappointment, but they redeemed themselves with the less proggy (apart from the final track) *Even In The Quietest Moments...* (1977) and hit pop paydirt with 1979's *Breakfast In America*.

Mike Oldfield bettered *Hergest Ridge* with *Ommadawn* (1975) and his magnum opus, 1978's *Incantations*. Camel released their most celebrated album, *Music Inspired By The Snow Goose*, in 1975 and the excellent *Moonmadness* the year after. And Robert Wyatt continued to release quirky, idiosyncratic albums that have resulted in him becoming something of a national treasure.

As for Frank Zappa, he never really cared about having 'commercial potential'. He just did what he wanted and managed to release some fabulous albums as a result. *One Size Fits All* (1975), *Sheikh Yerbouti* and *Joe's Garage* (both 1979) are essential listening.

As for prog itself, well, we all know what happened around 1977 when a bunch of spikey-haired yobs with a desire to share their saliva with anyone within range started storming the charts. But, as my previously published book on 1977 shows, some prog bands defied the punks and survived. You probably need to get that one next.

Above: Kraftwerk in 1974 during the recording of *Autobahn*.

Below: The perennially uncomfortable-looking Focus with dungaree-clad English drummer Colin Allen (far right) in 1974.

Also available from Sonicbond

On Track series

AC/DC – Chris Sutton 978-1-78952-307-2

Aerosmith – Andrew Rooney 978-1-78952-364-5

Allman Brothers Band – Andrew Wild 978-1-78952-252-5

Tori Amos – Lisa Torem 978-1-78952-142-9

Aphex Twin – Beau Waddell 978-1-78952-267-9

Asia – Peter Braidis 978-1-78952-099-6

Badfinger – Robert Day-Webb 978-1-878952-176-4

Barclay James Harvest – Keith and Monica Domone 978-1-78952-067-5

Beck – Arthur Lizie 978-1-78952-258-7

The Beat, General Public, Fine Young Cannibals – Steve Parry 978-1-78952-274-7

The Beatles 1962-1996 – Alberto Bravin and Andrew Wild 978-1-78952-355-3

The Beatles Solo 1969-1980 – Andrew Wild 978-1-78952-030-9

Black Sabbath The Dio Years – Chris Sutton 978-1-78952-409-3

Blue Oyster Cult – Jacob Holm-Lupo 978-1-78952-007-1

Blur – Matt Bishop 978-178952-164-1

Marc Bolan and T.Rex – Peter Gallagher 978-1-78952-124-5

David Bowie 1964 to 1982 – Carl Ewens 978-1-78952-324-9

David Bowie 1983 to 2016 – Don Klees 978-1-78952-351-5

Bucks Fizz – David Waterfield 978-1-78952-448-2

Kate Bush – Bill Thomas 978-1-78952-097-2

The Byrds – Andy McArthur 978-1-78952-280-8

Camel – Hamish Kuzminski 978-1-78952-040-8

Captain Beefheart – Opher Goodwin 978-1-78952-235-8

Caravan – Andy Boot 978-1-78952-127-6

Cardiacs – Eric Benac 978-1-78952-131-3

Wendy Carlos – Mark Marrington 978-1-78952-331-7

The Carpenters – Paul Tornbohm 978-1-78952-301-0

Nick Cave and The Bad Seeds – Dominic Sanderson 978-1-78952-240-2

The Chic Organisation – Chris Sutton 97801-78952-366-9

Eric Clapton Solo – Andrew Wild 978-1-78952-141-2

The Clash (revised edition) – Nick Assirati 978-1-78952-325-6

Leonard Cohen – Opher Goodwin 978-1-78952-359-1

Elvis Costello and The Attractions – Georg Purvis 978-1-78952-129-0

Crosby, Stills and Nash – Andrew Wild 978-1-78952-039-2

Creedence Clearwater Revival – Tony Thompson 978-1-78952-237-2

Crowded House – Jon Magidsohn 978-1-78952-292-1

The Cure – Matthew R. Davis 978-1-78952-347-8

The Damned – Morgan Brown 978-1-78952-136-8

Deep Purple and Rainbow 1968-79 (new ed)– Steve Pilkington 978-1-78952-411-6

Deep Purple from 1984 – Phil Kafcaloudes 978-1-78952-354-6

Def Leppard – Scott Robinson 978-1-78952-447-5

Depeche Mode – Brian J. Robb 978-1-78952-277-8

Dire Straits – Andrew Wild 978-1-78952-044-6

The Divine Comedy – Alan Draper 978-1-78952-308-9

The Doobie Brothers – Andrew Wild 978-1-78952-462-8
The Doors – Tony Thompson 978-1-78952-137-5
Dream Theater – Jordan Blum 978-1-78952-050-7
Duran Duran – Karen Windle 978-1-78952-368-3
Ian Dury – Opher Goodwin 978-1-78952-374-4
Bob Dylan 1962-1970 – Opher Goodwin 978-1-78952-275-2
Eagles – John Van der Kiste 978-1-78952-260-0
Earth, Wind and Fire – Bud Wilkins 978-1-78952-272-3
Electric Light Orchestra – Barry Delve 978-1-78952-152-8
Emerson Lake and Palmer – Mike Goode 978-1-78952-000-2
Fairport Convention – Kevan Furbank 978-1-78952-051-4
Focus 1969 to 1985 – Stephen Lambe 978-1-78952-463-5
Peter Gabriel – Graeme Scarfe 978-1-78952-138-2
Genesis – Stuart MacFarlane 978-1-78952-005-7
Gentle Giant – Gary Steel 978-1-78952-058-3
Gong (new edition)– Kevan Furbank 978-1-78952-340-9
Green Day – William E. Spevack 978-1-78952-261-7
Dave Grohl and Foo Fighters – Ben L. Connor 978-1-78952-363-8
Steve Hackett – Geoffrey Feakes 978-1-78952-098-9
Hall and Oates – Ian Abrahams 978-1-78952-167-2
Peter Hammill – Richard Rees Jones 978-1-78952-163-4
Roy Harper – Opher Goodwin 978-1-78952-130-6
Hawkwind (new edition) – Duncan Harris 978-1-78952-290-7
Jimi Hendrix – Emma Stott 978-1-78952-175-7
The Hollies – Andrew Darlington 978-1-78952-159-7
Horslips – Richard James 978-1-78952-263-1
The Human League and The Sheffield Scene – Andrew Darlington 978-1-78952-186-3
Humble Pie Robert Day-Webb 978-1-78952-2761
Ian Hunter – G. Mick Smith 978-1-78952-304-1
Iggy and the Stooges – Robert Day-Webb 978-1-78952-360-7
Iggy Pop 1977 to 1999 – Hans Meertens 978-1-78952-446-8
The Incredible String Band – Tim Moon 978-1-78952 107-8
INXS – Manny Grillo 978-1-78952-302-7
Iron Maiden (new ed) – Steve Pilkington 978-1-78952-380-5
Joe Jackson – Richard James 978-1-78952-189-4
The Jam – Stan Jeffries 978-1-78952-299-0
Jefferson Airplane – Richard Butterworth 978-1-78952-143-6
Jethro Tull – Jordan Blum 978-1-78952-016-3
J. Geils Band – James Romag 978-1-78952-332-4
Elton John in the 1970s – Peter Kearns 978-1-78952-034-7
Billy Joel – Lisa Torem 978-1-78952-183-2
Journey – Doug Thornton 978-1-78952-337-9
Judas Priest – John Tucker 978-1-78952-018-7
Killing Joke – Nic Ransome 978-1-78952-273-0
The Kinks – Martin Hutchinson 978-1-78952-172-6

The Smashing Pumpkins – Matt Karpe 978-1-7952-291-4
The Smiths and Morrissey – Tommy Gunnarsson 978-1-78952-140-5
Soft Machine – Scott Meze 978-1078952-271-6
Sparks 1969-1979 – Chris Sutton 978-1-78952-279-2
Spirit – Rev. Keith A. Gordon 978-1-78952- 248-8
Bruce Springsteen - David Starkey 978-1-78952-471-0
Stackridge – Alan Draper 978-1-78952-232-7
Status Quo the Frantic Four Years – Richard James 978-1-78952-160-3
Steeleye Span 1970-1989 – Darren Johnson 989-1-78952-369-0
Steely Dan – Jez Rowden 978-1-78952-043-9
The Stranglers – Martin Hutchinson 978-1-78952-323-2
Talk Talk – Gary Steel 978-1-78952-284-6
Talking Heads – David Starkey 978-178952-353-9
Tears For Fears – Paul Clark 978-178952-238-9
The Temptations 1960 to 1978 – George Haffenden 978-178952-373-7
The The –Brian J. Robb 978-178952-370-6
Thin Lizzy – Graeme Stroud 978-1-78952-064-4
Tool – Matt Karpe 978-1-78952-234-1
Toto – Jacob Holm-Lupo 978-1-78952-019-4
U2 – Eoghan Lyng 978-1-78952-078-1
UFO – Richard James 978-1-78952-073-6
Ultravox – Brian J. Robb 978-1-78952-330-0
Van Der Graaf Generator – Dan Coffey 978-1-78952-031-6
Van Halen – Morgan Brown 9781-78952-256-3
Suzanne Vega – Lisa Torem 978-1-78952-281-5
Jack White And The White Stripes – Ben L. Connor 978-1-78952-303-4
The Who – Geoffrey Feakes 978-1-78952-076-7
Steven Wilson – Insurgentes-To The Bone – Nick Holmes 978-1-78952-317-1
Wishbone Ash 1970 to 1982 978-1-78952-413-0
Roy Wood and the Move – James R Turner 978-1-78952-008-8
The Yardbirds – Andrew Darlington 978-1-78952-362-1
Yes (new edition) – Stephen Lambe 978-1-78952-282-2
Neil Young 1963 to 1970 – Oper Goodwin 978-1-78952-298-3
Frank Zappa 1966 to 1979 – Eric Benac 978-1-78952-033-0
Warren Zevon – Peter Gallagher 978-1-78952-170-2
The Zombies – Emma Stott 978-1-78952-297-6
10CC – Peter Kearns 978-1-78952-054-5

Decades Series
The Bee Gees in the 1960s – Andrew Mon Hughes et al 978-1-78952-148-1
The Bee Gees in the 1970s – Andrew Mon Hughes et al 978-1-78952-179-5
The Bee Gees in the 1980s – Andrew Mon Hughes et al 978-1-78952-497-0
Black Sabbath in the 1970s – Chris Sutton 978-1-78952-171-9
Britpop – Peter Richard Adams and Matt Pooler 978-1-78952-169-6
Phil Collins in the 1980s – Andrew Wild 978-1-78952-185-6

Doctor Who: The David Tennant Years – Jamie Hailstone 978-1-78952-066-8
James Bond – Andrew Wild 978-1-78952-010-1
Monty Python – Steve Pilkington 978-1-78952-047-7
Seinfeld Seasons 1 to 5 – Stephen Lambe 978-1-78952-012-5

Other Books

1967: A Year In Psychedelic Rock – Kevan Furbank 978-1-78952-155-9
1970: A Year In Rock – John Van der Kiste 978-1-78952-147-4
1972: The Year Progressive Rock Ruled The World – Kevan Furbank 978-1-78952-288-4
1973: The Golden Year of Progressive Rock – Geoffrey Feakes - 978-1-78952-165-8
1974: The Year Progressive Rock Came Of Age – Kevan Furbank 978-1-78952-473-4
1977: How Progressive Rock Defied Punk – Kevan Furbank - 978-1-78952-367-6
Apple Of My Eye: The Story Of Apple Records – Andrew Wild 978-1-78952-379-9
Eric Clapton Sessions – Andrew Wild 978-1-78952-177-1
Constellation Heroes – Hans Meertens 978-1-78952-498-7
Dark Horse Records – Aaron Badgley 978-1-78952-287-7
Derek Taylor: For Your Radioactive Children – Andrew Darlington 978-1-78952-038-5
Ghosts – Journeys To Post-Pop – Matthew Restall 978-1-78952-334-8
The Golden Age of Easy Listening – Derek Taylor 978-1-78952-285-3
The Golden Road: The Recording History of The Grateful Dead –
John Kilbride 978-1-78952-156-6
Hoggin' The Page – Groudhogs The Classic Years – Martyn Hanson 978-1-78952-343-0
Iggy and The Stooges On Stage 1967-1974 – Per Nilsen 978-1-78952-101-6
Jon Anderson and the Warriors – the Road to Yes – David Watkinson 978-1-78952-059-0
Magic: The David Paton Story – David Paton 978-1-78952-266-2
Misty: The Music of Johnny Mathis – Jakob Baekgaard 978-1-78952-247-1
Music in the 1980s – Peter Woolliscoft 978-1-78952-347-8
Nu Metal: A Definitive Guide – Matt Karpe 978-1-78952-063 7
Phish- Baker's Dozen – Brent Waltz 978-1-78952-361-4
Philip Lynott – Renegade – Alan Byrne 978-1-78952-339-3
Remembering Live Aid – Andrew Wild 978-1-78952-328-7
Thank You For The Days - Fans Of The Kinks Share 60 Years of Stories –
Ed. Chris Kocher 978-1-78952-342-3
The Making Of Abba – Joe Matera -978-178952-378-2
The Sonicbond On Track Sampler 978-1-78952-190-0
The Sonicbond Progressive Rock Sampler (Ebook only) 978-1-78952-056-9
Tommy Bolin: In and Out of Deep Purple – Laura Shenton 978-1-78952-070-5
Maximum Darkness – Deke Leonard 978-1-78952-048-4
The Twang Dynasty – Deke Leonard 978-1-78952-049-1
Van der Graaf Generator – Pawn Hearts – Paolo Carnelli 978-1-78952-357-7

... and many more to come!

Would you like to write for Sonicbond Publishing?

We are mainly a music publisher, but we also occasionally publish in other genres including film and television. At Sonicbond Publishing we are always on the look-out for authors, particularly for our two main series, On Track and Decades.

Mixing fact with in depth analysis, the On Track series examines the entire recorded work of a particular musical artist or group. All genres are considered from easy listening and jazz to 60s soul to 90s pop, via rock and metal.

The Decades series singles out a particular decade in an artist or group's history and focuses on that decade in more detail than may be allowed in the On Track series.

While professional writing experience would, of course, be an advantage, the most important qualification is to have real enthusiasm and knowledge of your subject. First-time authors are welcomed, but the ability to write well in English is essential.

Sonicbond Publishing has distribution throughout Europe and North America, and all our books are also published in E-book form. Authors will be paid a royalty based on sales of their book. Further details about our books are available from www.sonicbondpublishing.com. To contact us, complete the contact form there or email info@sonicbondpublishing.co.uk